Computer Item Generator

with

Standardized Test Practice

PRENTICE HALL

MIDDLE GRADES MATH

TOOLS FOR SUCCESS

Course 2

Prentice Hall
Needham, Massachusetts
Upper Saddle River, New Jersey

Your *Computer Item Generator* with *Standardized Test Practice* software is on the CD-ROM at the back of this book!

If you prefer diskettes,
call 1-800-468-8378,
and you will receive them at no charge.

PRENTICE HALL
Simon and Schuster Education Group

Printed in the United States of America.

ISBN 0-13-435404-4

1 2 3 4 5 6 7 8 9   03 02 01 00 99 98

Table of Contents

About Prentice Hall's Computer Item Generator with Standardized Test Practice

Contents of the Software

Items Corresponding to *Middle Grades Math* Student Editions

- Contains 10–15 items for *every* lesson in the Student Editions of Courses 1, 2, and 3
- Items arranged by chapter, lesson, and objective
- Items in Free-Response and Multiple-Choice formats

Items Corresponding to Standardized Test Objectives

- Contains 150–225 items for each of three levels of seven different standardized tests
- Items arranged according to test objectives
- Items in Multiple-Choice format

Standardized Test Practice

Do your students need preparation for standardized tests? Prentice Hall's unique Computer Item Generator with Standardized Test Practice provides you with practice exercises that have been correlated to the mathematics objectives of the following standardized tests:

A Prentice Hall Exclusive!

	Level of Prentice Hall *Middle Grades Math*		
	Course 1	**Course 2**	**Course 3**
California Achievement Tests, 5th Ed. (CAT5)	Level 16	Level 17	Level 18
Comprehensive Tests of Basic Skills (CTBS), Terra Nova	Level 16	Level 17	Level 18
Iowa Tests of Basic Skills, Form M (ITBS)	Level 12	Level 13	Level 14
Metropolitan Achievement Tests, 7th Ed. (MAT7)	Intermediate 1	Intermediate 2	Intermediate 3
Stanford Achievement Tests, 9th Ed. (SAT9)	Intermediate 2	Intermediate 3	Advanced 1
NC End-of-Grade	Grade 6	Grade 7	Grade 8
TAAS	Grade 6	Grade 7	Grade 8

To create worksheets for Standardized Test practice, simply select the test of your choice from the menu. Upon doing so, you'll find multiple-choice exercises, arranged according to the objectives of the test you've chosen. You can use all the regular Computer Item Generator features as you select individual exercises, groups of exercises, or randomly chosen exercises to make worksheets that will give your students practice in the skills they need to perform well on specific standardized tests.

No Computer? Use Dial-a-Test®

If you don't have access to a computer, one way to create worksheets or tests is to photocopy and paste exercises from this print version of the Computer Item Generator. A far less tedious way to is to use Prentice Hall's **free** Dial-a-Test® service. With Dial-a-Test®, you tell Prentice Hall which items you want on a test and let us create the test for you. For details, see page vii.

Create Tests and Worksheets Easily

Item Selection Options

- Select single items from any combination of textbook chapters or standardized tests.

- Select a range of exercises within one chapter or standardized test.

- Direct the software to randomly select exercises according to criteria you have chosen.

Output Options

- The Print Preview feature allows you to view and adjust pages before printing.

- Tests can be printed in one-column or two-column format.

- The software provides a customized answer key and a matching student answer sheet for each test or worksheet.

Dynamic Items—A Powerful Tool

Some of the items in the Computer Item Generator are dynamic. Dynamic items are very powerful and useful, because one item can be used to generate a practically unlimited number of different items. Here's how dynamic items work:

- Select any dynamic item and add it *several times* to the test file that you are working on.

  1. [TAAS 6,7,8+ 1.3.1.49]   Estimate with whole numbers and decimals.
  2. [TAAS 6,7,8+ 1.3.1.49]   Estimate with whole numbers and decimals.
  3. [TAAS 6,7,8+ 1.3.1.49]   Estimate with whole numbers and decimals.

- Print the test or choose Print Preview. You will see that the program automatically adjusts the item to appear differently each time.

  1. When all 5 runways are open, a large airport can handle 48 airplanes landing per hour. What is a good estimate for the number of planes that can land in a 6-hour period?

     [A] 350   [B] 50   [C] 200   [D] 300

  2. When all 5 runways are open, a large airport can handle 99 airplanes landing per hour. What is a good estimate for the number of planes that can land in an 8-hour period?

     [A] 700   [B] 800   [C] 1000   [D] 100

  3. When all 5 runways are open, a large airport can handle 97 airplanes landing per hour. What is a good estimate for the number of planes that can land in a 5-hour period?

     [A] 300   [B] 600   [C] 100   [D] 500

One dynamic item, therefore, represents a lot of opportunities for practice and assessment. In addition, if you use dynamic items to create an assessment, each time you print the assessment, you get a **different, yet equivalent form**, each with its own answer key.

Other Types of Items

Items that are not dynamic are called static items. The Computer Item Generator allows you to add your own exercises and to modify the exercises in the existing item bank. (All user-created items are static.) This functionality allows you to create tests and worksheets uniquely customized to your needs and preferences. On the software, item types and formats are indicated by these icons:

= **dynamic item** = **static item**

= **multiple-choice item** = **free response item**

= **item included with software** = **item customized by user**

User's Guide and On-Screen Help

The User's Guide for the Computer Item Generator with Standardized Test Practice describes the complete functionality of the software. The User's Guide appears in PDF format on the CD-ROM that contains the software. You will need to use Acrobat Reader™ to open and print the User's Guide. If you don't already have Acrobat Reader™ installed on your computer, you can install it from the CD-ROM.

The Computer Item Generator has an on-screen Help feature with easy-to-follow directions so that even novices can use the software immediately.

Another Middle Grades Math Resource to Help Prepare Students for Standardized Tests

You will also find the *Computer Item Generator with Standardized Test Practice* CD-ROM in the Middle Grades Math Assessment Success Kits for Courses 1, 2, and 3. Assessment Success Kits contain the Computer Item Generator CD-ROM plus pages of materials that give teachers everything they need to ready students for local, state, and national tests.

vi

About the Dial-A-Test® Service

If you do not have access to a computer or would like the convenience of designing your own tests without typing a word, you may want to take advantage of our free Dial-A-Test® Service. Available to all users of *Prentice Hall Math*, Dial-A-Test® is simple to use. At the right is an example of a filled-out form.

HERE'S HOW IT WORKS

1. Choose the questions you want from those listed in this book.

2. Enter the numbers of the questions in the order you want on a Dial-A-Test® Order Form (see page viii for a master that you may photocopy). Be sure to include the chapter number or the standardized test number on the form. For example, in the case of test question 17, taken from Chapter 1, mark the order form with the designation 1.17. Also be sure to check the box telling which objectives to use.

3. Use a separate Dial-A-Test® order form for each original test you request. You may use one form, however, to order multiple versions of the same original test.

4. If you would like another version of your original test with the questions scrambled, or put in another sequence, simply check the box labeled *Scramble Questions* on the order form. If you would like more than one scrambled version of your original test, note this on your order form or inform the Dial-A-Test® operator. Please note that Prentice Hall reserves the right to limit the number of tests and versions you can request at any one time, especially during the busier times of the year when midterms and finals are given.

5. Choose the method by which you would like to order your original test and/or multiple versions of your original test. To order by telephone, call toll free 1-800-468-8378 between 9:00 A.M. and 4:30 P.M. Eastern Standard Time and read the test question numbers to our Dial-A-Test® operator. To order by mail, send your completed Dial-A-Test® order form to the address listed below. Now you may also FAX your order to 1-614-771-7365.

6. You may order up to 100 questions per test by telephone on our toll-free 800 number or up to 200 questions per test by fax or by mail.

7. Please allow a minimum of two weeks for shipping, especially if you are ordering by mail. Although we process your order within 48 hours of your call or the receipt of your form by mail, mailing may take up to two weeks. Thus we ask you to plan accordingly and expect to receive your original test, any alternate test versions that you requested, and complete answer keys within a reasonable amount of time.

8. Tests are available all year. You can order tests before the school year begins, during vacation, or as you need them.

9. For additional order forms or to ask questions regarding this service, please write to the following address:

Dial-A-Test®, Prentice Hall School Division
4350 Equity Drive, Columbus, OH 43228

–ORDER FORM–
CTS

DIAL-A-TEST®
PRENTICE HALL SCHOOL DIVISION
CUSTOMIZED TESTING SERVICE
TOLL-FREE NUMBER 800-468-8378 (H O-T-T-E-S-T)

–ORDER FORM–
CTS

You may **call** the Dial-A-Test® toll-free number during our business hours (9:00 A.M.-4:30 P.M. EST).
Now you may also FAX your order to 1-614-771-7365 any time.

DIAL-A-TEST®
PRENTICE HALL SCHOOL DIVISION
4350 EQUITY DRIVE
COLUMBUS, OH 43228

FOR PH USE		DATE REC.	DATE SENT
__ PHONE __ MAIL __ FAX		_____	_____

EXACT TEXT TITLE/VOL. ___Middle Grades Math, Course 2___ **© DATE** ___1999___
CODE ___134354044___

CUSTOMER INFORMATION
NAME ___Ellen Mack___
SCHOOL ___Riverside High School___
ADDRESS ___700 River Road___
CITY ___Wells River___ STATE __TN__ ZIP __38578__
PHONE ___208-555-2717___ EXT. ___34___

DATE BY WHICH TEST IS NEEDED ___11/30/98___

OBJECTIVES TO USE (CHECK ONE)
X LESSON OBJECTIVES
__ STANDARDIZED TEST PRACTICE OBJECTIVES

VERSIONS (SEE REVERSE–INSTRUCTION #4)
(CHECK ONE)
__ 1. ORIGINAL   X 2. SCRAMBLE QUESTIONS

TEST IDENTIFICATION (This information will appear at the top of your test.)

Ellen Mack	EXAMPLE:	Mr. Holtzman
Math Period 2		Math, Period 5
Chapter 1 Test		Chapter Test

1 _1.3_	26 _1.74_	51 ____	76 ____	101 ____	126 ____	151 ____	176 ____
2 _1.5_	27 _1.80_	52 ____	77 ____	102 ____	127 ____	152 ____	177 ____
3 _1.6_	28 _1.81_	53 ____	78 ____	103 ____	128 ____	153 ____	178 ____
4 _1.7_	29 _1.82_	54 ____	79 ____	104 ____	129 ____	154 ____	179 ____
5 _1.11_	30 _1.83_	55 ____	80 ____	105 ____	130 ____	155 ____	180 ____
6 _1.12_	31 ____	56 ____	81 ____	106 ____	131 ____	156 ____	181 ____
7 _1.14_	32 ____	57 ____	82 ____	107 ____	132 ____	157 ____	182 ____
8 _1.17_	33 ____	58 ____	83 ____	108 ____	133 ____	158 ____	183 ____
9 _1.18_	34 ____	59 ____	84 ____	109 ____	134 ____	159 ____	184 ____
10 _1.21_	35 ____	60 ____	85 ____	110 ____	135 ____	160 ____	185 ____
11 _1.32_	36 ____	61 ____	86 ____	111 ____	136 ____	161 ____	186 ____
12 _1.34_	37 ____	62 ____	87 ____	112 ____	137 ____	162 ____	187 ____
13 _1.35_	38 ____	63 ____	88 ____	113 ____	138 ____	163 ____	188 ____
14 _1.38_	39 ____	64 ____	89 ____	114 ____	139 ____	164 ____	189 ____
15 _1.40_	40 ____	65 ____	90 ____	115 ____	140 ____	165 ____	190 ____
16 _1.41_	41 ____	66 ____	91 ____	116 ____	141 ____	166 ____	191 ____
17 _1.45_	42 ____	67 ____	92 ____	117 ____	142 ____	167 ____	192 ____
18 _1.47_	43 ____	68 ____	93 ____	118 ____	143 ____	168 ____	193 ____
19 _1.55_	44 ____	69 ____	94 ____	119 ____	144 ____	169 ____	194 ____
20 _1.57_	45 ____	70 ____	95 ____	120 ____	145 ____	170 ____	195 ____
21 _1.66_	46 ____	71 ____	96 ____	121 ____	146 ____	171 ____	196 ____
22 _1.67_	47 ____	72 ____	97 ____	122 ____	147 ____	172 ____	197 ____
23 _1.69_	48 ____	73 ____	98 ____	123 ____	148 ____	173 ____	198 ____
24 _1.70_	49 ____	74 ____	99 ____	124 ____	149 ____	174 ____	199 ____
25 _1.71_	50 ____	75 ____	100 ____	125 ____	150 ____	175 ____	200 ____

DIAL-A-TEST®
PRENTICE HALL SCHOOL DIVISION
CUSTOMIZED TESTING SERVICE
TOLL-FREE NUMBER 800-468-8378 (H O-T-T-E-S-T)

You may **call** the Dial-A-Test® toll-free number during our business hours (9:00 A.M.-4:30 P.M. EST).
Now you may also FAX your order to 1-614-771-7365 any time.

DIAL-A-TEST®
PRENTICE HALL SCHOOL DIVISION
4350 EQUITY DRIVE
COLUMBUS, OH 43228

FOR PH USE		DATE REC.	DATE SENT
__ PHONE __ MAIL __ FAX		_____	_____

EXACT TEXT TITLE/VOL. _____ Middle Grades Math, Course 2 _____ **© DATE** ___1999___
CODE ___134354044___

CUSTOMER INFORMATION
NAME _____
SCHOOL _____
ADDRESS _____
CITY _____STATE _____ ZIP _____
PHONE _____ EXT. _____

DATE BY WHICH TEST IS NEEDED _____

OBJECTIVES TO USE (CHECK ONE)

__ LESSON OBJECTIVES

__ STANDARDIZED TEST PRACTICE OBJECTIVES

VERSIONS (SEE REVERSE–INSTRUCTION #4)
(CHECK ONE)

__ 1. ORIGINAL   __ 2. SCRAMBLE QUESTIONS

TEST IDENTIFICATION (This information will appear at the top of your test.)

EXAMPLE: Mr. Holtzman
_____   Math, Period 5
_____   Chapter Test
_____
_____

1 ____	26 ____	51 ____	76 ____	101 ____	126 ____	151 ____	176 ____
2 ____	27 ____	52 ____	77 ____	102 ____	127 ____	152 ____	177 ____
3 ____	28 ____	53 ____	78 ____	103 ____	128 ____	153 ____	178 ____
4 ____	29 ____	54 ____	79 ____	104 ____	129 ____	154 ____	179 ____
5 ____	30 ____	55 ____	80 ____	105 ____	130 ____	155 ____	180 ____
6 ____	31 ____	56 ____	81 ____	106 ____	131 ____	156 ____	181 ____
7 ____	32 ____	57 ____	82 ____	107 ____	132 ____	157 ____	182 ____
8 ____	33 ____	58 ____	83 ____	108 ____	133 ____	158 ____	183 ____
9 ____	34 ____	59 ____	84 ____	109 ____	134 ____	159 ____	184 ____
10 ____	35 ____	60 ____	85 ____	110 ____	135 ____	160 ____	185 ____
11 ____	36 ____	61 ____	86 ____	111 ____	136 ____	161 ____	186 ____
12 ____	37 ____	62 ____	87 ____	112 ____	137 ____	162 ____	187 ____
13 ____	38 ____	63 ____	88 ____	113 ____	138 ____	163 ____	188 ____
14 ____	39 ____	64 ____	89 ____	114 ____	139 ____	164 ____	189 ____
15 ____	40 ____	65 ____	90 ____	115 ____	140 ____	165 ____	190 ____
16 ____	41 ____	66 ____	91 ____	116 ____	141 ____	166 ____	191 ____
17 ____	42 ____	67 ____	92 ____	117 ____	142 ____	167 ____	192 ____
18 ____	43 ____	68 ____	93 ____	118 ____	143 ____	168 ____	193 ____
19 ____	44 ____	69 ____	94 ____	119 ____	144 ____	169 ____	194 ____
20 ____	45 ____	70 ____	95 ____	120 ____	145 ____	170 ____	195 ____
21 ____	46 ____	71 ____	96 ____	121 ____	146 ____	171 ____	196 ____
22 ____	47 ____	72 ____	97 ____	122 ____	147 ____	172 ____	197 ____
23 ____	48 ____	73 ____	98 ____	123 ____	148 ____	173 ____	198 ____
24 ____	49 ____	74 ____	99 ____	124 ____	149 ____	174 ____	199 ____
25 ____	50 ____	75 ____	100 ____	125 ____	150 ____	175 ____	200 ____

CHAPTER 1

Lesson 1-1   Objective 1: Display data in a frequency table or line plot.

Dynamic Item

1. The numbers below represent the number of gallons of water used daily by ten people. Which line plot shows the data?
    26, 23, 22, 29, 24, 22, 29, 23, 21, 22

    [A]

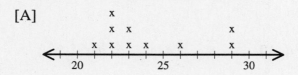

    [B]

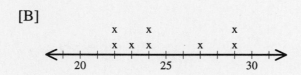

    [C]

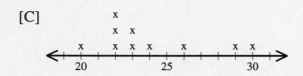

    [D]

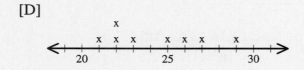

Dynamic Item

2. While shopping for tennis shoes, Jasmine compared prices of ten different brands. Use the prices she found to make a frequency table.
    $25.36, $40.60, $39.36, $28.98, $33.04,
    $32.83, $33.12, $31.87, $43.91, $22.74

3. Compare a histogram with a regular bar graph. Be sure to describe the way they are both alike and different.

4. The table below shows the number of public holidays in a number of different countries. Make a histogram to display the data. Explain how you chose the interval for your histogram.

Country	Number of Public Holidays
Canada	12
Denmark	8
France	9
Germany	10
Ireland	8
Italy	9
Japan	13
Norway	9
Portugal	14
Spain	14
Sweden	9
Switzerland	8
USA	11

How Many Books Have You Read During the Past Year?

3 ǁ	11 ǁǁǁǁǁ	18 ǁǁǁ
4 ǁǁǁ	12 ǁǁǁ	19 ǁ
6 ǁ	14 ǁǁǁǁǁǁǁǁ	20 ǁǁǁǁǁǁǁ
7 ǁǁǁǁ	15 ǁ	22 ǁ
9 ǁǁ	17 ǁ	24 ǁǁǁǁǁ

5. A survey was conducted among a group of seventh grade students to determine the average number of books a twelve-year-old reads yearly. The frequency table above shows the data collected from this survey. How many students participated in the survey? What was their most common response?

6. <u>How Many Books Have You Read During the Past Year?</u>

3 ||	11 ||||||	18 ||||
4 ||||	12 ||||	19 ||
6 ||	14 |||||||||	20 ||||||||
7 |||||	15 ||	22 ||
9 |||	17 |	24 ||||||

 A survey was conducted among a group of seventh grade students to determine the average number of books a twelve-year-old reads yearly. The frequency table above shows the data collected from this survey. Identify two possible choices of intervals for this data. Provide a reason for each interval selected.

7.
```
                X
                X
                X        X
                X        X
        X       X        X        X
        X       X        X        X        X
        X       X        X        X        X
        X       X        X        X        X
        X       X        X        X        X
   FOOTBALL  SOCCER  BASEBALL  BASKETBALL  TRACK
```

A class of 24 students was asked to identify a team sport in which they have participated. Their responses are shown in the line plot above. How many responses are recorded in the line plot? How does this compare with the number of students polled? Explain how this could occur.

CHAPTER 1

<u>**Lesson 1-1**</u>   Objective 2: Make a histogram.

Dynamic Item
 8. Draw a histogram for the intervals 17-19, 20-22, 23-25,
     and 26-28 using the following data: 21, 17, 19, 20, 23, 25, 19, 25, 25, 24,
     21, 28, 17, 17, 25, 19, 20, 19, 23, 26

[A] 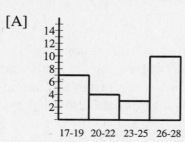   [B]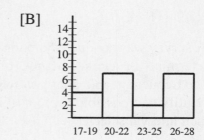

[C] 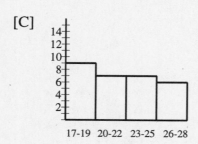   [D]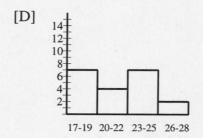

Dynamic Item
 9. Construct a histogram for the following frequency table.

Interval	Frequency
0.5 − 1.5	2
1.5 − 2.5	26
2.5 − 3.5	14
3.5 − 4.5	5
4.5 − 5.5	3

 10. Sixteen adults were asked the time they went to sleep the previous night.
      Their responses are shown below.

      10:15 P.M.   11:30 P.M.   1:00 A.M.   9:45 P.M.
      11:00 P.M.   10:15 P.M.   12:15 A.M.   10:45 P.M.
       9:30 P.M.   1:15 A.M.   11:45 P.M.   10:00 P.M.
      10:30 P.M.   12:30 A.M.   10:00 P.M.   11:00 P.M.

      Make a histogram.

CHAPTER 1

11. Twenty adults were asked how many radios were found in their homes. The responses are shown in the line plot below. Display this data in a frequency table.

```
                    X
                    X
          X         X
      X   X         X   X
      X   X   X     X   X
  X   X   X   X     X   X   X
  1   2   3   4   5   6   7
```

NUMBER OF RADIOS OWNED

12. Sixteen adults were asked the time they went to sleep the previous night. Their responses are shown below.

10:15 P.M.	11:30 P.M.	1:00 A.M.	9:45 P.M.
11:00 P.M.	10:15 P.M.	12:15 A.M.	10:45 P.M.
9:30 P.M.	1:15 A.M.	11:45 P.M.	10:00 P.M.
10:30 P.M.	12:30 A.M.	10:00 P.M.	11:00 P.M.

The interval size that would most accurately depict the information in a histogram is

[A] 30 minute intervals.   [B] 45 minute intervals.

[C] 1 hour intervals.   [D] 15 minute intervals.

13. How Many Books Have You Read During the Past Year?

3 II	11 IIIIII	18 IIII
4 IIII	12 IIII	19 II
6 II	14 IIIIIIIII	20 IIIIIIII
7 IIIII	15 II	22 II
9 III	17 I	24 IIIIII

A survey was conducted among a group of seventh grade students to determine the average number of books a twelve-year-old read yearly. The frequency table above shows the data collected from this survey. Make a histogram to represent the data.

14.

```
                        X
                        X
                        X             X
                        X             X
                        X             X             X
        X               X             X             X             X
        X               X             X             X             X
        X               X             X             X             X
        X               X             X             X             X
   FOOTBALL         SOCCER       BASEBALL     BASKETBALL       TRACK
```

A class of 24 students was asked to identify a team sport in which they have participated. Their responses are shown in the line plot above. Make a histogram to show this data.

Lesson 1-2   Objective 1: Make a bar graph.

Dynamic Item

15. The table below shows the number of games each team won last season. Choose the bar graph that best represents the data.

Team	Games Won
A	16
B	9
C	6

[A]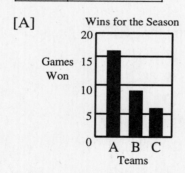

[B]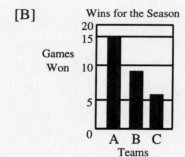

[C]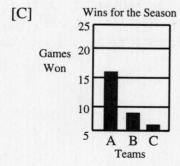

[D]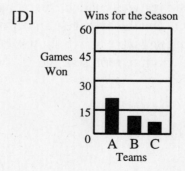

CHAPTER 1

Dynamic Item

16. Use the following information to draw a bar graph showing the number of participants in various school clubs.

Drama	45
Speech	55
Debate	90
Camera	95
Choir	75

17. The population of Readingville has increased by 6% each year during the past decade. If you want to represent this data on a graph, what type of graph would you use? Explain why.

18. Identify the main purpose of a bar graph. Describe two types of data that can be displayed on bar graphs.

19. Data from each of the following surveys can best be represented on a bar graph EXCEPT

   [A] the number of girls who walk to school.

   [B] the population in New Jersey in 1970, 1980, and 1990.

   [C] the total number of teachers versus students at your school.

   [D] the number of television stations in three different cities.

Country	Hourly Compensation (for Production Workers in U.S. $)
Brazil	$ 2.55
Canada	$17.31
Japan	$14.41
Mexico	$ 2.17
Spain	$12.65
United Kingdom	$13.42
United States	$15.45

(Source: The Universal Almanac 1993 p.345)

20. The table above shows the hourly compensation for production workers in 1991 in selected countries. The hourly compensation includes wages and all benefits. What type of graph would you make to display this data? Explain why.

21. The table above shows the hourly compensation for production workers in 1991 for selected countries. The hourly compensation includes all wages and all benefits. Create a graph to show the data in the table.

Lesson 1-2   Objective 2: Make a line graph and use a line graph to make predictions.

Dynamic Item

22. The hourly parking fees for the local airport from 1986 through 1996 are shown on the line graph below. Using this information, predict what the hourly parking fee was for 1997.

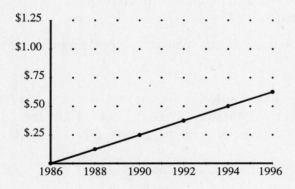

[A] $.62 per hour   [B] $1.00 per hour

[C] $.75 per hour   [D] $1.12 per hour

Dynamic Item

23. Draw a line graph to display the data in the table.

Month	Overcast Days
Jan	13
Feb	2
Mar	3
Apr	16
May	19

24. Suppose you wanted to graph the yearly population of your school during the past ten years. What type of graph would you use to display your data? Explain why.

CHAPTER 1

25. Data from each of the following surveys can best be represented on a line graph EXCEPT

    [A] the number of cars sold daily at a certain dealership during the past month.

    [B] the number of registered voters in the United States during the last five presidential elections.

    [C] the number of pupils who purchased lunch in the school cafeteria during a particular week.

    [D] the number of students absent versus those present on the first day of the school year.

26. The Capital School cafeteria sold 120 lunches on Monday, 101 lunches on Tuesday, 90 lunches on Wednesday, 119 lunches on Thursday, and 142 lunches on Friday. What type of graph would you create to show this data? Explain why.

27. The Capital School cafeteria sold 120 lunches on Monday, 101 lunches on Tuesday, 90 lunches on Wednesday, 119 lunches on Thursday, and 142 lunches on Friday. Display this information in a graph.

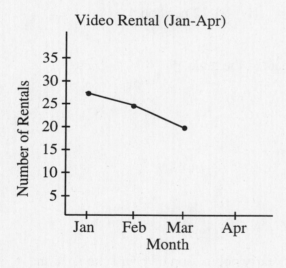

28. A clerk at a video store began creating a line graph to show the number of times a particular video was rented each month during the first four months of the year. However, he had to help a customer before he could complete the graph. Why did the clerk choose to show this data on the line graph in the figure above?

29.

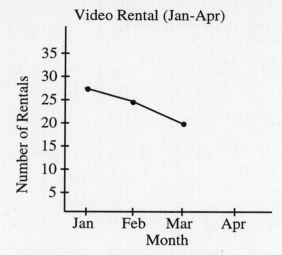

Video Rental (Jan-Apr)

A clerk at a video store began creating a line graph to show the number of times a particular video was rented each month during the first four months of the year. However, he had to help a customer before he could complete the graph. What information can you determine by studying the graph in the figure above? Predict what occurred during the last month.

Lesson 1-3   Objective 1: Use a spreadsheet to make graphs.

Dynamic Item

30.   In the spreadsheet below, what balance belongs in cell C3?

	A	B	C
	Date	Deposit / Checks	Balance
1	6 / 25		$255
2	6 / 28	−$310	−$55
3	6 / 29	$165	

[A] $310   [B] −$220   [C] $200   [D] $110

CHAPTER 1

Dynamic Item

31. What number goes in cell D4 in the spreadsheet below?

	A	B	C	D
1		Total	Males	Females
2	Southwest High School	1826	854	972
3	Marshall High School	1781		852
4	Washburn High School	1423	631	
5	Buena High School		532	508
6	Jefferson High School		748	812

	A	B	C
1	Hours Worked	Wages Earned by Otis	Money Earned by Tania
2	1	$5.00	$5.50
3	2	$10.00	$11.00
4	3	$15.00	$16.50
5	4	$20.00	$22.00
6	5	$25.00	$27.50

32. The spreadsheet above shows total pay for different hourly wages and hours worked. What is the value in cell C5?

33. What kind of graph would you draw to display the data in the spreadsheet above? Explain.

Lesson 1-3   Objective 2: Interpret and make double bar and double line graphs.

Dynamic Item

34. The comparison line graph compares rainfall, in centimeters, in Sydney and Canberra in March 1993. Determine which day the two cities had equal rainfall.

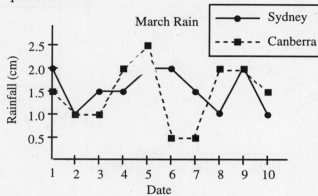

[A] March 4   [B] March 2   [C] March 3   [D] March 8

Dynamic Item

35. Display the data on a double bar graph.

Favorite Color	Boys	Girls
Purple	3	1
Green	8	7
Pink	4	9
Blue	2	6

CHAPTER 1

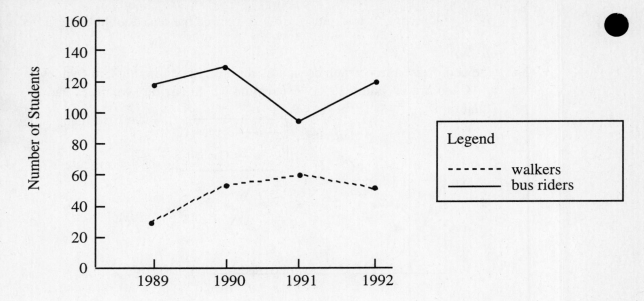

36. The line graph above shows the number of students who walked to Walker Elementary School and the number of students who rode buses to school each year from 1989 through 1992. What prediction can you make about the number of walkers versus bus riders in 1993?

37. The line graph above shows the number of students who walked to Walker Elementary School and the number of students who rode buses to the school each year from 1989 through 1992. What was the difference in the number of walkers and bus riders in 1991?

38. The line graph above shows the number of students who walked to Walker Elementary School and the number of students who rode the buses to the school each year from 1989 through 1992. In what year was the difference between number of walkers versus bus riders the greatest? What was the amount?

39. Which of the following types of information is not suited for display on a double bar graph?

    [A] The weekly interest rate for mortgages at a bank for the past year

    [B] Populations of boys and girls at three different schools

    [C] Number of records versus compact discs sold each week during a one-month period at Al's Music Den

    [D] Amount of hot and cold lunches sold each day in the school cafeteria during the first week of school

40. Which of the following types of information is suited for display on a double line graph?

    [A] All of these answers

    [B] Monthly sales of two different types of cars during a one-year period

    [C] Changes in Melody's height and weight from ages 5 to 10

    [D] Number of Democrats versus Republicans in the Senate during the past decade

Fiction Versus Non-Fiction Books

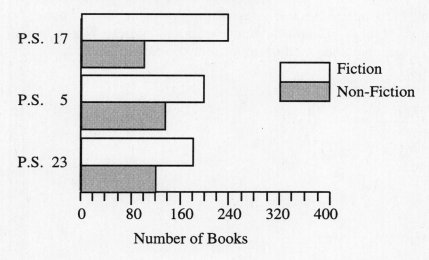

41. The double bar graph above compares the number of fiction and non-fiction books at three different elementary school libraries. What is the difference between the number of fiction and non-fiction books in the P.S. 23 school library according to the graph?

Fiction Versus Non-Fiction Books

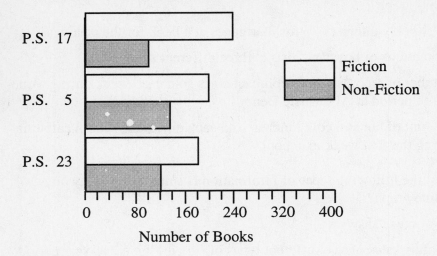

42. The double bar graph above compares the number of fiction and non-fiction books at three different elementary school libraries. Based on the graph, in which school is the difference between fiction and non-fiction books the greatest? What is the difference?

43. The double bar graph above compares the number of fiction and non-fiction books at three different elementary school libraries. Which school has the greatest combined total of fiction and non-fiction books according to the graph?

Day	Boys Absent	Girls Absent
1	14	12
2	11	18
3	19	11
4	13	15
5	25	25

44. The table above shows the number of boys and girls absent each day during the past week at a local high school. Make a graph to show this data. Explain why you chose to make a particular type of graph.

45.

Day	Boys Absent	Girls Absent
1	14	12
2	11	18
3	19	11
4	13	15
5	25	25

The table above shows the number of boys and girls absent each day during the past week at a local high school. Identify two conclusions illustrated by the data.

Lesson 1-4   Objective 1: Find the mean, the median, and the mode.

Dynamic Item
46. The number of patients treated at Dr. Jason's dentist office each day was recorded for eight days. Using the given data, find the mean, median, and mode for this sample.
8, 6, 14, 22, 21, 8, 10, 3

[A] 8, 9, 11.5   [B] 9, 11.5, 8   [C] 11.5, 9, 8   [D] 19, 11.5, 8

Dynamic Item
47. Find the mean, the median, and the mode of the data.
7, 6, 10, 6, 9, 6, 17, 14, 6

48. List the steps you would follow when identifying the mean of a set of numbers.

49. What is the difference between an outlier and a median?

50. What is the median of the following test grades: 95%, 92%, 78%, 88%, 80%, 95%, 100%, 96%, 88%, and 80%? Explain how you determined your answer.

51. For which of the following sets of data is the mode 5?

[A] 5, 0, 1, 2, 1, 4, 1, 0   [B] 3, 6, 5, 8, 1, 5, 9, 5

[C] 8, 4, 8, 8, 3, 5, 5, 1   [D] 2, 4, 1, 5, 7, 5, 2, 2

52. For which of the following sets of data is 14 an outlier?

[A] 12, 9, 11, 14, 14, 10, 16   [B] 18, 19, 14, 13, 14, 12, 14

[C] 2, 1, 0, 14, 3, 2, 0, 0   [D] 14, 18, 16, 16, 15, 17

Country	Average Hours Spent Socializing
France	8
Switzerland	7
Canada	11
Austria	9
Japan	3
Norway	13
Netherlands	10
United States	8
Finland	9

The table above shows the average number of hours an adult spends socializing each week in number of different countries.

53. What is the median of this data?

54. What is the mode of this data?

55. What is the mean of this data?

Country	Number of Vacation Days
United States	10
Italy	28
United Kingdom	22
Japan	10
Canada	10
Germany	18
Spain	22
Sweden	30

56. The table above shows the legal minimum number of vacation days enjoyed by workers in different countries. What is the median of this data?

57.

Country	Number of Vacation Days
United States	10
Italy	28
United Kingdom	22
Japan	10
Canada	10
Germany	18
Spain	22
Sweden	30

The table above shows the legal minimum number of vacation days enjoyed by workers in different countries. What is the difference between the mean and the mode of this data?

Lesson 1-4   Objective 2: Choose mean, median, or mode to describe data.

Dynamic Item

58. Bob was in charge of collecting contributions for the Food Bank. He received contributions of $10, $10, $20, $40, $70. The next potential contributor wanted to give an amount in line with the other contributions, so he asked "What is an acceptable amount to give?" If Bob uses the mode as the answer to the question, what amount will he tell the potential contributor?

[A] $ 10   [B] $ 20   [C] $ 70   [D] $ 30

Dynamic Item

59. You are in charge of collecting contributions for the Food Bank. You received contributions of $30, $40, $30, $50, $70. The next potential contributor wanted to give an amount in line with the other contributions, so he asked "What is an acceptable amount to give?" How much would you say is acceptable? Why?

60. Would you use the mean, median, or mode to determine the favorite subject of your math classmates? Explain why.

61.

Country	Average Hours Spent Socializing
France	8
Switzerland	7
Canada	11
Austria	9
Japan	3
Norway	13
Netherlands	10
United States	8
Finland	9

The table above shows the average number of hours an adult spends socializing each week in a number of different countries. Does this data contain an outlier? Explain your answer.

Lesson 1-5   Objective 1: Organize and display data using stem-and-leaf plots.

Dynamic Item

62. What data are represented by the stem-and-leaf plot below?

```
5 | 7 8 9
6 | 2 7 9
7 | 1 8
```

[A] 57, 58, 59, 62, 67, 69, 71, 78   [B] 75, 85, 95, 26, 76, 96, 17, 87

[C] 7, 8, 9, 2, 7, 9, 1, 8   [D] 57, 58, 59, 26, 76, 96, 17, 87

Dynamic Item

63. The list shows the final exam grades for Mr. Allen's science class.
76, 50, 79, 98, 91, 84, 72, 57, 65, 53,
64, 80, 75, 62, 77, 59, 56, 63, 61, 78
Construct a stem-and-leaf plot for the data.

64. Explain what the stems and leaves of a stem-and-leaf plot represent.

65. How can you determine the mode of data displayed on a stem-and-leaf plot? How can you identify the median?

Country	Percent of Households with Color Television
Australia	97%
Belgium	93%
Canada	69%
Denmark	95%
France	88%
Germany	94%
Greece	64%
Ireland	92%
Italy	88%
Japan	100%
Switzerland	91%
United States	97%

66. The table above shows the percent of households that own a color television set in a variety of different countries. Make a stem-and-leaf plot to display this data. Explain how you selected your stems and leaves.

67. The table above shows the percent of households that own a color television set in a variety of different countries. Find the median and mode of the data displayed in your stem-and-leaf plot.

```
10 | 0  0  0  0
 9 | 0  0  2  2  4  6  6  8  8
 8 | 0  4  4  6  6
   8 | 0   means 80
```

The stem-and-leaf plot above was created to show the test scores of a Science class.

68. What is the mode of this data?

    [A] 100   [B] 90   [C] 92   [D] 86

69.

```
10 | 0  0  0  0
 9 | 0  0  2  2  4  6  6  8  8
 8 | 0  4  4  6  6
```
        8 | 0   means 80

The stem-and-leaf plot above was created to show the test scores of a Science class. What is the mean of this data?

[A] 100　　　　　[B] 92.5　　　　[C] 87　　　　[D] 89.3

```
12 | 3  3  6  7  9  9
13 | 1  1  4  5  5
14 | 0  0  2  3  3  8  8  9
15 | 2  2  2  2  2  3  5  5  7
16 | 4  5  5  9  9
17 | 3  5
```
     12 | 3   means 12.3

The stem-and-leaf plot above shows kilometers walked during a benefit walk.

70. What do the stems represent? What do the leaves represent?

71. How many people participated in the walk? How many of the walkers traveled more than 14 kilometers?

72. What is the mean of this data? How does it compare to the median?

73.

Country	Active Recreational Time (Hours)
Austria	4.6
Canada	2.1
Finland	4.0
France	2.0
Japan	0.6
Netherlands	1.7
Norway	3.2
Switzerland	1.9
United Kingdom	1.2
United States	1.5

The table above shows the number of hours each week an average person spends on active recreational activities in a number of different countries. Make a stem-and-leaf plot to show this data.

Lesson 1-5   Objective 2: Find the range using stem-and-leaf plots.

Dynamic Item

74. The average number of days of thunderstorms at 16 Canadian airports are given.
5   11   21   6   24   25   28   29
15   16   2   21   3   26   2   28
a) Find the range.   b) Find the mean.

[A] a) range: 27 b) mean: 16.375   [B] a) range: 29 b) mean: 21

[C] a) range: 22 b) mean: 15   [D] a) range: 23 b) mean: 11.375

Dynamic Item

75. The average number of days of thunderstorms at 16 Canadian airports are given.
7   15   22   8   23   25   28   29
19   16   3   22   5   27   1   28
a) Construct a stem-and-leaf plot.
b) Find the mean and range.

76.

```
12 | 3  3  6  7  9  9
13 | 1  1  4  5  5
14 | 0  0  2  3  3  8  8  9
15 | 2  2  2  2  2  3  5  5  7
16 | 4  5  5  9  9
17 | 3  5
```

    12 | 3   means 12.3

The stem-and-leaf plot above shows kilometers walked during a benefit walk. Find the mode and the range of this data.

77.

Country	Active Recreational Time (Hours)
Austria	4.6
Canada	2.1
Finland	4.0
France	2.0
Japan	0.6
Netherlands	1.7
Norway	3.2
Switzerland	1.9
United Kingdom	1.2
United States	1.5

The table shows the number of hours each week an average person spends on active recreational activities in a number of different countries. Identify the mean and range of the data.

Lesson 1-6   Objective: Use logical reasoning to solve a problem.

Dynamic Item
78. Frederick, Ian, and Ho had 45 compact discs among them. Frederick gave 4 discs to Ian and Ho gave 5 discs to Frederick. Finally, Ian gave 6 discs to Frederick. They ended up with an equal number of discs. How many discs did each person start with?

   [A] Frederick: 22 discs, Ian: 13 discs, Ho: 10 discs

   [B] Frederick: 8 discs, Ian: 17 discs, Ho: 20 discs

   [C] Frederick: 15 discs, Ian: 15 discs, Ho: 15 discs

   [D] Frederick: 20 discs, Ian: 8 discs, Ho: 17 discs

Dynamic Item
79. In a marketing survey involving 1,000 randomly chosen people, it is found that 660 use brand P, 440 use brand Q, and 220 use both brands. How many people in the survey use brand Q and not brand P?

80. Explain what steps you would use to solve a problem using logical reasoning.

81. What is a logic table? How does it aid in solving a problem?

82. The top four scorers on a soccer team were Chris, Sean, Mia, and Erika. Mia scored one more goal than Erika. Chris scored half as many goals as Sean. Erika scored more goals than Chris but less than Sean. Organize this information in a logic table. Use the table to order these teammates from highest to lowest scorer.

83. The sum of all digits of a 5-digit number is 24. The digit in the ten-thousands' place is one-half the digit in the hundreds' place. The digit in the tens' place is one more than the digit in the ones' place. The digit in the ten-thousands' place is twice the value of the digit in the ones' place. If 2 is the digit in the ones' place, what is the number? Make a logic table to organize this information.

84. After taking five Math tests, Mila's mean test score is 91. His first score was 82%. His second test score was 13 points higher than his first but 5 points lower than his fourth test score. His fifth test score was 12 points lower than his fourth score. What was Mila's score on his third Math test?

85. The sum of the digits of a 5-digit number is 14. The ones' digit is one more than the thousands' digit. The tens' digit is one less than the thousands' digit. Three times the ones' digit is the value of the ten-thousands' digit. The hundreds' digit is five times the thousands' digit. If the number ends with a 2, what is the number?

86. After playing 5 games, the mean point total per game for the Charger football team is 19 points. In their fifth game, the Chargers scored one point less than the amount they scored in their opening game. In the fourth game of the season, the Chargers scored half as many points as the number scored in the fifth game, but one more than the points scored in the second game. If the Chargers scored 21 points in their opening game, how many points did the Chargers score in Game 3?

87. Martha's class is having a "Read-A-Thon" to raise money for a local charity. During the past month, Martha has read five more books than Theresa. Dan has read one less book than Martha, but half as many books as Scott. Eric has read one more book than Theresa. If Theresa has read 2 books, what is the mean number of books read by these students?

Year Women Received the Right to Vote

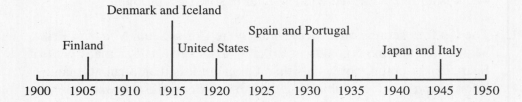

88. The time line above shows the year women got the right to vote in a number of different countries. Women in Germany received the right to vote before women in the United States but two years after women in the Soviet Union. If women in Iceland received the right to vote two years before women in the Soviet Union, when did German women acquire the right?

89. The time line above shows the year that women got the right to vote in a number of different countries. Seventy years after the Australian women, the Swiss women received the right to vote. The Italian women got their right 26 years before the Swiss women received their right to vote. In what year did the Australians receive the right to vote?

Lesson 1-7   Objective 1: Identify a random sample.

Dynamic Item
90. Which of the following is the best random sample for determining the number of houses in Sioux City with cedar siding?

   [A] Do a telephone survey of 1000 households across the city.

   [B] Phone all the houses in your neighborhood.

   [C] Interview people outside a hardware store.

   [D]   Mail a survey to 1000 households in each state.

Dynamic Item
91. Interview the people who wrote the ballot measure. Is this a random sample for predicting whether a state ballot measure will pass?

92. What is a random sample?

93. Why do statisticians often poll or survey a sample group instead of a certain population?

94. What is a biased question? How can a biased question affect the results of a survey?

95. A sales-clerk in a cosmetics department asks each customer who buys a particular brand of lipstick, "Which company makes the best type of lipstick?" Will the results of her survey be representative of all females? Explain.

96. Suppose you were conducting a survey to determine student evaluation of the quality of food served in a local school cafeteria. You decide to poll only those students who buy hot lunch on a particular day. Is your sample random? Explain.

97. Dana wants to identify the favorite professional baseball team of people in her community. She stood outside a local sporting goods store and asked every other person who entered, "What is the best professional baseball team?" Will the results of her survey be valid? Explain.

98. Ira wants to determine the fast food restaurant preferred by the majority of twelve-year-olds in his town. He decided to question all the twelve-year-olds who leave a particular hamburger restaurant. Is this a random sample? Explain.

CHAPTER 1

<u>Lesson 1-7</u>   Objective 2: Write survey questions.

Dynamic Item
99. Which survey question is unbiased?

 [A] "Which do you prefer with a meal, water or a syrupy sweet soft drink?"

 [B] "Which do you prefer with a meal, water or a soft drink?"

 [C] "Do you think mature students should be allowed to drive in spite of their age?"

 [D] "Do you think Jones is a good mayor in spite of his questionable character?"

Dynamic Item
100. Is the following survey question biased or unbiased?

 "Does the school board have a right to enforce a dress code?"

101. Give an example of a biased question and explain how it is biased.

102. Suppose you wanted to identify the soft drink most customers of the All Star Cafe order with dinner. How would you select a random sample? What question would you ask each member of your sample?

103. How would you go about surveying members of your community to identify the individual most citizens want to run for Mayor in the next election?

Lesson 1-8   Objective: Recognize how presentation of data can influence opinion.

Dynamic Item

104.   Both graphs represent the number of new clients signed up each month at Excelsior Realty. Which graph is misleading? Why?

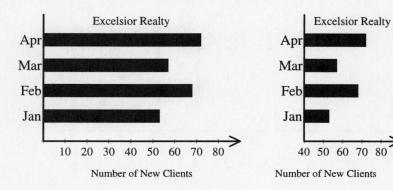

Dynamic Item

105.   Both graphs represent the number of new clients signed up each year at Sunnydays Insurance. Which graph is misleading? Why?

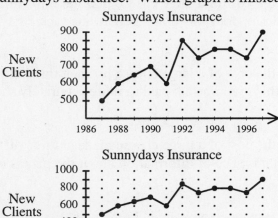

CHAPTER 1

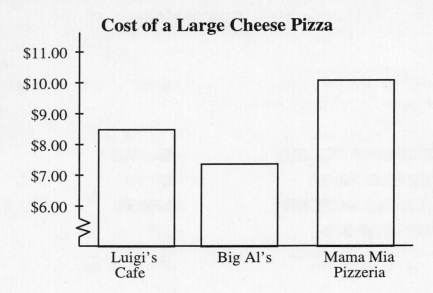

106. The graph above shows the cost of a large cheese pizza at three different restaurants. Explain how the size of the bars in the graph gives a false impression about the cost of a pizza at each restaurant.

107. The graph above shows the cost of a large cheese pizza at three different restaurants. Which restaurant does this graph benefit the most? Explain why.

108. The graph above shows the cost of a large cheese pizza at three different restaurants. How could this graph be adapted to more accurately show the information?

109. The graph above shows the cost of a large cheese pizza at three different restaurants. What important piece of information about the pizzas is missing from the graph?

110. Ted has the following scores on exams in his French class: 85, 79, 96, 95, 60, and 95. Should Ted use the mean, median, mode, or range of the exams to display his impressive knowledge of French?

    [A] mean   [B] mode   [C] range   [D] median

111. Ted has the following scores on exams in his French class: 85, 79, 96, 95, 60, and 95. Should Ted's French teacher use the mean, median, mode, or range of the exams to convince Ted he needs to study more regularly for his exams?

112. Ken asked 100 students "Should the lengthy school day which now extends for 7.5 hours be shortened to 6 hours?" Of the 50 responses he received, 48 were "yes". Are Ken's results unbiased? Explain.

113. A billboard advertises that a can of Coffee A is much less expensive than a can of Coffee B and therefore the consumer saves money by purchasing Coffee A. What additional information does a wise consumer need in order to evaluate the advertisement?

114. Mr. Stevens states "It is impossible to present misleading information in a graph that is drawn correctly." Do you agree with Mr. Stevens? Explain.

115. A federal law states that advertisers cannot print false claims in order to sell their products. How then is it possible for an advertisement to be misleading?

Lesson 1-9   Objective 1: Read scatter plots.

Dynamic Item
116. What type of relationship is shown by the scatter plot?

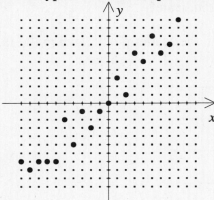

[A] negative   [B] positive   [C] not enough information   [D] none

CHAPTER 1

CHAPTER 1

Dynamic Item

117. The scatter plot shows how the length of the frost-free period in 15 western Canadian cities varies with their latitudes.

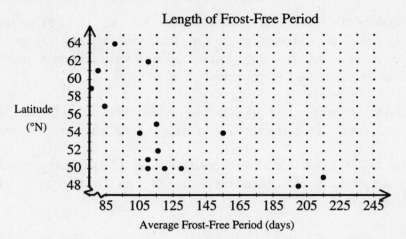

Length of Frost-Free Period

Latitude (°N)

Average Frost-Free Period (days)

The latitude of a city is 62°N. About how many frost-free days does this city have in a year?

118. What is a correlation? What does it indicate?

119. What type of correlation is shown in the scatter plot shown in the figure below? What does this indicate?

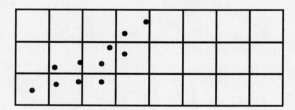

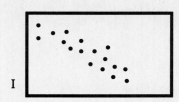 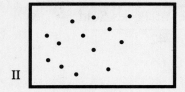 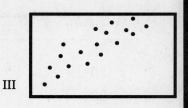

I   II   III

120. Kenneth created a scatter plot comparing the amount of calories he consumed each week with his body weight. Which of the three scatter plots above most likely represents this data?

[A] I   [B] II   [C] III   [D] none of these

121. Marcia created a scatter plot comparing the number of people who bought tickets to the school play and the amount of money raised by the event. Which of the three scatter plots above most likely represents this data?

[A] I   [B] III   [C] none of these   [D] II

122. Mrs. Stevens created a scatter plot comparing the test grades of boys and girls in her Math class. Which of the three scatter plots above most likely represents this data?

[A] I   [B] II   [C] III   [D] none of these

123. Describe the appearance of the points in a scatter plot having no correlation.

Temperature	Number of Cones Sold
76	42
80	66
84	72
88	87
92	90
96	92
100	94

124. The table above shows the relationship between temperature and the number of ice cream cones sold at a school cafeteria. Identify the labels and intervals you chose for the scatter plot. Explain why you selected each.

125. The table above shows the relationship between temperature and the number of ice cream cones sold at a school cafeteria. Identify any type of correlation shown in the scatter plot. What does it indicate?

126.

Student	Number of Movies Attended	Math Score
Brian	4	98%
Carole	1	88%
Dora	5	84%
Harry	7	100%
Juan	2	88%
Ilsa	3	98%
Maggie	6	100%

The table above compares the number of movies a student attended during the past six months and his/her score on a recent Math test. What type of correlation does the scatter plot show? What does this indicate?

Lesson 1-9   Objective 2: Draw scatter plots.

Dynamic Item

127. The table shows the study times and test scores for a number of students. Identify the scatter plot that corresponds to the given data.

Study Time (min)	11	14	20	24	29	31	33	40
Test Score	57	62	63	68	71	69	74	73

[A]

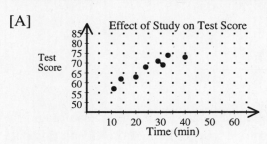

[B]

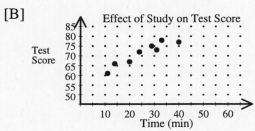

[C]

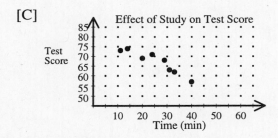

[D] none of these

Dynamic Item

128. Construct a scatter plot to show the relationship between minutes spent studying and test scores.

Study Time (min.)	13	18	25	32	36	39	42	45
Test Score	64	66	71	72	74	77	77	79

CHAPTER 1

129.

Temperature	Number of Cones Sold
76	42
80	66
84	72
88	87
92	90
96	92
100	94

The table above shows the relationship between temperature and the number of ice cream cones sold at a school cafeteria. Graph this data on a scatter plot.

130.

Student	Number of Movies Attended	Math Score
Brian	4	98%
Carole	1	88%
Dora	5	84%
Harry	7	100%
Juan	2	88%
Ilsa	3	98%
Maggie	6	100%

The table above compares the number of movies a student attended during the past six months and his/her score on a recent Math test. Make a scatter plot to display this data.

Lesson 2-1   Objective 1: Comparing and rounding decimals.

Dynamic Item
1. Arrange these decimal numbers from least to greatest: 0.02273, 0.03333, 0.01875, 0.06471.

    [A] 0.02273, 0.06471, 0.03333, 0.01875

    [B] 0.01875, 0.02273, 0.03333, 0.06471

    [C] 0.01875, 0.06471, 0.03333, 0.02273

    [D] 0.02273, 0.03333, 0.01875, 0.06471

Dynamic Item
2. Arrange from least to greatest:
    3.029   3.02   3.002

3. Explain how to compare and order decimals.

4. Write five numbers between the given numbers:
    a. 2.6 and 2.7
    b. 15 and 16

5. Which of the following decimals is represented by the number line shown below?

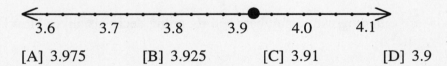

    [A] 3.975   [B] 3.925   [C] 3.91   [D] 3.9

6. During a gymnastics competition, five gymnasts received the following scores for their floor performance: 7.3, 8.75, 8.9, 8.7, 8.95. Which score was given to the third place gymnast?

    [A] 8.9   [B] 8.7   [C] 8.95   [D] 8.75

7. Using the symbols <, >, or =, compare and order the following: 0.810; 0.081; 0.8; 0.180; 0.82.

8. Given the digits 4, 8, 9, 2, 6 and using them only once, write the largest number less than 100.

9.

What changes would students make if they were principal for a day?	
Raise money for homeless	19.6%
Have a pizza party for lunch	19.9%
Cancel classes for the day	19.5%
New equipment / books	14.5%

Refer to the table above. If all of these decimals were rounded to the nearest whole amount, would this chart be helpful in comparing these changes? Explain.

Lesson 2-1   Objective 2: Round decimal numbers.

Dynamic Item
   10.   Round 0.452225 to the thousandths place.

   [A] 0.452   [B] 0.4522   [C] 0.4523   [D] 0.451

Dynamic Item
   11.   Round 0.338871 to the hundredths place.

   12.   A state charges 6 cents tax on each $1.00, so the proposed tax on $1.30 is
         7.8 cents. Explain what your actual tax on $1.30 is and why.

   13.   How are rounding whole numbers and rounding decimals alike? How do
         they differ?

   14.   Identify the place value of the underlined digit. Then round the decimal to
         the indicated place.
         a. 11.05<u>6</u>3
         b. 0.321<u>74</u>
         c. 67.0<u>0</u>6

15.

> What changes would students make if
> they were principal for a day?

Raise money for homeless	19.6%
Have a pizza party for lunch	19.9%
Cancel classes for the day	19.5%
New equipment / books	14.5%

Refer to the table above. Which two changes would students consider to be least important if they were principal for the day?

Lesson 2-2   Objective 1: Estimate sums and differences.

Dynamic Item
16. Estimate: $19.17 + $11.74

[A] $25   [B] $31   [C] $35   [D] $29

Dynamic Item
17. Estimate the difference using front-end estimation.   57.36
                                                          − 44.84

18. Explain how to use front-end estimation to estimate sums.

19. Describe the differences between the rounding method of estimating sums and the front-end method of estimating sums.

20. Which of the following choices show front-end estimation for the sum of: 9.327 + 5.72 + 4.132.

[A] 31   [B] none of these   [C] 19   [D] 19.36

21. Cluster to estimate: $142.25 + $141.75 + $141.59 + $142.15 = _____.

22. Use front-end estimation to find the sum:
a. 3.59 + 44.603 + 16.24
b. 13.40 + 36.61 + 125.042

Lesson 2-2   Objective 2: Estimate products and quotients.

Dynamic Item
23. Estimate. 49.4 × 61.71

Dynamic Item

24. Estimate. 43.1 ÷ 6.92

    [A] 7   [B] 60   [C] 6   [D] 35

25. Complete the following: You can estimate quotients by using _____.

26. Michael decided to estimate to find the quotient by changing 5,071 ÷ 62 to 5100 ÷ 60. Do you agree or disagree with his choices?

27. If the perimeter of a square is about 28 inches, which of the following could be the measurement of one of the sides?

    [A] 6.8   [B] 8.6   [C] 2.5   [D] 6.3

28. Use any estimation strategy to calculate. Tell which strategy you used and why.
    a. 163.28 − 120.1
    b. 19.22 × 185.13

29. You've earned $85.25. You'd like to buy several music videos. Estimate the number of videos you could purchase if each one costs $8.95.

30. Estimate the cost per ounce of the creamy peanut butter from the figure below. Decide which product is more economical. Why?

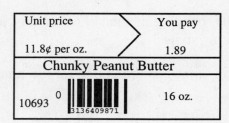

Unit price	You pay
11.8¢ per oz.	1.89
Chunky Peanut Butter	
10693 0 3136409871	16 oz.

Unit price	You pay
1.59 per lb.	1.99
Creamy Peanut Butter	
10732 0 3146509871	20 oz.

31. Look at the table below. Estimate the average score received by the Main Street Diving Team in the regional competition.

Member	Score
A	9.25
B	8.75
C	6.95
D	5.45
E	9.75

Lesson 2-3   Objective 1: Adding and subtracting decimals.

Dynamic Item
32. Subtract: $8.1 - 0.316$

   [A] 6.784   [B] 8.784   [C] 7.784   [D] 7.694

Dynamic Item
33. Add: $0.14 + 535 + 7.5 + 0.314$

34. Which of the addition properties would you use to find the sum of $0.45 + 30.05 + 10.25$ mentally?

35. Compare. Which of the following is a true statement?

   [A] $12.45 + 2.315 = 10.24 + 4.525$ [B] none of these

   [C] $0.01 < 0.0028 + 0.0072$ [D] $3.118 + 0.58 < 1$

36. If the sides of a rectangle measure 13.064 ft and 9.25 ft, what is the perimeter of the rectangle?

37. Compare. Use >, <, =. $145.2 - 95.63$ __ $163.04 - 85.236$.

38. At the Colorado ski meet, the French Canadian skier jumped 89.5234 meters. The American skier jumped 90.06 meters. How much farther did the American skier jump than the Canadian skier?

39. The Carlton family spent $1200.95 on air fare, $858.35 on hotels, $540.00 for meals, $52.64 for gifts and $42.05 for miscellaneous items on their recent vacation. What was the total cost of their trip?

40. Refer to the chart below. What is the difference between the percent of homes using natural gas and the homes using electricity and fuel oil?

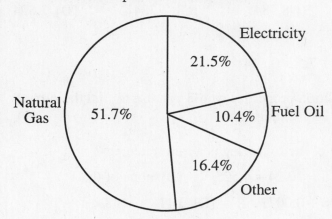

How People Heat Their Homes

41. Refer to the chart below. What is the difference between the average imagined age of people in the following age groups?
a. over 54 and 35 - 54 group
b. over 54 and 18 - 34 group
c. 35 - 54 and 18 - 34 group

| How old people say they feel relative to their real age: | |
Real Age Group	Average Imagined Age
18 - 34	1.5 years older
35 - 54	6.2 years younger
over 54	10.5 years younger

Lesson 2-3   Objective 2: Use the properties of addition.

Dynamic Item
42. Which property is illustrated by the following statement?
47.9 + (85 + 10) = (47.9 + 85) + 10

[A] addition property of zero   [B] commutative property of addition

[C] distributive property of addition

[D] associative property of addition

Dynamic Item

43. Is the equation true or false? If so, what addition property does it illustrate?
    $(61.5 + 43.2) + 0 = 61.5 + 43.2$

44. Explain how using the addition properties can help you solve a problem mentally.

45. Explain the commutative property of addition. Can this property be applied to subtraction problems? Explain.

46. How can the identity property be used to find $65.021 - 65.021 + 82.6514$?

47. Which of the following illustrates use of the associative property of addition?

    [A] $76 + ? = 52 + 76$ [B] $? + 17 = 17$

    [C] $5 \times (3 + 8) = ? + 40$ [D] $7 + (4 + 9) = ? + 9$

Lesson 2-4   Objective: Solve problems that have too much or too little information.

Dynamic Item

48. Thomas worked 6 hours more than Henry during the month of May. What more do you need to know to find how many hours Thomas worked in May?

    [A] the number of hours Thomas worked in June

    [B] the number of hours Thomas worked in April

    [C] the number of hours Henry worked in May

    [D] the number of hours Henry worked in June

Dynamic Item

49. Charles is purchasing prizes for the 5 races at the class picnic. There are 29 students in his class. He wants to have a first, second, and third place prize for each category. The prizes must cost less than $16 each. What information is **not** needed to find out how much Charles will spend?

50. In your own words, summarize the steps for solving a word problem.

51. Why is it necessary to focus on the information given when solving a word problem?

CHAPTER 2

52. Write a word problem which could be answered with some of the following information: Jessi plays piano 30 minutes each time she practices. Jessi practiced piano this week on Monday, Tuesday, and Thursday. Jessi's soccer team practices on Wednesday and Friday for $1\frac{1}{2}$ hours each day.

53. In the school fund-raising marathon, Robert walked 6.3 miles. Marie walked 4.15 miles and Scott walked 5.1 miles. How much farther did Robert walk than Scott?

    [A] 2.25 miles   [B] 2.15 miles   [C] 0.95 mile   [D] 1.2 miles

54. The local book store has a book sale every October. Mystery books cost $1.50, science-fiction cost $2.25, biographies cost $3.75, and reference books cost $5.95. How much will Alana have to pay for the books she will purchase?

    [A] $14.00   [B] $12.45   [C] not enough information   [D] $13.45

55. What information in the following problem is not necessary? Peter has 5 brothers and 5 sisters. Peter earned $50.00 last summer mowing lawns. If Peter worked for 5 hours each day for 5 weeks, how much did he average each week?

56. Solve, if possible. Two of the least populated cities in Virginia are Richmond and Lexington. There are about 14,232 people living in Richmond and Lexington. How many people are living in Lexington?

57. The Smith family would like to donate peanut butter sandwiches for a baseball fund-raiser day. They will need to purchase either a 16 oz jar of chunky peanut butter for $1.89 or a 20 oz jar of creamy peanut butter for $1.99. If they need 30 oz, how much could it cost to purchase the peanut butter?

58. The youngest president of the United States was John F. Kennedy. He was the 35th president. He was born on May 29, 1917, and died November 22, 1963. He became president at the age of 43. How old was he when he died?

59. Decide whether the table below provides enough information to solve the problem. If so, find the solution. If not, tell what information is needed. Only 7 of 184 U.N. member governments have paid their debts in full. What is the total amount of money owed by the U.N. member governments?

Here's what the top 5 countries owe:	
U.S.	$ 571
Russian Federation	$ 81
South Africa	$ 53
Ukraine	$ 34
Brazil	$ 31
	(millions)

Lesson 2-5   Objective 1: Multiply decimals.

Dynamic Item
60. Multiply: 0.006 × 8.4

   [A] 0.0504   [B] 5.04   [C] 0.00504   [D] 0.504

Dynamic Item
61. Multiply: 5.11 × 0.011

62. Suzanne needed material for her school project. She bought 2.75 yards of material selling for $3.82 a yard. What was the total cost of the material? Round to the nearest cent.

   [A] $105.50   [B] $11.53   [C] $9.50   [D] $10.51

63. If meat costs $3.29 per pound at the grocery store, what is the cost of 0.59 lb? Round to the nearest cent.

64. Mrs. Simons purchased 14 cans of mixed fruit at $0.85 each, 16 cans of light peaches at $0.79 each and 12 cans of light pears at $0.79 each. What was the total cost of her purchases?

65. Water makes up about 0.6 of the weight of the human body. How much water is contained in a person who weighs 127.5 lb?

CHAPTER 2

66. Which of the numbers below is the product of 9.6 x 0.3?

    [A] 28.8   [B] 0.288   [C] 2.88   [D] 288

67. Which of the multiplications below has the product 0.081?

    [A] 2.7 x 0.3   [B] 0.27 x 0.3   [C] 27 x 0.03   [D] 0.27 x 3

68. One cup of skim milk contains 0.3 g of fat. How much fat is in 2.5 qt?

Lesson 2-5   Objective 2: Use properties of multiplication.

Dynamic Item
69. What property is illustrated by the fact that $71.7 \cdot 1 = 71.7$?

    [A] zero property for multiplication

    [B] associative property for multiplication

    [C] identity property for multiplication

    [D] commutative property of multiplication

Dynamic Item
70. What property is illustrated by the fact that $(82.6 \cdot 72.7) \cdot 0 = 0$?

71. Explain what is meant by the statement: "There are several ways to indicate multiplication."

72. Complete: When multiplying two decimals, the sum of the decimal places in the factors is _____.

73. How are the properties of addition and multiplication alike? How are they different?

74. Explain the following property: $(ab) \times c = a \times (bc)$.

Lesson 2-6   Objective 1: Divide decimals by whole numbers.

Dynamic Item
75. $1.23 \div 3 =$

    [A] None of these   [B] 0.401   [C] 0.41   [D] 4.1   [E] 4.01

Dynamic Item
76. Divide: $86)\overline{0.602}$

77. Christine's family drove 523.4 mi from home to Lake Paradise. The trip took about 10 h. What was the average driving speed of the family car during this journey? Round to the nearest tenth.

78. What is the average percentage of claims settled for the companies in the chart below with the best records?

Businesses with the Best and Worst records for setting complaints filed with the Better Business (Percentage of claims settled)			
Best		Worst	
Book - record club	90.8%	Carpet Cleaners	32.7%
Products ordered from newspapers / magazines	88.4%	Paint / Wallpaper Contractors	44.8%
Banks	87.0%	Paving Contractors	46.5%

79. What is the average winning percentage of the top 5 football teams in the chart below?

Top high school football teams in the country for the past two seasons		
Team	Record	Percentage
Wilton	18 - 0	1.000
Arlington	17 - 1	.944
Bishop	17 - 1	.944
Hanson	16 - 2	.889
Cambridge	16 - 2	.889

80. A car has traveled 135.75 miles in 3 hours. What was its average speed in miles per hour?

81. Suppose you paid $4.14 for 6 pounds of bananas. About how much was the price per pound? Explain how you got your answer.

82. You have 3.5 liters of orange juice to share with your class. Counting you, there are 22 students. How much juice will each classmate get?

CHAPTER 2

Lesson 2-6   Objective 2: Divide decimals by decimals.

Dynamic Item
83. 0.4)‾1.08

   [A] 2.7   [B] 0.27   [C] 2.3   [D] 0.207

Dynamic Item
84. Divide: 46.292 ÷ 6.52

85. If a car traveled 275 miles in 5.25 hours, how far would it travel in 1 hour?
     Round to the nearest tenth.

   [A] 0.524   [B] 52.3   [C] 52.4   [D] 0.523

86. If tomatoes cost $1.06 per pound, and you paid $0.93, how many pounds
     did you purchase?

87. Which number below is the quotient of 6.25 ÷ 0.5?

   [A] 12.5   [B] 125   [C] 0.125   [D] 1.25

88. Write an exercise dividing a decimal by a decimal that has the quotient 30.

89. A stack of quarters is 5.92 cm high. The thickness of 1 quarter is 0.16 cm.
     How many quarters are in the stack?

Lesson 2-7   Objective 1: Investigate division using a calculator.

Dynamic Item
90. Use a calculator to find the quotient. Use a bar to show repeating
     decimals.
     7 ÷ 33

   [A] $0.\overline{22}$ [B] $0.0\overline{21}$ [C] $0.\overline{21}$ [D] 0.2121

Dynamic Item
91. Use a calculator to find the quotient. Use a bar to show repeating decimals.
     66 ÷ 90

92. Which of the following fractions represent these decimals:
     (0.11, 0.22, 0.33)?

   [A] $\frac{1}{9}, \frac{2}{9}, \frac{3}{9}$ [B] $\frac{1}{11}, \frac{1}{22}, \frac{1}{33}$ [C] $\frac{1}{11}, \frac{2}{11}, \frac{3}{11}$ [D] none of these

93. Which of the following decimals represents the fraction $\frac{5}{11}$?

    [A] 0.515   [B] 0.511   [C] 0.45   [D] 0.11

94. What will you see displayed on a calculator when you convert a fraction to a repeating decimal?

95. Use a calculator.

    a. Express as decimals: $\frac{1}{9}, \frac{2}{9}, \frac{3}{9}, \frac{4}{9}$

    b. Name the next two decimals without using the calculator for $\frac{5}{9}, \frac{6}{9}$.

96. Divide. Use a bar to show repeating decimals:
    a. $1 \div 0.9$
    b. $2 \div 0.9$
    c. $5 \div 6$

97. Write each mixed number as a decimal:
    a. $2\frac{1}{3}$

    b. $3\frac{3}{5}$

    c. $5\frac{5}{6}$

CHAPTER 2

98. Look at the table below. Find the missing numbers to complete the table.

	Dividend	Divisor	Quotient
a.	30	100	
b.	30	10	
c.	30	1	
d.	30	0.1	
e.	30	0.01	
f.	30		
g.	30		
h.	30		
i.	30		
j.	30		

Lesson 2-7   Objective 2: Classify decimals as repeating or terminating.

Dynamic Item
99. Find the quotient.
    $9 \div 18$
    Is the quotient a terminating or repeating decimal?

Dynamic Item
100. Find the quotient.
     $9 \div 15$
     Is the quotient a terminating or repeating decimal?

     [A] $0.\overline{6}$ repeating   [B] 0.4 terminating

     [C] $0.58\overline{3}$ repeating   [D] 0.6 terminating

101. Define, in your own words, a repeating decimal.

102. Define, in your own words, a terminating decimal.

103. What is true of fractions whose denominators are 3 and 9?

104. Write the fractions as decimals. Use a bar to show repeating decimals.

a. $\dfrac{2}{3} =$ _____

b. $\dfrac{5}{6} =$ _____

c. $\dfrac{41}{99} =$ _____

105. Which decimals in the figure below are repeating decimals?

Fraction	Decimal
$\dfrac{1}{10}$	0.1
$\dfrac{1}{11}$	$0.\overline{09}$
$\dfrac{1}{12}$	$0.08\overline{33}$
$\dfrac{1}{13}$	0.0769231
$\dfrac{1}{14}$	0.0714286
$\dfrac{1}{15}$	$0.0\overline{66}$
$\dfrac{1}{16}$	0.0625
$\dfrac{1}{17}$	0.0588235
$\dfrac{1}{18}$	$0.0\overline{55}$

Lesson 2-8   Objective 1: Use order of operations.

Dynamic Item
106. Write the missing operation signs to make the following statement true.

  1.9 ⑦ 10.2 ⑦ 3.4 = 4.9

  [A] $1.9 + 10.2 \div 3.4 = 4.9$ [B] $1.9 \div 10.2 + 3.4 = 4.9$

  [C] $1.9 \times 10.2 \div 3.4 = 4.9$ [D] $1.9 - 10.2 + 3.4 = 4.9$

Dynamic Item
107. Simplify: $5.3 \times 4.9 + 1.2 \div 3.0$

108. Explain how the distributive property helps you solve a problem such as 5×64 mentally.

109. How is the left side of this equation different from the right side?
  $6(2.3) + 6(1.4) = 6(2.3 + 1.4)$

110. How can you explain $2(2 + 6) = 2(2) + 2(6)$? You may use pictures.

111. Explain how you could use the distributive property in at least two ways to calculate $5(120.5)$.

112. Eric spends 2.5 hours each weekday on his homework and 1.25 hours each weekday practicing soccer. Which of the following equations shows the total amount of time he spends on both activities for 5 days?

  [A] $5(1.50) = 7.50$ [B] $5(1.25) + 5(2.5) = 19.75$

  [C] $5(1.25 + 2.5) = 18.75$ [D] $5(3.75) = 20$

113. If Michele spends $1.60 for lunch and $0.80 for snacks each day, what does she spend in 5 days? Use the distributive property.

114. Solve and draw a picture to illustrate: $(5 \times 4) + (8 \times 4) = (5 + 8)4$

115. The soccer team requires each player to sell 6 packs of ball-point pens, 5 packs of pencils and 4 packs of lined paper. If there are 15 players on each team, how many packs of pens, pencils, and paper does a team sell? Use the distributive property.

116. Four students each ordered the following for lunch: chicken nuggets--$2.89, french fries--$1.19, juice--$1.09. Use the distributive property to find the total cost of lunch.

117. Use the table below. Use the distributive property to determine the total cost of 6 bags of each type of snack.

Snack	Cost
popcorn	$2.87
rice cakes	$3.07
granola bars	$3.25

118. Use the table below. Use the distributive property to determine the total cost of buying 4 jars of each type of pickle.

Pickles	
Garlic	$2.50
Sweet	$3.02
Dill	$2.49
Bread & Butter	$2.67

Lesson 2-8   Objective 2: Use the distributive property.

Dynamic Item
119. $4 \times (8 + 3) =$

[A] $(4 \times 8) + 3$ [B] $(4 \times 8) + (4 \times 3)$

[C] $(4 + 8) + 3$ [D] $(4 + 8) \times (4 + 3)$

Dynamic Item
120. What number would make the number sentence true?
$? \times (15 + 3) = (2 \times 15) + (2 \times 3)$

121. Find the missing number: $8.4(1.5 + 2.3) = 12.6 + ?$

[A] 8.45   [B] 14.67   [C] 19.32   [D] 25.33

Lesson 3-1   Objective 1: Evaluate variable expressions.

Dynamic Item
1. Evaluate $20 + s$ for $s = 6$.

    [A] −26   [B] 26   [C] 14   [D] −14

Dynamic Item
2. Evaluate $6d + 3e$, where d is 7.3 and e is 7.5.

3. Complete: "To evaluate an expression with a variable, you... ."

4. Can a number such as 23 be expressed as xy if $x = 2$, $y = 3$? Explain.

5. Evaluate the expression: Let $x = 4$, $y = 2$. $x^2 y^2$.

    [A] 64   [B] 32   [C] 12   [D] 16

6. Explain how to evaluate the expression $3x^2 - 5$ for $x = 2$.

7. The length of a rectangle is represented by L ft and the width is 2 ft less than the length. Evaluate the expression for finding the perimeter when $L = 5$ ft ($P = 2L + 2W$).

8. Evaluate the expression: $\dfrac{a^2 + b^2 - c^2}{2ab}$ when $a = 4$, $b = 3$, and $c = 5$.

Lesson 3-1   Objective 2: Write variable expressions.

Dynamic Item
9. Write as a variable expression: a number plus 17

    [A] $x - 17$ [B] $17x$ [C] $17 - x$ [D] $x + 17$

Dynamic Item
10. Write a word phrase for the expression $2n$.

11. Define "variable expression" in your own words.

12. Use words to explain the following variable expression: $10x - 5$

13. Use the following symbols to create a variable expression. Explain your variable expression in words: 4, -, 2, +, *s*, 8

14. Write a variable expression for: "two less than six times a larger number divided by two times a smaller number".

15. Write each variable expression in words:

    a. $\dfrac{n+2}{2}$

    b. $n - 3$

    c. $2n + 1$

16. If a major league baseball player chews 50 pieces of gum per game, write a variable expression to show how many pieces of gum he might chew in "*n*" number of games.

Lesson 3-2   Objective 1: Graph and order integers.

Dynamic Item

17. Write the integers 3, –13, 19, 17, –1, in order from least to greatest.

    [A] –13, –1, 3, 17, 19   [B] –13, –1, 3, 19, 17

    [C] 19, 17, 3, –1, –13   [D] 3, –13, 19, 17, –1

Dynamic Item

18. Graph –5, +5, –2, and +8 on a number line.

19. A weather map for Alaska shows the temperature in Anchorage to be -10°F and for Juneau to be +10°F. Explain how these temperatures are different and how they are alike.

20. Explain what is meant by the "absolute value of an integer." Can -5 be the absolute value of a number? Explain why or why not.

21. Which expression is NOT equivalent to the opposite of +7?

    [A] –7   [B] $-|7|$ [C] $-(-|-7|)$ [D] $-|-7|$

CHAPTER 3

<u>Lesson 3-2</u>   Objective 2: Find the opposite and absolute value of an integer.

Dynamic Item
22. Evaluate. $|3|$

   [A] 3   [B] −3   [C] $\frac{1}{3}$ [D] $-\frac{1}{3}$

Dynamic Item
23. Find the opposite of 161.

24. Replace each ☐ with the closest integer to the given integer to make a true statement.

   a. $-19 <$ ☐

   b. $171 >$ ☐

   c. $-3 >$ ☐

   d. ☐ < 0

25. Explain how using a number line can help you to order a set of integers.

26. What is the sum of: $|-8| + |-7| + 3$

   [A] 12   [B] 4   [C] 18   [D] 59

27. Draw a number line and graph the following points: -2, 10, -5, 7, 0.

28. Name the integer represented by each of the points A, B, C and D on the number line in the figure below.

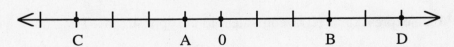

29. Suppose you mow a neighbor's lawn and receive a payment of $5.00. Your friend helps and you pay her $2.00. Draw a number line to represent these 2 amounts as they relate to you.

30. The temperature in St. Louis is -5° F in the early morning. The weather man predicts it will be +10°F by late afternoon. Draw a number line to find the difference between these two temperatures.

31. The graph below shows the profit or loss for the Bob's Bike Repair company. To show a loss, it uses a bar that goes below zero. Find the difference between January and June for profit/loss.

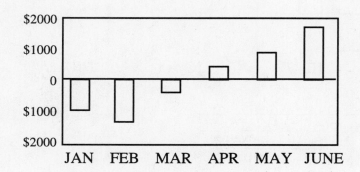

32. The chart below shows the lowest recorded temperatures for February in selected cities. Using the data, find the difference between the February lowest temperature in Wichita and Miami.

Record Low Temperatures (Feb.)	
City	Temperature (°F)
Wichita	- 21°
Boston	- 4°
Little Rock	- 5°
Portland	- 3°
Miami	32

Source: U.S. Statistical Abstract, 1992

Lesson 3-3   Objective 1: Use models to add integers.

Dynamic Item

33. Use a number line to help you find the sum of: −1 + 17

   [A] −16   [B] 18   [C] 16   [D] −18

Dynamic Item

34. Use tiles to find the sum. −6 + 8

CHAPTER 3

CHAPTER 3

35. Explain how algebra tiles are combined to make zero pairs.

36. What integer is represented by 18 positive tiles and 22 negative tiles?

    [A] 22   [B] 4   [C] 40   [D] -4

37. Which integer is represented by the following set of algebra tiles?

    [A] -1   [B] 7   [C] +1   [D] 0

38.

Extreme Elevations in Selected States		
State	Name	Elevation
AK	Mt. McKinley	6,198 m
HI	Puu Wekiu	4,208 m
SD	Big Stone Lake	295 m
LA	New Orleans	− 2 m
CA	Death Valley	− 86 m

Source: <u>U.S. Statistical Abstract 1992</u>

The table above gives the elevation above or below sea level of selected places in the United States, including the lowest and highest places. Find the difference between the elevation of Mt. McKinley and Death Valley.

39. Explain how the two addition models shown below are alike and how they are different.

Lesson 3-3   Objective 2: Use absolute value to add integers.

Dynamic Item
40.   Add: −20 + 2

[A] 22   [B] −22   [C] −18   [D] 18

Dynamic Item
41.   Add: 3 + (−13)

42.   Find two integers whose sum is 24. Can you find other pairs of integers whose sum is 24? Give at least three other examples.

43.   The temperature in your town is 29°F. The radio announcer says that the temperature will drop 30 degrees. Which sum can be used to compute the predicted temperature?

[A] −29 + 30   [B] −30 + (−29)   [C] −30 + 29   [D] 30 + (−29)

44.   During the day, the temperature in Nome, Alaska rose 23°. The low temperature for the day was -38°F. What was the high temperature for the day?

[A] 30°   [B] 15°   [C] -61°   [D] -15°

45.   Suppose your friend borrowed $10.00 from you on Saturday, then, on Monday borrowed $3.00 more. Tuesday, she paid you $2.00. Use an equation with absolute values to compute what your friend now owes you.

46.   A rocket support is removed 3 minutes before take-off. The countdown is started 10 minutes before takeoff. How long after the countdown is begun, does the support get removed?

CHAPTER 3

47. The water level indicator measures the rise and fall in meters of the water level at a reservoir. The 0 on the gauge indicates the normal water level in the reservoir. What was the water level at the end of the summer? at the end of the winter? Find the difference between these two levels.

Water Level Indicator

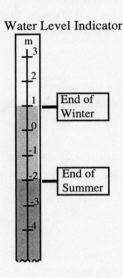

48. A Canadian student used the graph to track temperatures in his home town for a week. The solid line connects the daily high temperatures. The dashed line connects the daily low temperatures. What are the high and low temperatures for Monday? Explain how you can use algebra tiles to find the difference between the high and low on Monday. On what day was there the smallest difference between the high and low temperatures? the largest difference?

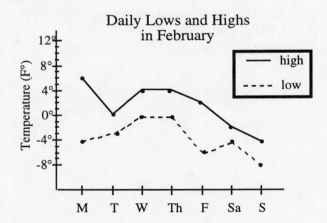

Chapter 3: Integers and Equations

Lesson 3-4   Objective 1: Use models to subtract integers.

Dynamic Item
  49. Which model shows the difference 1 − 2?

[A] 3   [B] 1

[C] 〔model〕 −3   [D] 〔model〕 −1

Dynamic Item
  50. Draw a model to find the difference 3 − 5.

  51. Jamie borrowed $5.00 from you, then he borrowed $3.00 a few days later. Which of the following may be used to compute Jamie's total debt?

[A] 5 − 3   [B] −3 + 5   [C] −5 + 3   [D] −5 + (−3)

  52. Find the change in altitude when you go from one place which is 15 feet below sea level to a place which is 95 feet above sea level.

  53. In a game, Shawn is in debt 35 points. How many points must he make to have a score of 150 points?

Lesson 3-4   Objective 2: Use a rule to subtract integers.

Dynamic Item
  54. (+13) − (−3) =

[A] 10   [B] −16   [C] −10   [D] 16

Dynamic Item
  55. Subtract: 8 − 19

  56. Suppose your friend's calculator is broken. The minus key is the only key that doesn't work. Explain to your friend why she can still use her calculator to subtract.

  57. Explain the 2 different uses of the symbol "−" in numerical expressions.

  58. Is it true that subtraction problems can be reordered? Explain with examples.

  59. Write a rule for subtracting integers. Write three subtraction examples. Apply the rule to each of the examples and explain how you can find each difference.

60. Which of the following statements is always true?
I. A negative integer plus a negative integer equals a negative integer.
II. A negative integer minus a negative integer equals a negative integer.

    [A] II only   [B] Both I and II   [C] I only   [D] Neither I nor II

61. Meghan had $12.00 at the beginning of the week. At the end of the week, she was $5.00 in debt. How much did she spend during the week?

62. On a given day, the lowest temperature in the United States was −12°F at Chandalar, Alaska. The highest temperature was 93°F at Fort Myers, Florida. What is the difference between these two temperatures?

63. Use the chart below to determine how many passes the Wawasee High School football team has attempted.

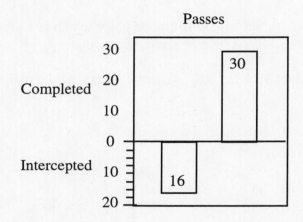

64. Refer to the figure below. The altitude of Death Valley is –282 feet. What is the altitude of Mt. Whitney?

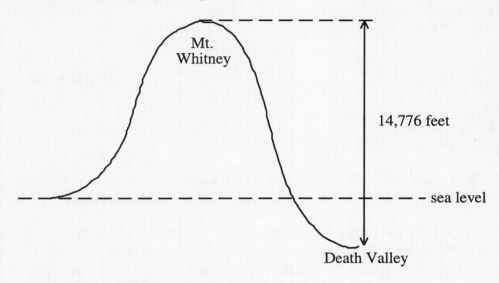

Lesson 3-5 Objective 1: Multiply integers.

Dynamic Item
65. Multiply: –6 · (–53)

   [A] –318   [B] 328   [C] –328   [D] 318

Dynamic Item
66. Multiply: –6 · (–6)

67. Explain the rule for multiplying two negative integers. Use a number line or algebra tiles to illustrate three examples. Make a sketch of your work.

68. Two integers have a product of –42. How many different pairs whose product is –42 also have a sum whose absolute value is 1?

   [A] 2   [B] more than 2   [C] none   [D] 1

69. Your local gas stations are having a price war. During the past 7 days they have lowered the price of regular, unleaded gas by $0.02 a day. What is the total change in the price?

70. You are playing a computer trivia game. Each right answer is worth 100 points. For each second that passes before the answer is entered, 5 points are deducted. You answer the first 5 questions correctly. You take 90 seconds total. What is your score?

Lesson 3-5   Objective 2: Divide integers.

Dynamic Item
71. Divide. $-10 \div (-2)$

[A] -5 [B] $-\dfrac{1}{5}$ [C] $\dfrac{1}{5}$ [D] 5

Dynamic Item
72. Divide. $(-330) \div (-6)$

73. Explain the rules for dividing signed integers. How are they alike or different than the rules for multiplying two signed integers?

74. You decide to buy a stock only if it shows an overall increase for the next thirty days. The first 10 days it has an average increase of $0.30. The next 10 days it has an average decrease of $0.45. The last 10 days it has an average increase of $0.25. Do you buy the stock? Explain your answer.

75. The temperature on Mars reaches 27°C during the day and −125°C at night. What is the average temperature?

[A] $-49°$C   [B] $+76°$C   [C] $+49°$C   [D] $-76°$C

76. Complete the spreadsheet below for your club's annual sale of greeting cards.

	Boxes		
	100	200	400
Variable cost per box	$50	a. ☐	$200
Fixed Cost	b. ☐	$200	$200
Total Cost	c. ☐	$300	d. ☐

77. A plane descends at a rate of 30 feet per second. If the plane is at an altitude of 1500 feet, how many seconds will it take the plane to reach an altitude of 300 feet?

78. Your cousin is coming for a visit. She writes and asks what the average temperature will be for her visit. You find that last year, for the same week, the temperatures were −7°F, 3°F, 12°F, −9°F, −10°F, 2°F and −5°F. What was the average temperature for that week?

79. Find the average temperature for the week, using the data in the graph below.

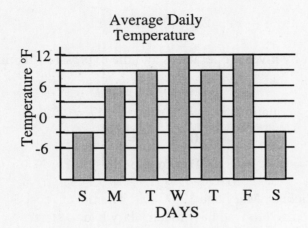

80. Use models to solve $w - 6 = 12$.

Lesson 3-6   Objective 1: Use models to solve addition and subtraction equations.

Dynamic Item
80. Use models to solve $w - 6 = 12$.

    [A] 6   [B] 18   [C] −18   [D] −11

Dynamic Item
81. Use models to solve $3 + 2 = f$.

82. Explain what is meant by the expression "keeping an equation balanced."

83. Your friend weighs 84 pounds and you weigh 91 pounds. Explain how you and your friend can keep a see-saw in balance.

84. Explain when using algebra tiles may not be practical to solve a problem. Write at least one example.

Lesson 3-6   Objective 2: Use inverse operations to solve addition and subtraction equations.

Dynamic Item
85. Solve: $4 + y = 1$

[A] 4   [B] –4   [C] –3   [D] –6

Dynamic Item
86. Solve. a) $d + 14 = 27$ b) $e - 11 = 2.9$ c) $f + 5 = 11.7$

87. Explain what is meant by inverse operations and the expression "isolate the variable."

88. Which of the following equations is equivalent to $x - 17 = -22$?

[A] $x - 15 = -20$ [B] $x - 15 = 20$

[C] $x - 19 = -20$ [D] None of these

89. After buying 2 raffle tickets, Mary had $3.00 left. The tickets cost $4.00. Which equation can be used to find how much Mary had to start?

[A] $2 + x = 4$ [B] $-3 + x = 4$ [C] $6 + x = 4$ [D] $-4 + x = 3$

90. A lab technician reduced the heat under a sample by 17°C to 7°C. Write an equation and find the original temperature.

91. A lab is using 155 mice to test a vaccine. Kim has injected 55 mice with a 5 mg dose and 42 mice with a 15 mg dose. The remaining mice make up the control group. Write an equation and find the number of mice in the control group.

92. Draw a bar graph to display the sales for two companies. Company A sales were $100 and Company B sales were $55 lower.

93. A concrete and gravel mixture will be used to fill a form with a volume of 1,500 m^3 . Write an equation, and find the volume of the gravel that must be mixed with 975 m^3 of cement to fill the form.

94. Use the table below to write an equation and find the difference between the average spent annually in the United States and Canada.

Average spent annually on toys and games per child around the world

Germany	$429
U.S.A.	$384
Japan	$355
Canada	$187
China	$0.92

95. Use the table below to write an equation and find the difference in games coached between Hayden Fry and Bobby Bowden.

College football coaches (Division 1-A) who have coached the most games:

Hayden Fry	358
Joe Paterno	324
Jim Sweeney	318
Bobby Bowden	315
Johnny Majors	296

__Lesson 3-7__   Objective 1: Solve equations by dividing.

Dynamic Item

96. Solve. a) $7e = 28$ b) $4f = 6.8$

   [A] a) 196   b) 1.7   [B] a) 196   b) 27.2

   [C] a) 4   b) 1.7   [D] a) 4   b) 27.2

Dynamic Item

97. Solve. a) $8b = 16$ b) $4c = 12.4$

98. How are the equations $5 + x = 20$ and $5x = 20$ alike? How are they different?

99. After falling for y seconds, a penny dropped from a bridge will have a speed of $16y$ ft/s. Which equation can be used to find the number of seconds it will take for the penny to reach a speed of 80 ft/s?

    [A] $y = 80 \times 16$ [B] $16y = 80$ [C] $\dfrac{y}{16} = 80$ [D] $16 + y = 80$

100. $10 \cdot |z| = y$ Which statement is true?

    [A] z will always be negative.   [B] z and y will always be positive.

    [C] y will always be positive.   [D] z will always be positive.

101. Objects on the moon weigh about $\dfrac{1}{6}$ as much as they weigh on Earth. If Kristen weighs 22 pounds on the moon, what is her weight on Earth?

102. At the local drugstore, it costs $0.35 to get a negative of a picture developed. If Lauren spent $3.85 getting negatives developed, how many did she get?

103. A computer prints mailing labels at a rate of 5 per minute. How many minutes will it take to print 1,000 labels?

104. Refer to the chart below. Use the variable m to represent the percent of employees in retailing covered by a health plan. Write an expression, using m, to represent the percent of employees covered in transportation/communications.

% Employees Covered by Their Employers' Health Care Plan (companies of 200 or more workers)	
High Technology	89%
Manufacturing	82%
Transportation / Communications	78%
Retailing	39%

Lesson 3-7   Objective 2: Solve equations by multiplying.

Dynamic Item

105.   Solve. a) $\dfrac{s}{6} = 7$ b) $\dfrac{t}{2} = 3.8$

   [A] a) $\dfrac{7}{6}$ b) 7.6   [B] a) 42   b) $\dfrac{19}{10}$

   [C] a) 42   b) 7.6   [D] a) $\dfrac{7}{6}$ b) $\dfrac{19}{10}$

Dynamic Item

106.   Solve: $\dfrac{p}{4} = 9$

107.   Explain the mathematical statement: If $a = b$, then $ac = bc$.

108.   A number is multiplied by a positive integer, the result is -22. Explain what you know about the first number and why.

109.   Stuart solved the equation $\dfrac{x}{5} = -100$ and got $x = -20$. Explain how he might have gotten this answer. How would you help him correct his mistake?

110.   You are 3 times older than your younger sister and you are 12 years old. Write an equation to solve for your sister's age. Will you be 3 times her age next year?

111.   Refer to the line graph below. Using x to represent the horizontal value, write an expression (in terms of x) to find the vertical value.

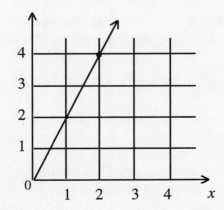

Lesson 3-8   Objective: Write equations.

Dynamic Item
112.   The product of –7 and an unknown number is –70. Which equation matches this situation?

[A] $\dfrac{x}{-70} = -7$ [B] $-70x = -7$ [C] $-7x = -70$ [D] $\dfrac{-7}{x} = -70$

Dynamic Item
113.   Write the following as an equation. When a number is increased by 15, the result is 18.

114.   Make up two different word problems that can be solved by the equation $y - 25 = 175$.

115.   Explain the steps in writing a word problem as an equation.

116.   Rewrite each of the following sentences in two ways, replacing the capitalized word(s) with other word(s) without changing the meaning of the sentence.
a. A number DECREASED by six EQUALS four.
b. Seven PLUS a number IS negative ten.
c. Three TIMES a number EQUALS fifteen.
d. ONE HALF a number IS negative eight.

117.   Which equation could be used to solve: Find a number that is 3 less than 5 times some number is 22?

[A] $5n - 3 = 22$ [B] $3 - 5n = 22$ [C] $5n = 3 - 22$ [D] $\dfrac{22}{5}n = 3$

118.   Erin spends 10 hours a week doing homework. This is 1 hour less than 5 times the amount she spends at practicing the piano. How long does Erin spend at piano practice?

[A] 1.8 hours   [B] 11 hours   [C] 2.2 hours   [D] 2 hours

119.   Meghan wrote the equation $12 = 5 - n$ for the problem "12 is 5 less than a certain number." Explain why this is incorrect.

120.   Draw a diagram to represent the following problem. Two friends live 28 miles apart on a straight road. One can bicycle 3 miles per hour faster than the other. They start at the same time and meet after cycling for 2 hours. What rate did each cycle?

121. A computer has been programmed in BASIC to perform a series of steps. For all integer values of x from 1 to 10,000, the computer calculates the value of (a) using the formula (a) = $3x + 1$. If (a) = 400, the computer prints "I found it." The program continues until $x = 10,000$ and then it ends. Determine how many values of x are tried before the computer prints "I found it." Will it print "I found it" more than once? Explain.

122. A dietitian is preparing a dessert which contains 150 calories. This will be 60 calories less than $\frac{1}{2}$ the number of calories in a regular serving of apple pie and ice cream. How many calories in a regular serving of apple pie and ice cream?

123. Sound travels through silver at a rate of 2,680 m/s and through steel 2,530 m/s faster. Write an equation and determine how fast sound travels through steel.

124. The original cost of a very old statue, x, is $24,000. The cost to clean and refurbish it is $720,000. Represent the cost to clean and refurbish the statue in terms of x.

125. Use the table below. Represent the number of Girls' Scout Troops in 1987 (in thousands) by x. Write a variable expression to represent the number of troops in 1990 in terms of x.

Total Number of Girls' Scout Troops (in thousands): 1985 – 1990	
1986	174
1987	180
1988	189
1989	196
1990	202

Lesson 3-9   Objective: Solve two-step equations.

Dynamic Item

126. $\dfrac{y}{5} - 10 = 4$

    [A] 70   [B] –30   [C] 30   [D] 200

CHAPTER 3

Dynamic Item

127. Solve: $2x + 8 = -6$

128. Explain how you solve the equation $3t + 11 = -10$.

129. Explain how you solve the equation $\frac{j}{4} + 3 = -7$.

130. Josh bought packs of baseball cards for $0.79 each and a card container for $3.98. The total cost of Josh's purchases was $7.93. Which equation can you use to determine how many packs of cards Josh bought?

   [A] $\$3.98C + \$0.79C = \$7.93$ [B] $\$7.93 - \$3.98C = \$0.79$

   [C] $\$0.79C + \$3.98 = \$7.93$ [D] $\$0.79 + \$3.98 = \$7.93$

131. Mrs. Baker purchased a number of juice packs at a cost of $0.30 each and a loaf of bread that cost $1.19. The total cost of her purchases was $2.99. Which equation would you use to determine how many juice packs Mrs. Baker purchased?

   [A] $\$1.19j + \$0.30j = \$2.99$ [B] $\$0.30j + \$2.99 = \$1.19$

   [C] $\$2.99 - \$1.19j = \$0.30$ [D] $\$0.30j + \$1.19 = \$2.99$

132. Write a two-step equation using the variable x whose solution is 8.

133. Write a two-step equation using the variable y whose solution is -6.

134. Write and solve an equation for the sentence: "six more than three times a number is eighteen."

135. Write and solve an equation for the sentence: "ten more than a number divided by 4 equals 5."

136. Write and solve an equation for the sentence: "five more than a number divided by -6 is -11."

137. In 1992, women with a Masters degree earned a median wage of $35,081 and women who only completed high school earned a mean wage of $18,648. Write an equation to find the income of women with Masters degrees if a woman with a high school education earns y.

138. Use the table below. Let x = the percent of homes in the West that carve pumpkins. Then, using x, represent the percents for the other regions.

Number of U.S. homes who make
jack o' lanterns for Halloween

West	47%
Midwest	52%
South	43%
Northeast	56%

Lesson 3-10   Objective: Solve a problem by making a table.

Dynamic Item

139. A coin is tossed. If a head turns up, a spinner that can land on any of the numbers from 1 to 7 is spun. If a tail turns up, the coin is tossed a second time instead of spinning the spinner. What are the possible outcomes?

[A] (T, H), (T, T), (H, 1), (H, 2), (H, 3), (H, 4), (H, 5), (H, 6), (H, 7)

[B] (T, H), (H, H), (T, 1), (T, 2), (T, 3), (T, 4), (T, 5), (T, 6), (T, 7)

[C] (T, H), (H, H), (H, 1), (H, 2), (H, 3), (H, 4), (H, 5), (H, 6), (H, 7)

[D] (T, H), (T, T), (T, 1), (T, 2), (T, 3), (T, 4), (T, 5), (T, 6), (T, 7)

Dynamic Item

140. Jill went to the mall to buy a shirt for a friend. Her choices for the shirt were henley and v-neck. Both of the choices came in yellow, purple, and blue. Create an organized list showing the different choices Jill could have.

CHAPTER 3

Lesson 4-1   Objective 1: Use models to explore fractions.

Dynamic Item

1. What fraction of the circles are black?

   [A] $\dfrac{3}{5}$ [B] $\dfrac{2}{5}$ [C] $\dfrac{3}{2}$ [D] $\dfrac{2}{3}$

Dynamic Item

2. Draw a diagram to show $\dfrac{5}{8}$ as part of a whole.

3. Describe a model for the fraction $\dfrac{2}{5}$.

4. Lia identified the shaded portion of the diagram below as $\dfrac{1}{3}$ of the circle. Was she correct? Explain.

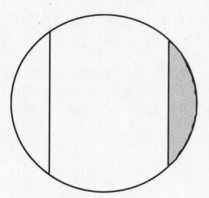

5. Identify two real-life situations in which you have used fractions.

6. Use fractions to describe the time you spend at work or in school, sleeping, eating, doing homework, and at leisure.

7. 3 h is equivalent to

   [A] $\dfrac{10}{24}$ day.   [B] $\dfrac{3}{24}$ day.   [C] $\dfrac{5}{24}$ day.   [D] $\dfrac{1}{24}$ day.

CHAPTER 4

8. 2.5 ft² is equivalent to

[A] $2\frac{5}{100}$ ft².   [B] $2\frac{5}{10}$ ft².   [C] $2\frac{1}{50}$ ft².   [D] $2\frac{1}{5}$ ft².

Lesson 4-1   Objective 2: Model mixed numbers.

Dynamic Item
9. What mixed number is pictured below?

[A] 4   [B] $3\frac{2}{3}$ [C] 8   [D] $3\frac{5}{6}$

Dynamic Item
10. Name the fraction or the mixed number marked by the arrow.

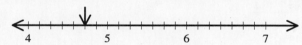

11. $3\frac{6}{12}$ is equivalent to

[A] $3+\frac{12}{6}$.   [B] $3+\frac{1}{12}$.   [C] $3+\frac{6}{12}$.   [D] $3+\frac{6}{10}$.

12. The fraction bars could NOT represent

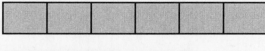

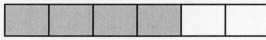

[A] $1\frac{2}{3}$.   [B] $1\frac{4}{6}$.   [C] $\frac{10}{6}$.   [D] $\frac{4}{3}$.

Rainfall	Intensity (in./h)
Cloudburst	4
Excessive Rain	$1\frac{6}{10}$
Heavy Rain	$\frac{6}{10}$
Moderate Rain	$\frac{15}{100}$
Light Rain	$\frac{4}{100}$
Drizzle	$\frac{1}{100}$
Mist	$\frac{2}{1000}$
Fog	$\frac{5}{1000}$

Source: Old Farmer's Almanac 1994

13. Use the table above. The radio announcer said that $1\frac{1}{10}$ in. of rain fell in an hour. What kind of rain was it?

14. Use the table above. There is heavy rain over your school for an hour. Draw a model that shows the amount of rain that fell.

15. Use the table above. How long would there have to be drizzle for the equivalent of 1 h of light rain to fall?

16. Use the table above. Draw a model that shows the number of inches of excessive rain that falls in an hour.

Lesson 4-2   Objective 1: Find factors and multiples of numbers.

Dynamic Item
17. Find the least common multiple of 72 and 24.

[A] 72   [B] 144   [C] 36   [D] 216

Dynamic Item
18. List all the factors of 54.

19. Describe the relationship between 3, 7, and 21 using the terms factor and multiple.

20. Can a number ever be both a factor and a multiple of itself? Explain using examples.

21. Describe the difference between a factor and a multiple.

22. All of the following are factors of 24 EXCEPT

[A] 4   [B] 9   [C] 12   [D] 6

23. All of the following are factors of 96 EXCEPT

[A] 48   [B] 3   [C] 36   [D] 16

24. All of the following are multiples of 8 EXCEPT

[A] 160   [B] 100   [C] 104   [D] 120

25. All of the following are multiples of 15 EXCEPT

[A] 250   [B] 45   [C] 300   [D] 225

26. What is the least number of dancers that are needed if a choreographer wants to arrange them in groups of 4, 5, or 6 with none left over?

27. Randall rented two sizes of tables for a banquet. One size seats 5 people and the other seats 8 people. He plans to seat 79 people at less than 12 tables. If there are no empty places, how many tables of each size will there be?

CHAPTER 4

Lesson 4-2   Objective 2: Write equivalent fractions.

Dynamic Item

28.   Which of the following fractions is equal to $\frac{6}{3}$?

[A] $\frac{78}{12}$ [B] $\frac{24}{39}$ [C] $\frac{3}{6}$ [D] $\frac{24}{12}$

Dynamic Item

29.   Write two fractions equivalent to $\frac{5}{9}$.

30.   Explain a method of determining if two fractions are equivalent.

Mimi's Computer Disks Week's Sales	
Spreadsheets	35
Word Processing	55
Tax Packages	40
Games	80

31.   Refer to the list above of a recent week's sale for Mimi's Computer Disks. What fraction of the sales is word processing?

32.   Refer to the list above of a recent week's sale for Mimi's Computer Disks. What fraction of sales is tax packages?

Lesson 4-3   Objective 1: Compare fractions.

Dynamic Item

33.   Compare: $\frac{3}{8}$ ◯ $\frac{1}{2}$

[A] $\frac{1}{2} < \frac{3}{8}$ [B] $\frac{3}{8} > \frac{1}{2}$ [C] $\frac{3}{8} = \frac{1}{2}$ [D] $\frac{3}{8} < \frac{1}{2}$

Dynamic Item

34.   Compare $\frac{2}{3}$ and $\frac{1}{2}$ using <, >, or =.

35. Explain how to compare two fractions with different denominators.

36. Explain how to compare two fractions with like denominators.

37. Which fraction is greater than $\frac{2}{5}$?

    [A] $\frac{4}{10}$ [B] $\frac{5}{10}$ [C] $\frac{1}{10}$ [D] $\frac{1}{5}$

38. Casey got 32 out of 40 questions correct on her social studies test. Last week she got 24 out of 30 questions correct. Which score was better? Explain.

39. During a soccer game, Erin scored 3 out of 7 goals attempted. Lauren scored 7 out of 10 goals attempted. Show the fraction that represents each and compare to determine who was the most successful.

40. Mark's family spends $\frac{3}{8}$ of their day traveling to a vacation home. Justin's family spends $\frac{5}{6}$ of their day traveling to a different vacation home. Which family spends more of their day traveling?

41.

State	Uninsured Population (Approximate)
New Jersey	1 out of 10
Mississippi	1 out of 5
Iowa	8 out of 100
Florida	9 out of 50
New York	3 out of 25
Pennsylvania	5 out of 50

Health Care Uninsured, 1990
(Selected States in the U.S.A.)

Source: The 1993 Information Please Almanac

Use the table above to determine which two states have the same fraction of the population that is uninsured.

CHAPTER 4

Lesson 4-3   Objective 2: Order fractions.

Dynamic Item

42.   Which of the following fractions has the greatest value?

[A] $\dfrac{15}{43}$ [B] $\dfrac{13}{21}$ [C] $\dfrac{27}{32}$ [D] $\dfrac{23}{33}$

Dynamic Item

43.   List the fractions in order from greatest to least.

$\dfrac{9}{34}$, $\dfrac{18}{13}$, $\dfrac{27}{32}$, and $\dfrac{13}{21}$

44.   Write three fractions that are equivalent to one another.

45.   Write two fractions that are less than $\dfrac{3}{4}$, but greater than $\dfrac{1}{3}$.

46.   Which of the following fractions are in order from least to greatest?

[A] $\dfrac{3}{10}$, $\dfrac{3}{8}$, $\dfrac{3}{6}$, $\dfrac{3}{5}$ [B] $\dfrac{5}{7}$, $\dfrac{5}{8}$, $\dfrac{2}{3}$, $\dfrac{6}{21}$

[C] $\dfrac{1}{2}$, $\dfrac{2}{5}$, $\dfrac{3}{8}$, $\dfrac{3}{10}$ [D] $\dfrac{1}{2}$, $\dfrac{3}{8}$, $\dfrac{1}{8}$, $\dfrac{5}{8}$

47.   Mia rode her bike 1.6 km on Saturday. Max rode his bike $1\dfrac{2}{3}$ km on Sunday. Who rode farther? Explain.

48.

Health Care Uninsured, 1990 (Selected States in the U.S.A.)	
State	Uninsured Population (Approximate)
New Jersey	1 out of 10
Mississippi	1 out of 5
Iowa	8 out of 100
Florida	9 out of 50
New York	3 out of 25
Pennsylvania	5 out of 50

Source: The 1993 Information Please Almanac

Rank the states listed in the table above according to the fraction of the population uninsured from least to greatest.

Lesson 4-4   Objective 1: Write numbers with exponents.

Dynamic Item
49. Write as a power: $2 \times 2 \times 2$

[A] 2^3 [B] 2^4 [C] $(3)^2$ [D] 2^{-3}

Dynamic Item
50. Simplify: 2^5

51. Complete the chart:
Standard form: 1,000,000   100,000   10,000   1,000   100
Power of 10: _____ _____ _____ _____ ___

52. Describe the pattern in the chart below. Use this pattern to solve
$13^6 \times 13^2 = x$. You can express the answer as an exponent.
$2^3 \times 2^2 = 2^5$
$3^2 \times 3^4 = 3^6$
$5^2 \times 5^2 = 5^4$

53. Write the expressions below using exponents.
    i) $3 \cdot 4 \cdot 3 \cdot 5 \cdot 4 \cdot 3 \cdot 5$
    ii) $x \cdot y \cdot y \cdot y \cdot x \cdot x \cdot 4$

Lesson 4-4 Objective 2: Evaluate expressions with exponents using the order of operations.

Dynamic Item
54. Use a calculator to evaluate: $81 \div 3^3 - 2 + 5^2$

    [A] 26　　　　[B] 19,692　　　[C] 12　　　　[D] 19,706

Dynamic Item
55. Simplify: $90 \div 0.02 - 21 \times (0.2 + 8.2)^2$

56. Explain how to read 3.2^2, and then write in standard form.

57. Summarize the order of operations for evaluating expressions.

58. Explain how to find the value of $16 + 8 \div 4(3)$.

59. Write two numbers in exponential form that are between the values of 4^2 and 4^3.

60. Choose the standard form for 5.3^3.

    [A] 15.9　　　　[B] 142　　　　[C] 159　　　　[D] 148.877

61. Evaluate the expression: $4(1.5 + 3.5)^3$.

    [A] 60　　　　[B] 800　　　　[C] 500　　　　[D] 50

62. Write an expression and solve for: the cost of 5 juices at $0.89 each and 6 personal pizzas at $2.98 each.

63. Mike's running times were 1.5 min, 2.2 min, 1.8 min, 1.9 min. Write an expression that represents his average running time. Solve the expression.

Lesson 4-5   Objective 1: Find the prime factorization of a number.

Dynamic Item
64. Find the prime factorization of 11,011.

[A] 11 · 11· 91   [B] 1 · 13 · 77 ·11

[C] 7 · 11· 143   [D] 11 · 11· 13 · 7

Dynamic Item
65. Make a factor tree of 150.

66. Explain the difference between a prime number and a composite number. Give an example of each.

67. Determine whether 321 is prime or composite.

68. Determine whether 652 is prime or composite.

69. Determine whether 198 is prime or composite.

70. Determine whether 71 is prime or composite.

Lesson 4-5   Objective 2: Find the greatest common factor (GCF) of two numbers.

Dynamic Item
71. What is the greatest common factor of 40 and 30?

[A] 120   [B] 10   [C] 2   [D] 24

72. The local reader's club has a set of 18 hardback books and a set of 24 paperbacks. Each set can be divided equally among the club members. What is the greatest possible number of club members?

73. Suppose you have a collection of 36 model cars and 21 model boats. You want to arrange them on shelves with the same number of models on each shelf. What is the smallest number of shelves you will need?

74. The Easton High School marching band has 52 members and the Weston High School marching band has 65 members. They are going to march in a parade. How can they be arranged so that each row has the same number of players? The players from each school have to be separate.

75. Which pair of numbers does not have the same GCF as the other pairs?

    [A] 6, 12   [B] 4, 10   [C] 2, 8   [D] 18, 22

Dynamic Item
76. What is the greatest common factor of 40 and 24?

Lesson 4-6   Objective 1: Write fractions in simplest form.

Dynamic Item
77. Write $\dfrac{24}{36}$ in simplest form.

    [A] $\dfrac{8}{12}$ [B] $\dfrac{2}{3}$ [C] $\dfrac{1}{6}$ [D] $\dfrac{6}{7}$

Dynamic Item
78. Simplify: $\dfrac{2}{20}$

79. Explain how to simplify a fraction.

80. All of the following fractions are in simplest form EXCEPT

    [A] $\dfrac{12}{35}$ [B] $\dfrac{14}{70}$ [C] $\dfrac{3}{245}$ [D] $\dfrac{11}{111}$

81. All of the following fractions are in simplest form EXCEPT

    [A] $\dfrac{36}{180}$ [B] $\dfrac{71}{99}$ [C] $\dfrac{23}{40}$ [D] $\dfrac{2}{221}$

CHAPTER 4

Favorite Professional Baseball Team	
Team	Number of Responses
Chicago Cubs	8
Toronto Blue Jays	7
Philadelphia Phillies	6
New York Yankees	4
San Francisco Giants	5
Atlanta Braves	8
Pittsburgh Pirates	4
Texas Rangers	8

82. Matt conducted a survey to determine his classmates' favorite professional baseball team. After polling 50 classmates, Matt arranged his data in the table above. What fraction of the people that Matt surveyed named the New York Yankees as their favorite team? Write the fraction in simplest form.

83. Matt conducted a survey to determine his classmates' favorite professional baseball team. After polling 50 classmates, Matt arranged his data in the table above. What fraction of the people that Matt surveyed named the Philadelphia Phillies or the Pittsburgh Pirates as their favorite team? Write the fraction in simplest form.

84. Matt conducted a survey to determine his classmates' favorite professional baseball team. After polling 50 classmates, Matt arranged his data in the table above. Three teams received an equal number of votes. What are these teams? Write a fraction in simplest form to show the fraction of the people who identified any of these three teams as their favorite.

85. Matt conducted a survey to determine his classmates' favorite professional baseball team. After polling 50 classmates, Matt arranged his data in the table above. If you were to write a fraction for each team listed in the table, only one fraction would appear in simplest form. What team does this fraction represent? What is the fraction?

Lesson 4-6   Objective 2: Use the greatest common factor (GCF) to write fractions in simplest form.

Dynamic Item

86. Find the GCF of the numerator and denominator of the fraction. Write the fraction in simplest form.

$$\frac{60}{72}$$

[A] $\frac{20}{24}$ [B] $\frac{5}{6}$ [C] $\frac{15}{18}$ [D] $\frac{5}{18}$

Dynamic Item

87. Find the GCF of the numerator and denominator of the fraction. Write the fraction in simplest form.

$$\frac{6}{8}$$

88. Use a divisibility test to write $\frac{27}{144}$ in simplest form. Tell which divisibility test you used.

89. When simplifying a particular fraction, Ian had to divide the numerator and denominator two separate times. Did Ian use the GCF of the numbers? How do you know?

90. How can GCF help when simplifying a fraction?

91. Which of the following sets of numbers does NOT have a GCF of 12?

[A] 12, 72   [B] 36, 48   [C] 60, 84   [D] 24, 32

92. Which of the following sets of numbers does NOT have a GCF of 15?

[A] 15, 35   [B] 15, 30   [C] 30, 105   [D] 45, 60

Lesson 4-7   Objective: Solve problems by looking for a pattern.

Dynamic Item

93. The total number of horses and people at the riding academy for the Sunday session was 43. The total number of legs at the academy that day was 124. How many horses were at the riding academy that Sunday?

[A] 20   [B] 24   [C] 23   [D] 19

94. A large number of red marbles, blue marbles, and green marbles are to be divided into three bags. The first bag contains 6 red marbles, 4 blue marbles, and 2 green marbles. The second bag contains 4 red marbles, 2 blue marbles, and 6 green marbles. If this pattern is continued, how many of each type of marble will the third bag contain?

95. At the school store, 2 pens cost the same as 1 notebook. Five pencils cost the same as 1 pen. If a pencil costs $0.10, how much does a notebook cost?

96. The Wilson School Cafeteria offers three different types of drinks and four different lunches every day. How many different lunch combinations are available to students?

97. What is the perimeter of the fifth square in this pattern?

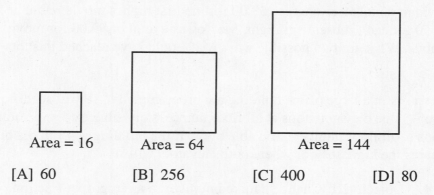

Area = 16   Area = 64   Area = 144

[A] 60   [B] 256   [C] 400   [D] 80

98. Sixteen students from Lunch Table 1 line up in the Hot Lunch line. When given the signal, Students 1 through 7 enter the kitchen. As Student 1 leaves the kitchen, Students 8 and 9 enter it. As Student 2 leaves, Students 10 and 11 enter. If this process is repeated, when should the last student in line enter the kitchen?

99. A local fast-food restaurant generally serves an average of 84 customers per hour between 8:00 and 11:00, and twice that number of customers each hour between 11:00 and 2:00. On an average day, how many customers does the restaurant serve between 10:00 and 1:00?

100. A science class of 28 students were given the option of designing an experiment or preparing an oral report for extra credit. Six students decided not to do an extra credit assignment. Fourteen students chose to design an experiment and 12 selected an oral report. How many students will complete two extra credit assignments?

101. What is the area of the sixth rectangle in this pattern?

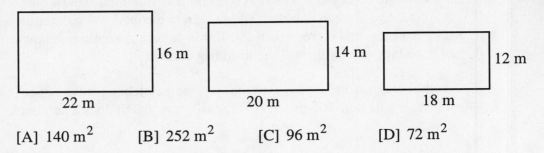

[A] 140 m^2 [B] 252 m^2 [C] 96 m^2 [D] 72 m^2

102. Cinema I holds a maximum capacity of 144 people while Cinema II holds only 84 people. Movies are scheduled three times a day in Cinema I and six times a day in Cinema II. Estimate the total number of people who will view movies in the cinemas on a day when every show is sold out.

103. A video rental store charges $3.00 for the first night's movie rental and $1.50 for each subsequent night. Max owes a total of $9.00 for movie rentals. What are two possible ways Max could have reached this total?

Dynamic Item
104. Elevators in a large office building are programmed to stop at specific floors. One elevator stops at all floor numbers divisible by 4 and another stops at all floor numbers divisible by 7. If the building is 95 floors high, what is the highest floor where both elevators will stop?

Lesson 4-8   Objective 1: Change a mixed number to an improper fraction.

Dynamic Item
105. Write $6\frac{2}{3}$ as an improper fraction.

[A] $\frac{20}{3}$ [B] $\frac{16}{3}$ [C] $\frac{18}{3}$ [D] $\frac{62}{3}$

Dynamic Item
106. Name a fraction that is equal to $3\frac{4}{7}$.

107. Explain when any fraction $\frac{a}{b}$ is improper.

108. Describe a situation where you would use a mixed number, and a different situation where you would use an improper fraction.

109. Each of the following fractions is equal to the mixed number $1\frac{1}{4}$ EXCEPT

    [A] $\frac{15}{12}$.   [B] $\frac{25}{20}$.   [C] $\frac{7}{3}$.   [D] $\frac{30}{24}$.

110. Each of the following fractions is equal to the mixed number $2\frac{3}{5}$ EXCEPT

    [A] $\frac{38}{15}$.   [B] $\frac{52}{20}$.   [C] $\frac{91}{35}$.   [D] $\frac{26}{10}$.

111. A pizza parlor sold $30\frac{1}{8}$ pizzas during a dinner hour. If each pizza contained 8 slices, how many slices of pizza were sold?

112. A recipe calls for $2\frac{1}{2}$ cups of sugar. If you only have a $\frac{1}{4}$ cup measurer available, how many times will you need to fill it with sugar?

113. Mia baby-sat for $3\frac{1}{2}$ h and Joe baby-sat for an additional $1\frac{3}{4}$ h. Write the total time they spent baby-sitting as a mixed number and improper fraction.

Lesson 4-8   Objective 2: Change an improper fraction to a mixed number.

Dynamic Item

114. Choose the mixed number that is equal to $\frac{23}{5}$.

    [A] $3\frac{1}{5}$ [B] $4\frac{5}{3}$ [C] $4\frac{3}{5}$ [D] $4\frac{1}{5}$

Dynamic Item

115. Write $\frac{15}{6}$ as a mixed number.

116. Explain how to change an improper fraction to a mixed number.

117. Describe 2 real-life situations where $1\frac{1}{2}$ as an answer would make the most sense.

CHAPTER 4

118. Each of the following fractions is greater than 2 but less than $2\frac{1}{2}$ EXCEPT

    [A] $\frac{30}{13}$.   [B] $\frac{23}{11}$.   [C] $\frac{26}{10}$.   [D] $\frac{35}{17}$.

119. Each of the following fractions is less than 5 EXCEPT

    [A] $\frac{84}{17}$.   [B] $\frac{69}{14}$.   [C] $\frac{111}{22}$.   [D] $\frac{79}{16}$.

120. Minnie worked on a term paper for a total of 525 minutes. Express this in hours.

Lesson 4-9   Objective 1: Change fractions to decimals.

Dynamic Item

121. Write $4\frac{1}{8}$ as a decimal.

    [A] 4   [B] 0.401   [C] 4.125   [D] 4.01

Dynamic Item

122. Write $\frac{19}{20}$ as a decimal.

123. Explain how to write a fraction as a decimal.

124. Explain the difference between a terminating and a repeating decimal.

125. Name three unequal decimals in between $\frac{3}{8}$ and $\frac{2}{5}$.

126. Which of the following is the number closest to 0.327?

    [A] $\frac{13}{40}$ [B] $\frac{1}{2}$ [C] $\frac{3}{4}$ [D] $\frac{6}{40}$

127. Sam worked on his math homework for 45 minutes, on his Spanish homework for 30 minutes, and on his science project for 50 minutes during the weekend. What fraction of his homework time did he spend on each subject? Write each of these fractions as decimals.

128. Three friends went on a hiking trip on Saturday. Each person packed a knapsack with his or her own food and the same size canteen filled with water. Every hour, they stopped for a water break and at noon they sat down and ate lunch. After lunch, Jenn said that she only had $\frac{2}{5}$ of her water left. Rick said he had $\frac{3}{8}$ of his water, and Lori said that she had $\frac{5}{14}$ of her water. Use decimal equivalents to find out who had the most water left and who had the least.

129. Find the decimal equivalents for the following fractions: $\frac{1}{11}$; $\frac{2}{11}$; $\frac{3}{11}$; $\frac{4}{11}$. Predict from the pattern found what the decimal equivalents would be for $\frac{5}{11}$, $\frac{6}{11}$.

130.

Leading Pitchers - National League 1987 - 1992			
Year	Pitcher and Team	W	L
1987	Dwight Gooden, NY	15	7
1988	David Cone, NY	20	3
1989	Mike Bielecki, Chicago	18	7
1990	Doug Drabek, Pittsburgh	22	6
1991	John Smiley, Pittsburgh	20	8
	Jose Rijo, Cincinatti	15	6
1992	Bob Tewksbury, St. Louis	16	5

Source: <u>Sports Illustrated 1993 Sports Almanac</u>

The table above shows the leading pitchers in the National League from 1987 to 1992. What fraction of the total number of games pitched did each pitcher win? Change each fraction to its equivalent decimal. Use these decimals to rank the pitchers according to their record.

Lesson 4-9   Objective 2: Change decimals to fractions.

Dynamic Item
131. Express 3.79 as a mixed number and as an improper fraction in lowest terms.

[A] $3\frac{79}{100}, \frac{349}{90}$ [B] $3\frac{79}{90}, \frac{349}{90}$ [C] $3\frac{79}{100}, \frac{379}{100}$ [D] $3\frac{79}{90}, \frac{379}{100}$

Dynamic Item
132. Write 3.05 as a mixed number.

133. Describe a situation in which decimals are used more often than fractions. Explain why.

134. Which of the following is equivalent to 0.225?

[A] $\frac{225}{100}$ [B] $\frac{25}{40}$ [C] $\frac{9}{40}$ [D] $\frac{8}{40}$

135. One bank is advertising a savings account interest rate of $3\frac{1}{2}\%$. Another bank is advertising a rate of 3.45%. Which is the better rate? Explain how you got your answer.

136. When you are comparing rates, is it easier to change the fraction to a decimal, or the decimal to a fraction?

Chapter 5: Applications of Fractions

Lesson 5-1   Objective 1: Estimate sums and differences.

Dynamic Item

1. Estimate: $8\dfrac{2}{5} + 4\dfrac{2}{9}$

   [A] 13   [B] 1   [C] 8   [D] 14

Dynamic Item

2. Estimate. $9\dfrac{2}{5} - \dfrac{2}{3}$

3. Explain how to estimate sums or differences of fractions and of mixed numbers.

4. Write two unequal fractions whose estimated sum is 1.

5. Mr. Li went to the meat market to buy cold cuts. He bought $1\dfrac{1}{2}$ lb of bologna, $\dfrac{3}{4}$ lb of boiled ham, $1\dfrac{1}{8}$ lb of Swiss cheese, $1\dfrac{2}{5}$ lb of roast beef, and $\dfrac{7}{8}$ lb of salami. Estimate how many pounds of cold cuts Mr. Li bought.

6. Devi and Sharda are buying fruit to make a fruit salad for the end-of-the-year school picnic. Devi bought three cantelopes weighing $1\dfrac{1}{4}$ lb each, one pineapple weighing $2\dfrac{5}{8}$ lb, and two watermelons weighing $6\dfrac{1}{2}$ lb each. Sharda bought two bags of oranges weighing 28 oz each and $4\dfrac{1}{2}$ lb of grapes. Estimate how many pounds of fruit they bought. The girls estimate that they need about $\dfrac{1}{4}$ lb of fruit per person. Did they buy enough fruit for 100 people? Explain.

7.

State	Normal Annual Precipitation
New York	$35\frac{3}{4}$ inches
New Jersey	$41\frac{9}{10}$ inches
Pennsylvania	$39\frac{1}{10}$ inches
Maryland	$41\frac{8}{10}$ inches
Delaware	$41\frac{3}{10}$ inches

Use the table above to estimate the difference in average annual precipitation between the state that has the greatest annual precipitation and the state that has the least annual precipitation.

Lesson 5-1   Objective 2: Estimate products and quotients.

Dynamic Item

8. Estimate to the nearest whole number. $40\frac{1}{3} \div 4\frac{1}{2}$

[A] 9   [B] 8   [C] $3\frac{1}{3}$ [D] $\frac{5}{121}$

Dynamic Item

9. Estimate: $6\frac{2}{3} \times \frac{3}{4}$

10. Explain how to estimate products or quotients of mixed numbers.

11. Write two unequal mixed numbers whose quotient would be estimated to be 14.

12. Estimate the product of $2\frac{3}{7}$ and $1\frac{1}{5}$.

[A] 3   [B] $1\frac{1}{2}$ [C] $2\frac{1}{2}$ [D] 2

13. Choose a reasonable estimate for $6\frac{3}{8} \div 2\frac{1}{2}$.

    [A] 3   [B] 4   [C] 5   [D] 2

14. On a Pacific Island, the rainfall during the months of June, July and August was $6\frac{3}{4}$ inches, $3\frac{5}{6}$ inches, and $7\frac{1}{6}$ inches. About how much was the average monthly rainfall for these three months?

15. A box of rice makes about 25 c of cooked rice. If you must use $1\frac{1}{2}$ c of uncooked rice for 5 to 6 servings, would you have enough rice to make 12 servings for 6 different rice dishes? Estimate.

16.

State	Normal Annual Precipitation
New York	$35\frac{3}{4}$ inches
New Jersey	$41\frac{9}{10}$ inches
Pennsylvania	$39\frac{1}{10}$ inches
Maryland	$41\frac{8}{10}$ inches
Delaware	$41\frac{3}{10}$ inches

Use the table above to estimate to find the average annual precipitation for these Mid-Atlantic states.

Lesson 5-2 Objective 1: Add fractions.

Dynamic Item

17. Add: $\frac{3}{25} + \frac{3}{20}$

    [A] $\frac{2}{15}$ [B] $\frac{27}{100}$ [C] $\frac{7}{25}$ [D] $\frac{6}{45}$

Dynamic Item

18. Add: $\frac{3}{20} + \frac{4}{15}$

19. Explain how to add or subtract fractions with different denominators.

20. Explain what you can do if you are having difficulty finding the LCD.

21. Name three unequal fractions with different denominators whose LCD is 24.

22. Make up and solve a word problem which involves addition or subtraction of fractions or mixed numbers.

23. Which model in the figure shows an addition problem?

    I) 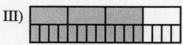   II)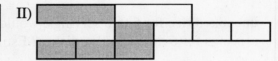

    III)

    [A] III   [B] all of the above   [C] II   [D] I

Lesson 5-2   Objective 2: Subtract fractions.

Dynamic Item

24. Subtract: $\frac{19}{20} - \frac{13}{24}$

    [A] $\frac{197}{480}$ [B] $\frac{1}{3}$ [C] $\frac{49}{120}$ [D] $\frac{33}{80}$

Dynamic Item

25. Subtract: $\frac{15}{16} - \frac{1}{24}$

26. You are baking muffins that require $\frac{1}{2}$ cup of vegetable oil. You only have $\frac{1}{3}$ cup left. How much more do you need?

27. You have to find the difference $\frac{7}{12} - \frac{5}{8}$. What common denominator should you use? Why?

Lesson 5-3   Objective 1: Add mixed numbers.

Dynamic Item

28. Add: $4\frac{1}{3} + 7\frac{3}{4}$

[A] $11\frac{4}{7}$ [B] $11\frac{1}{12}$ [C] $28\frac{1}{4}$ [D] $12\frac{1}{12}$

Dynamic Item

29. Add: $6\frac{1}{3} + 2\frac{3}{5}$

30. Mark ran $3\frac{3}{4}$ miles the first day of the race, $6\frac{1}{2}$ miles the second day of the race, and $5\frac{1}{5}$ miles the third day of the race. How many miles did he run?

31. Cyndi is making a pillow in her sewing class. She needs $1\frac{1}{3}$ yds of light printed fabric, $2\frac{1}{2}$ yds of solid fabric, and $1\frac{3}{4}$ yds of dark printed fabric. How much fabric does Cyndi need for her pillow?

32. You want to put a desk and a bookshelf in a $7\frac{1}{2}$ ft space. The bookcase is $3\frac{1}{4}$ ft long and the desk is $4\frac{1}{3}$ ft long. Will they fit in the space?

33. Your friend is having trouble adding mixed numbers, especially when the sum of the fractions is greater than 1. Explain how to do it.

34. A bread recipe calls for $2\frac{1}{2}$ cups of white flour and $3\frac{2}{3}$ cups of whole wheat flour. How much flour is that all together?

CHAPTER 5

Lesson 5-3   Objective 2: Subtract mixed numbers.

Dynamic Item

35. Subtract: $5\frac{1}{5} - 4\frac{3}{7}$

   [A] $1\frac{4}{35}$ [B] $\frac{27}{35}$ [C] $\frac{4}{35}$ [D] $1\frac{2}{35}$

Dynamic Item

36. Subtract: $9\frac{1}{7}$

   $- 5\frac{5}{8}$

37. Find the difference: $19\frac{2}{3} - 8\frac{8}{9}$.

   [A] $10\frac{8}{9}$ [B] $11\frac{2}{9}$ [C] $10\frac{7}{9}$ [D] $10\frac{2}{9}$

38. Gregg spends $5\frac{3}{4}$ hours mowing lawns on Saturday. If his parents will only allow him to work a total of 13 hours on the weekend, how many more hours could Gregg mow lawns?

39. The table below shows the mileage that two runners ran one week while training. Who ran farther? How much farther?

	Mon (miles)	Tues (miles)	Wed (miles)	Thu (miles)	Fri (miles)
Marissa	2	$3\frac{1}{2}$	3	2	3
Mark	3	2	2	3	$3\frac{1}{8}$

40. You have a piece of fabric $3\frac{1}{3}$ yd long. You need $1\frac{7}{8}$ yd for a pillow. How much will be left?

41. Your new puppy weighs $4\frac{1}{8}$ pounds this week. Last week she weighed $3\frac{3}{4}$ pounds. How much weight has she gained this week?

Lesson 5-4   Objective 1: Solve one-step equations by adding.

Dynamic Item

42. Solve and check: $x - \dfrac{2}{10} = \dfrac{3}{11}$

   [A] $4\dfrac{8}{11}$ [B] $\dfrac{26}{55}$ [C] $5\dfrac{1}{5}$ [D] $\dfrac{1}{22}$

Dynamic Item

43. Solve: $x - \dfrac{3}{14} = \dfrac{2}{14}$

44. Explain why you can add or subtract the same fraction from both sides of an equation to solve the equation.

45. Explain how to solve the equation $n - \dfrac{3}{4} = 5\dfrac{1}{2}$.

46. Write a subtraction equation whose solution is $9\dfrac{7}{15}$.

47. For which equation is n greater than 1?

   [A] $\dfrac{3}{5} - n = \dfrac{3}{5}$ [B] $\dfrac{7}{10} + n = 1\dfrac{4}{5}$ [C] $\dfrac{2}{6} + n = 1$ [D] None of these

48. Choose the equation for the sentence: $6\dfrac{3}{4}$ less than a number, n, equals twenty.

   [A] $20 - n = 6\dfrac{3}{4}$ [B] $6\dfrac{3}{4} - n = 20$

   [C] $n - 6\dfrac{3}{4} = 20$ [D] $n = 20 - 6\dfrac{3}{4}$

49. Eight and one-half years ago, Steven was 7 years old. How old is he now? Solve by writing an equation.

50. Marissa has a piece of calico cloth that is $4\frac{1}{3}$ yd long. She needs $2\frac{3}{4}$ yd for her school project. How many yards is the length of the cloth that she will have left? Solve by writing an equation.

51.

New York Stock Exchange Tuesday, Dec. 28, 1993		
Stock	Close	Chg
Merck	$35\frac{1}{4}$	–
MerryGo	$3\frac{3}{4}$	$+\frac{1}{2}$
Walmart	$26\frac{1}{8}$	$+\frac{3}{8}$
Amer T& T	54	$-\frac{1}{2}$
MayDS	$39\frac{5}{8}$	$+\frac{3}{8}$
SearsRoeb	$51\frac{7}{8}$	$-\frac{3}{8}$
QuestValCap	24	$+\frac{1}{8}$

Source: USA Today, Dec. 29, 1993

The table above shows the results of stock trading on Dec. 28, 1993. The closing stock price for Merck was $35.25. This is recorded under the column "Close," as the mixed number $35\frac{1}{4}$. The "-" under the column "Chg" indicates that the Tuesday's closing price was the same as the closing price on Monday. Write and solve an equation to find the closing price of Amer T&T on Monday, Dec. 27, 1993. Express your answer as a mixed number and as a decimal.

Lesson 5-4 Objective 2: Solve one-step equations by subtracting.

Dynamic Item

52. Solve: $N + \frac{1}{2} = \frac{2}{3}$

[A] $\frac{1}{5}$ [B] $\frac{1}{6}$ [C] $1\frac{1}{6}$ [D] $1\frac{1}{2}$

Dynamic Item

53. Solve: $N + \dfrac{1}{4} = \dfrac{4}{5}$

54. Write an addition equation whose solution is $6\dfrac{7}{30}$.

55. Solve for n. Show your steps.

    (a) $4 + n = 12\dfrac{3}{4}$

    (b) $n - 1\dfrac{5}{6} = 2\dfrac{1}{2}$

56. If Jason spends $2\dfrac{1}{4}$ hours more at the camp, he will complete 9 hours of camp counseling. How many hours has he worked as a counselor so far? Solve by writing an equation.

57.

New York Stock Exchange		
Tuesday, Dec. 28, 1993		
Stock	Close	Chg
Merck	$35\frac{1}{4}$	–
MerryGo	$3\frac{3}{4}$	$+\frac{1}{2}$
Walmart	$26\frac{1}{8}$	$+\frac{3}{8}$
Amer T& T	54	$-\frac{1}{2}$
MayDS	$39\frac{5}{8}$	$+\frac{3}{8}$
SearsRoeb	$51\frac{7}{8}$	$-\frac{3}{8}$
QuestValCap	24	$+\frac{1}{8}$

Source: USA Today, Dec. 29, 1993

The table above shows the results of stock trading on Dec. 28, 1993. The closing stock price for Quest Val Cap was $24.00. The $\frac{1}{8}$ under the "Chg" column indicates that this price is $\frac{1}{8}$ of a dollar or $0.125 more than the preceding day's closing price. Write and solve an equation to find the closing price for Monday, Dec. 27, 1993. Express your answer as a mixed number and as a decimal.

Lesson 5-5   Objective 1: Multiply fractions.

Dynamic Item

58. Multiply: $\frac{3}{55} \cdot \frac{15}{9}$

[A] $\frac{1}{5}$ [B] $\frac{9}{165}$ [C] $\frac{1}{11}$ [D] $\frac{4}{33}$

Dynamic Item

59. Evaluate: $\frac{2}{63}$ of 14

60. Explain how to multiply fractions or a fraction and a whole number.

61. Explain how simplifying factors before multiplying fractions can be useful.

62. When multiplying two fractions which are less than 1:

[A] the product is greater than each factor.

[B] the product is less than each factor.

[C] none of these   [D] the product is equal to each factor.

63. When multiplying a fraction less than 1 by a whole number, the

[A] product is less than each of the factors.

[B] product is greater than each of the factors.

[C] product is less than the whole number, but greater than the fraction.

[D] product is less than the fraction, but greater than the whole number.

64. A department store is selling its compact discs for $\frac{1}{3}$ off the regular $12.00 price. How much would Emma pay if she bought 10?

65.   A seventh grade math class has 32 students. $\frac{1}{4}$ of the students are boys. How many students are boys? How many are girls?

66. How much of each ingredient would you need to make 4 times the recipe below?

Baked Apple Recipe
10 medium apples
$\frac{1}{2}$ c sugar
$\frac{1}{2}$ tbsp. butter
1 tsp. cinnamon
$\frac{1}{3}$ c raisins
$\frac{1}{2}$ c water

Lesson 5-5   Objective 2: Multiply mixed numbers.

Dynamic Item

67. Multiply: $1\frac{1}{2} \cdot 4\frac{2}{3}$

   [A] $5\frac{1}{11}$ [B] $2\frac{4}{11}$ [C] 7   [D] $2\frac{2}{3}$

Dynamic Item

68. Multiply: $4\frac{2}{7} \cdot 7\frac{1}{2}$

69. Explain how to multiply two mixed numbers.

70. Explain how you can use the distributive property for multiplying a whole number by a mixed number.

71. Mario's car gets $21\frac{1}{2}$ miles per gallon of gasoline. How far can he drive if he has $10\frac{3}{4}$ gallons of gasoline in his tank?

72. Ben and Eric walked over to a neighbor's house to help with some yard work. Ben worked $\frac{2}{3}$ the amount of time that Eric worked. Eric started at 1:00 P.M. and stopped at 4:45 P.M. At what time did Ben stop working?

73. The table below represents Jason's work schedule and earnings. What is the total he earned this week? Round your answer to the higher cent.

Day	Hours Worked	Amount Earned
Mon	1:00 P.M. – 5:30 P.M.	$4.50 / hr
Wed	12:30 P.M. – 2:45 P.M.	$4.50 / hr
Fri	1:30 P.M. – 5:15 P.M.	$4.50 / hr
Sat	10:00 A.M. – 2:30 P.M.	$6.75 / hr

Chapter 5: Applications of Fractions

Lesson 5-6   Objective 1: Divide fractions.

Dynamic Item

74. Divide: $20 \div \frac{2}{5}$

    [A] 50   [B] 100   [C] $\frac{1}{50}$ [D] $\frac{1}{100}$

Dynamic Item

75. Divide: $\frac{2}{7} \div \frac{10}{3}$

76. What is a reciprocal of a number? Give two examples.

77. Name a situation where dividing fractions would be preferred to converting fractions to decimals and then dividing.

78. Do all numbers have reciprocals? Explain.

Lesson 5-6   Objective 2: Divide mixed numbers.

Dynamic Item

79. Divide: $4\frac{1}{5} \div 1\frac{1}{8}$

    [A] $2\frac{2}{3}$ [B] $3\frac{11}{15}$ [C] $1\frac{19}{21}$ [D] $1\frac{9}{13}$

Dynamic Item

80. Find the quotient. $1\frac{1}{4} \div 2\frac{6}{7}$

81. Explain how to divide two mixed numbers.

82. Mark completed his bike race in $2\frac{1}{3}$ hours. What was Mark's race time in hours and minutes?

    [A] 2 h 30 min   [B] 1 h 43 min   [C] 2 h 20 min   [D] 3 h 20 min

83. Choose the numerical expression that is NOT equal to $\frac{5}{6}$.

    [A] $6\frac{2}{3} \div 4\frac{1}{2}$ [B] $2\frac{1}{12} \div 2\frac{1}{2}$ [C] $\frac{1}{2} \div \frac{3}{5}$ [D] $\frac{1}{4} \div \frac{3}{10}$

84. A dance teacher is cutting two pieces of ribbon to decorate her students' tap shoes for recital. Each piece must be $10\frac{3}{4}$ inches long. She bought two rolls of ribbons of 15 yd each. Does she have enough for 50 students? Explain.

85. Suzanne bought $2\frac{2}{3}$ pounds of carrots at the store. She wanted to divide the carrots among her friends, giving each friend $\frac{1}{3}$ pound. How many friends can she share with?

86. Melanie has a piece of cloth $11\frac{1}{3}$ yd long. How many $2\frac{5}{6}$ yd pieces can be cut from this cloth?

87. If the average serving size for rice is $1\frac{1}{4}$ cups, how many servings are there in $6\frac{1}{2}$ cups of rice?

88. The recipe below has been adapted to serve three people. If you cook this recipe, how much chicken will each person get in his or her serving? how much potato?

Chicken Neopolitan Recipe	
$1\frac{1}{2}$ lbs chicken	$\frac{1}{4}$ clove garlic
$\frac{1}{4}$ large onion	$\frac{3}{8}$ teaspoon salt
$1\frac{1}{2}$ potatoes	$\frac{1}{16}$ teaspoon pepper (pinch)
$\frac{1}{2}$ peppers	$\frac{3}{16}$ teaspoon basil
$\frac{1}{12}$ c parsley	$\frac{1}{2}$ lb tomato sauce

89. Use the table below to find how many full Snac-Paks can be made out of $2\frac{1}{2}$ lb of raisins. Explain how you can solve this problem using decimals and mixed numbers.

Usual Dried Fruit Package Sizes
Raisins $1\frac{1}{2}$ oz (42.5 g) Snac-Paks

Source: <u>The World of Food</u>, Prentice Hall, 1990

<u>Lesson 5-7</u>   Objective: Solve a problem by working backward.

Dynamic Item
90. A feature film runs 2 h 13 min. The theater requires 11 min between performances, and has 11 min of previews and short subjects to show before the feature. If the third showing of the feature film ends at 11:34, when did the first preview begin?

    [A] 3:34   [B] 2:34   [C] 4:00   [D] 4:45

Dynamic Item
91. Stuart is playing in a volleyball game. The game is to start at 9:00. The coach wants the players to be at the gym 30 min before the game starts. It takes 55 min for Stuart to get to the gym. Before he leaves for the game, Stuart needs 30 min to eat and get ready, and he allows 5 min to stop for gas. What time must Stuart get up the day of the game?

CHAPTER 5

92. A number, added to 6, then multiplied by 8 is 144. What is the original number?

[A] 22   [B] 72   [C] 6   [D] 12

93. A movie is scheduled to begin at 3:00 P.M. It takes 15 minutes to travel from Miako's house to his friend's home and another 10 minutes to get to the theatre. What is the latest time that Miako can leave his home and still make the 3 o'clock movie on time?

[A] 2:45   [B] 2:55   [C] 2:40   [D] 2:35

Checking Account Register

Date	Transaction	Payment / Debit	Deposit / Credit	Balance
11/19	Deposit		$60.00	$____
11/19	Cash	$100.00		$____
11/20	Al's Mart	$39.98		$377.35

94. Use the checking account register above. What was the balance of the checking account before the first transaction shown in the register?

95. Use the checking account register above. The balance shown on the checkbook statement for 11/20 was recorded incorrectly. It should be $317.35. Find the balance after each of the transactions on 11/19.

96. After shopping at a local mall, John had $5.60 left. He spent $2.50 of his money on bus fare to the mall and $1.25 for a folder and notebook at a stationery store. How much money did John have when he left home?

97. If you multiply a certain number by 11, and then add 6, the result is 127. What is the original number?

98. Jon is thinking of a number. If he adds 12 to the number and doubles the sum, the result is 38. What number is Jon's number?

99. The trip from Ellie's home to the soccer field takes 20 minutes. After playing in a game that lasted 1 hour and 25 minutes, Ellie went directly home. If it was 4:40 P.M. when she reached her front door, what time did Ellie leave her home?

100. Greg is scheduled for a piano lesson at 4:00 P.M. On his way to the lesson, Greg intends to stop at a friend's home. What time must he leave home if he plans to spend 20 minutes with his friend and the walk to the piano school takes 35 minutes?

101. A book store opened with 1,024 copies of a best-seller. After every 10 minute period, half of the total copies of the book were sold. If the last two copies of the book were purchased at 2:40 P.M., when did the store open?

Lesson 5-8   Objective 1: Change units of length and capacity.

Dynamic Item
102. Complete: 440 yd = _____ mi

    [A] $\frac{1}{4}$ mi   [B] 72 mi   [C] $2\frac{5}{6}$ mi   [D] 18 mi

Dynamic Item
103. Convert 16 cups to quarts.

104. Describe a situation when you need to change one unit of measurement into another. Explain the process you would use.

105. What is the best unit for measuring each of the following quantities:
    (a) the height of your school building
    (b) the weight of a car
    (c) the capacity of a swimming pool
    Explain each answer.

106. Which of the following is equivalent to 8,400 ft?

    [A] 700 yd   [B] 2 mi   [C] 2,800 yd   [D] 700 in.

107. Which of the following is NOT equivalent to $3\frac{3}{4}$ gal?

    [A] 13 qt   [B] 60 c   [C] 30 pt   [D] 15 qt

108. A rectangular yard is 6 yards wide and 4 yards 2 feet long. What is the perimeter of the yard?

109. Mark walked 660 yards while Steve walked $\frac{1}{3}$ mile. Which boy walked farther? What was the difference in the length of their walks? Round to the nearest yard.

110. The cream of barley soup recipe below is for 8 servings. Find the amount of each ingredient needed to serve 12 people.

Ingredient	8 Servings
Barley	1 c
Onion	1 c
Celery	1 c
Leeks	$\frac{1}{2}$ c
Ham Hocks	3 small
Chicken Stock	$3\frac{1}{2}$ qt
Heavy Cream	1 pt

Lesson 5-8   Objective 2: Change units of weight.

Dynamic Item
111. 19 ounces = _____ lb _____ oz

[A] 1 lb 3 oz   [B] 1 lb 9 oz   [C] 1 lb 7 oz   [D] 2 lb 3 oz

Dynamic Item
112. Convert 3 tons to pounds.

113. Explain how to convert 80 oz to pounds.

114. Describe a situation in which estimating weight would be an acceptable procedure. Compare this with a situation in which determining actual weight is necessary.

115. Tomatoes cost $1.56 a pound. If Suzanne purchased 36 ounces of tomatoes, how much did she pay? Round to the nearest cent.

116. A box of spaghetti weighs 1 pound. Lindsay cooked 9 oz of the spaghetti. Will she be able to make another meal of equal size with the remainder of the box?

117. The table below shows the solid waste collected per capita and the population of selected cities. Find the city which collected the most waste. How many tons were collected in this city?

Solid Waste Collected (per capita)

City	Population	Lb per year
Buffalo	328,123	380
El Paso	515,342	920
Denver	467,610	1,000
Oakland	372,242	1,600
Honolulu	365,272	2,200
Miami	358,548	2,560
Wichita	304,011	2,880

Source: The 1993 Information Please Almanac

Lesson 5-9   Objective 1: Solve equations using multiplication.

Dynamic Item

118. Solve. $\dfrac{x}{4} = \dfrac{1}{2}$

[A] 2   [B] $\dfrac{1}{8}$ [C] $\dfrac{9}{10}$ [D] $\dfrac{1}{10}$

Dynamic Item

119. Solve for y: $2y = \dfrac{13}{12}$

120. Explain how to solve the equation $\dfrac{m}{2} = 8$.

121. How can inverse operations help you solve an equation?

122. Write two different equations with a solution of $1\dfrac{1}{4}$.

123. Which of these equations has a solution of $\frac{3}{4}$?

    [A] $3y = 4$ [B] $8 = 6x$ [C] $\frac{3}{8}x = \frac{1}{4}$ [D] $\frac{1}{6}z = \frac{1}{8}$

124. Steve's family traveled $\frac{1}{5}$ the distance that Mike's family traveled. If Steve's family traveled 15 miles, how far did Mike's family travel?

125. Lenny's dog weighs 6 times as much as Dennis' dog. If Lenny's dog weighs 96 pounds, how much does Dennis' dog weigh?

126. Four-fifths a number is 28. Write and solve an equation to find the number.

127.

North American Dinosaurs			
Name	Length*	Height*	Food
Allosaurus	11 m	5 m	Meat
Brachiosaurus	23 m	12 m	Plant
Diplodocus	27 m	7 m	Plant
Orniholestes	2 m	1 m	Meat
Stegoceras	1 m	1 m	Plant
Parasaurolophus	10 m	6 m	Plant
Tyrannosaurus	14 m	6 m	Meat
Triceratops	9 m	6 m	Plant

*Lengths and heights are estimates
Source: Arithmetic Teacher, Vol. 38, Sept. 1990
 The table shows the estimated length and height of selected dinosaurs found in North America. The Apatosaurus, better know as the Brontosaurus, is a plant eater that was found in Colorado, Oklahoma, Utah, Montana, Texas, Wyoming, and Mexico. The length of the Tyrannosaurus is $\frac{2}{3}$ the length of the Apatosaurus. The height of the Brachiosaurus is $1\frac{1}{3}$ times the height of the Apatosaurus. Write and solve equations to find the height and length of the Apatosaurus.

Lesson 5-9   Objective 2: Solve equations using division.

Dynamic Item
128. Solve: $27 = 9y$

    [A] 2   [B] 3   [C] 36   [D] $\dfrac{1}{3}$

Dynamic Item
129. Solve for c. $4c = \dfrac{1}{14}$

130. Explain how to solve the equation $3x = 9$.

131. Which of these equations does NOT have a solution of $\dfrac{2}{3}$?

    [A] $\dfrac{1}{2}t = \dfrac{1}{3}$ [B] $6x = 4$ [C] $\dfrac{4}{3}a = \dfrac{1}{2}$ [D] $12 = 18y$

132. The Tyrannosaurus with a height of 6 m is twice as tall as the Pentaceratops. Write and solve an equation to find the height of the Pentaceratops.

CHAPTER 5

133.

North American Dinosaurs

Name	Length*	Height*	Food
Allosaurus	11 m	5 m	Meat
Brachiosaurus	23 m	12 m	Plant
Diplodocus	27 m	7 m	Plant
Orniholestes	2 m	1 m	Meat
Stegoceras	1 m	1 m	Plant
Parasaurolophus	10 m	6 m	Plant
Tyrannosaurus	14 m	6 m	Meat
Triceratops	9 m	6 m	Plant

*Lengths and heights are estimates
Source: <u>Arithmetic Teacher</u>, Vol. 38, Sept. 1990

The table above shows the estimated length and height of selected dinosaurs found in North America. The Euophocephalus is a plant eater found in Alberta. The length of the Parasaurolophus is $1\frac{2}{3}$ times the length of the Euophocephalus. The height of the Triceratops is 3 times the heights of Euophocephalus. Write and solve equations to find the length and height of the Euophocephalus.

Chapter 6: Using Proportions and Percents

Lesson 6-1   Objective 1: Write ratios.

Dynamic Item
1. A history class consists of 11 boys and 16 girls. Find the ratio of girls to boys.

    [A] $\dfrac{11}{27}$ [B] $\dfrac{16}{27}$ [C] $\dfrac{11}{16}$ [D] $\dfrac{16}{11}$

Dynamic Item
2. A class is attended by 28 boys and 24 girls. Write the ratio of girls to students in the class as a fraction in lowest terms.

3. What is a ratio? Give an example of a ratio using subjects that you observe frequently.

4. A student reported that the amount of shaded area in the figure below is one-third of the circle. Is this true? What ratio did the student use to get his answer?

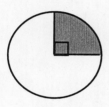

5. You sleep 8 hours per day. Find the ratio of the number of hours you sleep to the number of hours in one day.

6. Emma studies dance 3 days a week and practices soccer 5 days a week. Which ratio equals the number of dance days to soccer days over a 3-week period?

    [A] 9:15   [B] 15:15   [C] 12:15   [D] 6:15

7. There are twenty students in a particular class. Sixteen students are right-handed and four are left-handed. Explain a ratio that can be given to show the number of right-handed to left-handed students, and a ratio for the number of right-handed students to the total of students.

8. While picking a basketful of thirty apples, Mojo noticed that six apples had worm holes and had to be thrown away. What is the ratio of good apples to bad apples that were picked?

CHAPTER 6

9. While picking a basketful of thirty apples, Mojo noticed that six apples had worm holes and had to be thrown away. What is the ratio of good apples to the total number of apples picked?

Lesson 6-1   Objective 2: Find equal ratios.

Dynamic Item

10. Write three ratios equal to $\dfrac{4}{16}$.

   [A] $\dfrac{4}{1}, \dfrac{2}{8}, \dfrac{12}{3}$ [B] $\dfrac{1}{4}, \dfrac{8}{2}, \dfrac{3}{12}$ [C] $\dfrac{1}{4}, \dfrac{2}{8}, \dfrac{3}{12}$ [D] $\dfrac{4}{1}, \dfrac{8}{2}, \dfrac{12}{3}$

Dynamic Item

11. Write the ratio 4:16 in two other ways.

12. Use the set = (4, 7, 12, 16, 17, 22, 25, 28). Write as a decimal the ratio of even numbers to odd numbers. Round to the nearest tenth.

13. Use the set = (4, 7, 12, 16, 17, 22, 25, 28). Write as a decimal the ratio of odd numbers to even numbers. Round to the nearest tenth.

Estimated Costs for Class Picnic

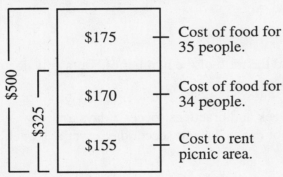

$500 $325

$175 — Cost of food for 35 people.

$170 — Cost of food for 34 people.

$155 — Cost to rent picnic area.

14. The diagram shows estimated costs for a class picnic. What is the ratio of the cost of a picnic for 34 people to the cost of a picnic for 69 people?

15. The diagram shows estimated costs for a class picnic. What is the ratio of the cost to rent the picnic area to the cost of a picnic for 69 people?

Lesson 6-2   Objective 1: Find unit rates.

Dynamic Item

16. A writer was paid $14,000 for a 2,000-word article. Find the rate per word.

    [A] $1.43 per word   [B] $0.14 per word

    [C] $7.00 per word   [D] $70.00 per word

17. What is a rate? Suppose you took a test that allowed you to answer as many questions as you could in ten minutes. By the end of the ten minutes you answered fourteen questions. How would you apply a rate to this occurrence?

18. Shannan, who lives in Pennsylvania, has visited her Aunt Susan in Illinois seven times over the last seven years. The rate you would apply to her visits is $\dfrac{\text{seven visits}}{\text{seven years}}$. Can you conclude that Shannan visited her aunt every year during the last seven years? Explain.

19. What is a unit rate? Suppose you took a test that allowed you to answer as many questions as you could in ten minutes. By the end of the ten minutes you answered fourteen questions. How would you apply a unit rate to this occurrence?

20. The state of Georgia is made up of 159 counties and 58,056 square miles. What is the unit rate of square miles per county? Round your answer to the nearest mile.

    [A] 365   [B] 159   [C] 318   [D] 274

21. The unit rate of 80 feet/20 seconds is _____.

    [A] 40 ft/sec   [B] 20 ft/sec   [C] $\dfrac{1}{4}$ ft/sec   [D] 4 ft/sec

22. Derrike Cope won the 1990 Daytona 500, covering the 500 mile race in 3 hours and 1 minute. What was his average miles per hour in this race? Round your answer to the nearest tenth.

23. A farm stand sells pumpkins for $4.00 each and the price drops to $2.50 for every pumpkin you buy after the third one. What is the average price per pumpkin if you buy five?

24. A farm stand sells pumpkins for $4.00 each and the price drops to $2.50 for every pumpkin you buy after the third one. What is the average price per pumpkin if you buy ten?

25. During his hockey career, Gordie Howe played 1,767 games, scoring 801 goals and making 1,049 assists. If goals and assists each count as one point, what was his average points earned per game? Round to the nearest hundredth point.

26. During his hockey career, Gordie Howe played 1,767 games, scoring 801 goals and making 1,049 assists. What was the average number of goals Gordie Howe scored per game? Round to the nearest hundredth.

27. Solve for n. $\dfrac{\frac{1}{4}}{4} = \dfrac{n}{1}$.

Dynamic Item
28. A factory can produce 1,092 parts in 4 h. What is the unit rate in parts per hour?

Lesson 6-2   Objective 2: Compare unit pricing.

Dynamic Item
29. Find each unit price to decide which is the better buy.

[A] 8 granola bars for $5.52   [B] 7 granola bars for $4.69

[C] 12 granola bars for $8.64   [D] 9 granola bars for $6.30

Dynamic Item
30. Which salsa is the better buy?

$22.23 for 9 cans of salsa or $19.60 for 8 cans of salsa

31. An 18 ounce box of cereal costs $1.79. A 36 ounce box of the same cereal costs $3.50. Find the unit price for each size and explain which is the better buy.

Lesson 6-3   Objective 1: Use cross products.

Dynamic Item
32. Do the ratios $\dfrac{3}{4}$ and $\dfrac{12}{16}$ form a true proportion?

Dynamic Item

33. Which of the following proportions is NOT true?

    [A] $\dfrac{3}{4} \overset{?}{=} \dfrac{15}{20}$ [B] $\dfrac{3}{4} \overset{?}{=} \dfrac{12}{16}$ [C] $\dfrac{24}{32} \overset{?}{=} \dfrac{3}{4}$ [D] $\dfrac{3}{4} \overset{?}{=} \dfrac{12}{20}$

34. How would you explain the proportion $4 = \dfrac{16}{4}$ using cross products?

35. Write the steps for solving the proportion $\dfrac{4}{n} = \dfrac{n}{16}$.

36. How would you show that $\dfrac{16}{19} = \dfrac{32}{39}$ is not a proportion? Which number in these ratios would you change to form a proportion?

37. Which of the following pairs of ratios do NOT form a proportion?

    [A] $\dfrac{27}{9}, \dfrac{12}{4}$ [B] $\dfrac{36}{30}, \dfrac{7}{6}$ [C] $\dfrac{52}{13}, \dfrac{4}{1}$ [D] $\dfrac{2}{7}, \dfrac{8}{28}$

38. Explain how you would find n in this proportion: $\dfrac{33}{36} = \dfrac{99}{n}$.

Lesson 6-3   Objective 2: Use proportions to solve problems.

Dynamic Item

39. If 3 cans of tomatoes cost $2.22, how many cans of tomatoes can you buy for $8.14?

    [A] 11   [B] 3   [C] 33   [D] 10

Dynamic Item

40. Solve: $\dfrac{10}{13} = \dfrac{x}{36}$

41. In a deck of playing cards, what is the ratio of total cards to the suit of hearts? What is the ratio of aces to the ace of spades? Can these ratios form a proportion?

42. Jeff's car gets 444 miles with a full tank of gas. If his gas tank holds twelve gallons, how many miles per gallon is his car getting?

    [A] 34   [B] 44.4   [C] 12   [D] 37

43. At Mario's Pizza Parlor, each piece of the special pizza contains four slices of pepperoni. If a pizza is made up of eight pieces, how many slices of pepperoni would be in half a pizza?

44. Find n in the proportion and give another ratio that also equals $\dfrac{14}{28}$.

    Express this ratio as a percent. $\dfrac{n}{7} = \dfrac{14}{28}$

45. Show your steps in solving the proportion to find n: $\dfrac{1}{n} = \dfrac{n}{4}$.

46. Find n in this proportion and give another ratio which also equals $-\dfrac{3}{8}$: $-\dfrac{3}{8} = \dfrac{n}{32}$

47. Find n in this proportion and give another ratio which equals $\dfrac{12}{13}$: $\dfrac{12}{13} = \dfrac{42}{n}$

48. Use a proportion to express $\dfrac{3}{4}$ as a percent.

49. Will n be a positive or negative number? Explain your answer and solve for n. $\dfrac{-8}{11} = \dfrac{24}{n}$

Lesson 6-4   Objective 1: Discover the properties of similar figures.

Dynamic Item
50. Which best represents a pair of similar figures?

[A]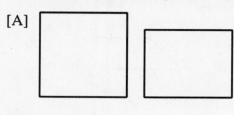

[B]

[C]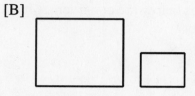

[D]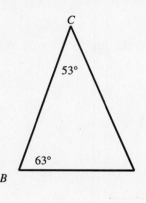

Dynamic Item
51. Triangle *BCD* is similar to triangle *EFG*. Find the measure of *x*.

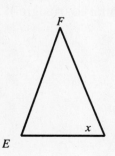

52. The ratios of the corresponding sides of the figures below are equal. Must these two figures be similar? Why or why not?

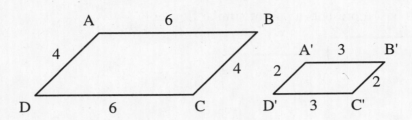

53. The corresponding angles of the figures below are congruent. Must these two figures be similar? Why or why not?

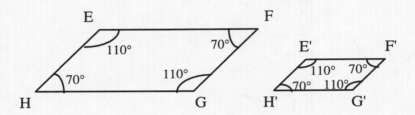

54. Name at least two sets of similar figures on an American flag.

55. Is each stripe on an American flag similar to all the others? Explain.

56. Fill in the blank. Different sized squares are _____ similar.

   [A] rarely   [B] never   [C] always   [D] usually

Lesson 6-4   Objective 2: Use proportions to find missing lengths in similar figures.

Dynamic Item

57. Triangle *TUV* is similar to triangle *WXY*. Find the length of side *WX*.

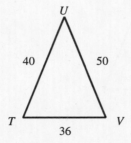 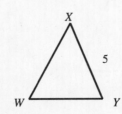

Dynamic Item

58. Two ladders are leaning against a wall at the same angle as shown.

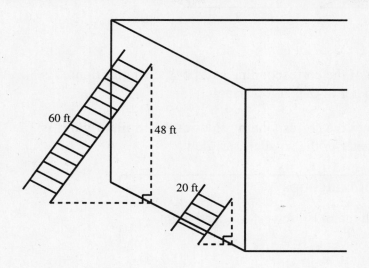

How far up the wall does the shorter ladder reach?

[A] 16 ft   [B] 32 ft   [C] 12 ft   [D] 14 ft

59. If the figures below are similar, what is the perimeter of the smaller figure?

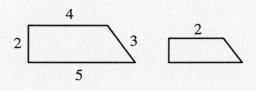

[A] 6   [B] 14   [C] 10   [D] 7

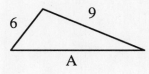   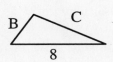

60. The ratio of the corresponding sides of the similar figures is 3:2. What is the length of Side A?

61. The ratio of the corresponding sides of the similar figures is 3:2. What is the length of Side C?

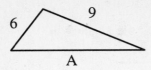 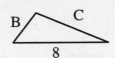

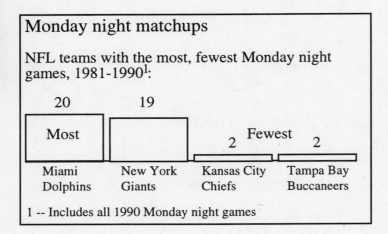

62. The ratio of the corresponding sides of the similar figures is 3:2. What is the perimeter of the larger triangle?

63. The ratio of the corresponding sides of the similar figures is 3:2. What is the perimeter of the smaller triangle?

Monday night matchups

NFL teams with the most, fewest Monday night games, 1981-1990[1]:

20	19	Fewest	
Most		2	2
Miami Dolphins	New York Giants	Kansas City Chiefs	Tampa Bay Buccaneers

1 -- Includes all 1990 Monday night games

64. The diagram illustrates activity on Monday night football as rectangles. Which two football teams are represented by similar figures?

65. The diagram illustrates activity on Monday night football as rectangles. Do the rectangles relating to the Miami Dolphins and the N.Y. Giants represent similar figures? Why or why not?

Lesson 6-5   Objective: Use proportions to solve problems involving scale.

Dynamic Item

66. A map has a scale of 1:2,800,000. If two cities are 12 cm apart on the map, what is the actual distance between the two cities?

[A] 2.3 km   [B] 336 km   [C] 3360 km   [D] 0.4 km

Dynamic Item

67. Find the perimeter of the actual object using the scale factor shown on the blueprint.

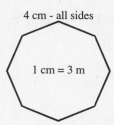

4 cm - all sides

1 cm = 3 m

68. In your own words, define scale drawing.

69. What happens on a map as the scale approaches 1:1?

70. Suppose you were given equal size maps of the states of Texas, Delaware, Indiana, and Oregon. Which state's map scale would be closest to actual size? Which would be farthest from actual size?

71. Why would a pocket map of New Jersey have a scale of 1 cm:15 mi and one of Pennsylvania have a scale of 1 cm:60 mi?

72. A scale drawing of a town park has a scale of 1 inch:100 feet. What is the actual length for each 1 foot on the drawing?

[A] 1000 ft.   [B] $\dfrac{1}{1200}$ in.   [C] 1200 ft.   [D] none of these answers

73. Which of the following would be the most appropriate subject if you were drawing it at a scale of 1:1?

[A] New Jersey   [B] a baseball

[C] a micro-organism   [D] a bedroom

74. On a map, the mileage scale is 1 cm:30 mi. The border of Utah and Wyoming measures 3.7 cm. Approximately how many miles is the border of Utah and Wyoming? Round your answer to the nearest ten miles.

75. On a map, the mileage scale is 1 cm:30 mi. Approximately how many miles is the southern border of Utah if it measures 9.5 cm on the map? Round to the nearest ten miles.

76. A scale drawing of a flea is 1 in: 3 mm. If a flea actually occupies a space 3 mm×3 mm, how large would a drawing of 36 fleas be if drawn to scale?

77. A scale drawing has a scale of $\frac{1}{2}$ in:10 km. What is the length of the drawing if the actual length is 200 km?

78. If the scale of a map is 0.5 cm:15 km, then 4.0 cm = _____ km.

79. If the scale of a map is 1 in:20 mi, then 6.5 in = _____ mi.

Lesson 6-6   Objective 1: Model percents.

Dynamic Item
80. What percent of the figure is shaded?

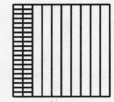

[A] 50%   [B] 80%   [C] 2%   [D] 20%

Dynamic Item
81. What percent of the figure is shaded?

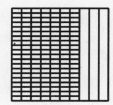

82. Give an example of a daily observation or activity that can be represented using percents.

83. What percent of probability would a meteorologist apply to her prediction if she is absolutely certain that it will rain?

84. If you work with a 5 × 5 graph to determine percents instead of 10 × 10, what percent would each square represent? Explain.

85. What percent of the graph above is represented by the shaded area?

86. What percent of the graph above does each square represent?

87.

What percent of the graph is represented by the shaded area?

<u>Lesson 6-6</u>   Objective 2: Write percents using equal ratios.

Dynamic Item
88. Of every 2 hot dogs Lester sold, 1 had sauerkraut. What percent had sauerkraut?

[A] 50%   [B] $\frac{1}{2}$%   [C] 5%   [D] 0.5%

Dynamic Item
89. Write $\frac{9}{10}$ as a percent.

90. While drawing a picture of a checkerboard, which should be 8 x 8 in size, you realize that you actually drew it 10 x 10. What percent of your drawing must be removed to return it to its proper size? What percent of the length and width must be removed? Explain.

91. The ratio $\frac{10}{1}$ is equal to which of the following percents?

[A] 0.1%   [B] 10%   [C] 1,000%   [D] 1%

92. The ratio $\dfrac{1}{1000}$ is equal to which of the following percents?

    [A] 10%   [B] 1,000%   [C] 1%   [D] 0.1%

93.

    What ratio would represent the comparison of one square to the entire graph?

94. If Kara's soccer team has won all but 2 of their 8 games, what percent has the team won?

95. Thomas walked his dog for 12 minutes today, 2 more minutes than yesterday. Express as a percent his walking time today compared with his walking time yesterday.

Lesson 6-7   Objective 1: Write fractions as percents and percents as fractions.

Dynamic Item
96. Write $\dfrac{17}{50}$ as a percent. Round to the nearest tenth.

    [A] 340.0%   [B] 3.4%   [C] 3.0%   [D] 34.0%

Dynamic Item
97. Write 99% as a fraction in simplest form.

98. Of fractions, decimals and percents, which two forms are the most alike? Explain your answer.

99. If you spend three hours per day studying, which form, fraction, decimal or percent, would you prefer to use to explain this portion of the day? Explain.

100. Convert the fraction $\dfrac{1}{3}$ to a percent. Round to the nearest tenth.

101. Convert the fraction $\dfrac{2}{3}$ to a percent. Round to the nearest tenth.

102. Convert 150% to a fraction.

Lesson 6-7   Objective 2: Write decimals as percents and percents as decimals.

Dynamic Item
103. What is 42% as a decimal?

  [A] 0.042   [B] 0.0042   [C] 0.42   [D] 4.2

Dynamic Item
104. Write 0.0047 as a percent.

105. If you spend eight hours of your day asleep, which form, fraction, decimal
      or percent, would be most exact in relating this activity? Explain.

106. Use a fraction, decimal, or percent to illustrate the relationship of one star
      to all the stars and one stripe to all the stripes on the American flag.
      Explain your choice.

107. Which of the following does NOT represent three equal forms?

  [A] 36%, $\dfrac{36}{100}$, 0.36   [B] 20%, $\dfrac{1}{5}$, 0.20

  [C] 5%, $\dfrac{50}{100}$, 0.05   [D] 15%, $\dfrac{15}{100}$, 0.15

108. The value of "one-in-a-thousand" is equal to which of the following?

  [A] $\dfrac{10}{1000}$ [B] 0.1%   [C] both $\dfrac{10}{1000}$ and 0.01   [D] 0.01

109. Convert the decimal 0.01 to a fraction.

CHAPTER 6

MEDICAID RECIPIENTS AND EXPENDITURES, 1990

Status	Recipients (Thousands)	Expenditures[1] (Millions)
Aged	3,202	$ 21,508
Blind	83	$ 434
Disabled	3,635	$ 23,969
Dependent children under 21	11,220	$ 9,100
Adults in families with dependent children	6,010	$ 8,590
Other	990	$ 1,051
Total	25,255	$ 64,859

Note: A small number of recipients are in more than one category

(Source: The Universal Almanac 1993)

110. Using the data, express the number of aged medicaid recipients to the total, in fraction, decimal and percent.

111. Using the data, express the relationship between total expenditures paid to aged recipients, to the total paid to all recipients, in fraction, decimal and percent.

Lesson 6-8   Objective: Solve a problem by using multiple strategies.

Dynamic Item
112. Chris and two of her friends wrote a book on horse grooming. In May, they received a royalty check for $6,000. They shared this money evenly. Chris also received $210 for boarding 3 horses on her property and $240 for teaching riding classes. How much money did Chris receive in May?

[A] $2,450   [B] $2,150   [C] $6,450   [D] $2,210

Dynamic Item
113. Donald wants to buy a car when he is sixteen. He has saved $635 for this purpose. He can afford to pay $21 a week. His grandparents will sell him their car for $1,370. In how many weeks will he fully pay for the car?

114. Imagine a graph made up of 100 by 100 squares. Explain how you would determine the total number of squares in this graph using only mental math.

115. The figure is known as a magic square. Explain how you would find the value of *x* and *y*.

x	9	2
3	5	7
8	1	*y*

116. Long ago, there lived a farmer whose land was in the shape of a square, 50 meters per side. Upon doing a kind deed for the price of the kingdom, he was notified that the king allowed the farmer to double the size of his farm, but only under the condition that the shape of the farm remain a square. Explain and draw a diagram to show how the farmer was able to accomplish this. Hint: drawing diagonals on the square may help you solve this problem.

117. Estimate the value of the figure's shaded area in square inches. Explain the procedure you used in getting this value. Round your answer to the nearest tenth.

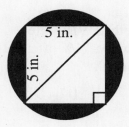

118. What three consecutive numbers have a sum of 51?

[A] 16, 17, 18   [B] 17, 18, 19   [C] 17, 17, 17   [D] 15, 17, 19

119. Four pennies are placed 2 by 2 to form a square. How many more pennies must be added to form a square 3 by 3?

[A] 7   [B] 3   [C] 1   [D] 5

120. Stan rode his bike on a square course covering six miles. If his brother Mike also rode a square course and covered twelve miles, how much farther, per side of the square, did Mike travel than Stan?

121. What three different even numbers total twelve?

122. What is the least number of coins that can total $0.49? Name the coins.

123. Using only the digits 1, 2, and 3, find all 3-digit numbers that are divisible by 3. You may use a digit only once in each number. How many numbers did you find?

Lesson 6-9   Objective 1: Use a percent to find part of a whole.

Dynamic Item
124. What is 25% of 36?

 [A] 0.9   [B] 9   [C] $\dfrac{25}{36}$ [D] NG

Dynamic Item
125. What is 26% of 61?

126. The population of the country of Haiti is 6.6 million. 72% of the population live in rural parts of the country. How many people live in non-rural, or urban, areas of Haiti? Explain your procedure for determining this amount.

127. An NCAA survey of 802 four-year colleges offering women's intercollegiate sports shows that 96% offer basketball, 91% offer volleyball, 89% offer tennis, 82% offer cross country, 71% offer softball, and 69% offer track. How many schools offer softball?

 [A] 802   [B] 569   [C] 71   [D] 233

128. An NCAA survey of 802 four-year colleges offering women's intercollegiate sports shows that 96% offer basketball, 91% offer volleyball, 89% offer tennis, 82% offer cross country, 71% offer softball, and 69% offer track. If the same results were obtained by surveying a set of 508 2-year colleges, how many colleges would offer tennis?

 [A] 89   [B] 714   [C] 452   [D] 508

Lesson 6-9   Objective 2: Find discount prices.

Dynamic Item
129. An article regularly selling for $32.11 is advertised at 10% off. Find the sale price.

 [A] $28.90   [B] $31.79   [C] $3.21   [D] $35.32

Dynamic Item
130. An article regularly selling for $18.51 is advertised at 15% off. Find the sale price.

CHAPTER 6

131. You buy a pair of running shoes for a discount of 12% from the regular selling price of $69.95. How much do the shoes cost? Round to the nearest cent.

132. In November, a pair of skis costing $80 was increased in price by 25%. In March, the skis were marked down 25%. Was the price in March the same, less than, or more than the original price?   Find the March price.

133. You want to find the cost of a CD that is on sale for 15% off its regular $12.95 price. Which expression below gives you the cost (C)?

    [A] C = 12.95(0.85)   [B] C = 12.95 ÷ 0.15

    [C] C = 0.15(12.95)   [D] C = $12.95 + 0.15(12.95)

134. The Book Barn is having a sale. All hardback books are 20% off, and all paperbacks are 10% off. Suppose you buy four paperbacks that originally cost $9 each and two hardbacks that originally cost $20. What percent of the total have you saved? Round to the nearest percent.

135. You buy a book at a 20% off sale. Your state has a sales tax of 4.5%. If the book normally costs $22.50, how much do you pay for it, including tax?

136. Which costs less: a pair of $95 skis on sale for 10% off, or a $120 pair, at 25% off?

Lesson 6-10   Objective 1: Find what percent one number is of another.

Dynamic Item
137. What percent of 15 is 3?

    [A] none of these   [B] 0.2%   [C] 15%   [D] 20%

Dynamic Item
138. What percent of 300 is 126?

139. Dave's Gift Shoppe has an advertisement in the newspaper for holiday wreaths. The cost is $8.00 per wreath, plus tax. There is an additional $3.00 shipping and handling charge. Can you determine, with the information given, the percent of your total payment that is for the wreath only? Explain.

CHAPTER 6

140. A recipe for pancakes calls for one cup of water and $\frac{3}{4}$ cup of pancake mix to make seven pancakes. Explain the procedure for determining the percent of one cup of pancake mix in this particular recipe necessary to make one pancake. Round to the nearest tenth percent.

141. While visiting your cousin, who lives in another state, you buy a souvenir for $12.00. Upon entering the purchase price into the cash register, the sales clerk advises you that the total amount due, including tax, is $12.72. What is the sales tax in this state? Explain how you would figure out the tax rate using the information given.

142. If Chelsey increased her total bowling score from 200 to 250, what percent of her new score is her old score?

    [A] 1.25   [B] $\frac{5}{4}$ [C] 250%   [D] 125%

143. Two American states are not part of the continental United States. What is the percent of states that are included in the continental United States?

    [A] 96%   [B] 48%   [C] 13%   [D] 2%

144. In the 1980 census, Ohio was listed as having 88 counties, 41,004 square miles of land and a population of 10,797,603. What was the average percent of population living in each county? Round your answer to the nearest tenth percent.

145.

Expenditures for New Plant and Equipment[1]
(in billions of dollars)

Year	Manufacturing	Transportation[2]	Total Nonmanufacturing	Total
1950	$ 7.73	$2.87	$18.08	$25.81
1955	12.50	3.10	24.58	37.08
1960	16.36	3.54	32.63	48.99
1965	25.41	5.66	45.39	70.79
1970	36.99	7.17	69.16	106.15
1975	53.66	9.95	108.95	162.60
1980	112.60	13.56	205.48	318.08
1985	152.88	14.57	302.05	454.93
1986	137.95	15.05	309.16	447.11
1987	141.06	15.07	320.45	461.51
1988	163.45	16.63	344.77	508.22
1989	183.80	18.84	380.13	563.93
1990	192.61	21.47	399.34	591.96
1991	183.61	22.69	405.13	588.74

(1) Data exclude agriculture. (2) Transportation is included in total manufacturing. Source: Department of Commerce, Bureau of the Census The chart above details, in billions of dollars, the amounts spent in the United States for new plants and equipment. The column labelled "transportation" is included with the "total non-manufacturing" amounts. What percent of the total expenditures in 1990 was for manufacturing equipment only? Round to the nearest percent.

Lesson 6-10   Objective 2: Find a number when you know a percent and a part.

Dynamic Item
146. 80% of what number is 136?

[A] 1.7   [B] 108.8   [C] 170   [D] 10,880

Dynamic Item
147. 24 is 20% of what number?

148. Cutters 'n Things is offering a seasonal set of cookie cutters for $6.50, plus 6% tax. There is also a $3.00 non-taxed shipping and handling charge. If you ordered a set of cookie cutters to be sent to your home, what percent of the total payment would be for the cookie cutters only? Round to the nearest percent.

149. Cutters 'n Things is offering a seasonal set of cookie cutters for $6.50, plus 6% tax. There is also a $3.00 non-taxed shipping and handling charge. If you ordered two sets of cookie cutters and the total shipping and handling charge was $3.00, what percent of your total payment would be for the cookie cutters only? Round to the nearest percent.

150. What number would you have to add to 50 to get 120% of 50?

151. A poll of 1,600 golfers shows that 42% are college graduates, 26% are high school graduates, 28% attended some college, and 4% do not have a high school diploma. Explain how you would determine the proportion of those surveyed who graduated high school. What is this proportion?

152. Two percent of American states have both the Atlantic Ocean and the Gulf of Mexico as coastline. What fraction of the states is that? Can you name them?

Lesson 6-11   Objective 1: Find percent of increase.

Dynamic Item
153. The wholesale price for an item that regularly sells for $22.23 is $19.50. What is the percentage markup for this item?

   [A] 12.28%   [B] 273%   [C] 2.73%   [D] 14%

Dynamic Item
154. The sales of Jetta sneakers rose from $4 million to $4.4 million. Find the percent increase to the nearest whole percent.

155. Mario bought a pizza cut into eight pieces. He ate one slice every five minutes. At the end of ten minutes, Mario ate two pieces, or 25% of the pizza. Explain how you would determine the percent increase of the pizza eaten during the following five minutes. What is the increase?

156. The diagram shows the performance of the NASDAQ stock index from the period 9/13 (740) to 10/15 (787). What is the percent of increase during this period? Do any periods show a decrease from the 9/13 index? Explain.

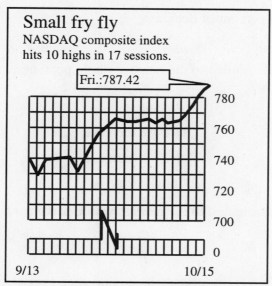

Source: USA Today 10/18/93

157. Day $X = 33$; Day $Y = 44$. Which of the following is the percent of change from Day X to Day Y?

    [A] $33\frac{1}{3}\%$ decrease   [B] 25% decrease

    [C] 25% increase   [D] $33\frac{1}{3}\%$ increase

158. A worker receives a raise of $1,400 a year from his salary of $20,000. What is the percent of change?

159. What is the percent of change from $\frac{7}{8}$ to 1.6? Round to the nearest percent.

160. On January 3, 1959, Alaska became the nation's 49th state. What is the percent of change in the number of states represented by this action? Round to the nearest percent.

161. In 1959, Alaska and Hawaii became the nation's 49th and 50th states. What is the percent of change in the number of states from the end of 1958 to the end of 1959? Round your answer to the nearest tenth percent.

Lesson 6-11   Objective 2: Find percent of decrease.

Dynamic Item
162. Find the percent of change, rounded to the nearest whole percent. Describe the change.
$8.95/h to $7.15/h

[A] 21% decrease   [B] 20% increase

[C] 20% decrease   [D] 21% increase

Dynamic Item
163. Find the percent of change, rounded to the nearest whole percent. Describe the change.
$10.00/h to $9.10/h

164. Mario bought a pizza cut into eight pieces. He ate one slice every five minutes. At the end of fifteen minutes, Mario ate three pieces of the pizza. After forty minutes, the whole pizza was eaten. Explain the procedure to determine the percent of change of pieces eaten after fifteen minutes to the number eaten during the first fifteen minutes. What is the percent of change?

165. The Military National Defense budget for the United States was about $291 billion and $276 billion for the years 1991 and 1992. What is the percent of change from 1991 to 1992? How much would have to be added to the 1993 budget to reflect a 1 percent increase to the 1992 budget? Explain. Round your answer to the nearest percent.

166. Day $X = 44$; Day $Y = 33$. Which of the following is the percent of change from Day Y to Day X?

[A] $33\frac{1}{3}\%$ increase   [B] 25% decrease

[C] 25% increase   [D] $33\frac{1}{3}\%$ decrease

167. Find the percent of change of a store item's price from $22.00 to $17.60. State whether the change is an increase or a decrease.

168. Due to company cutbacks, all salaries must be decreased by 5%. What decrease must an employee earning $18,000 expect?

CHAPTER 6

Lesson 7-1   Objective: Comparing and rounding decimals.

Dynamic Item
1. If the pattern indicated below is continued, what would be the total number of cubes in the 8th stage of the pattern?

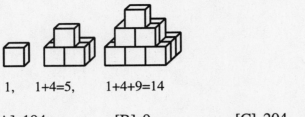

    1,   1+4=5,   1+4+9=14

    [A] 194   [B] 9   [C] 204   [D] 81

Dynamic Item
2. How many dots will be in the eighth figure of this pattern?

    ```
              • • •
        • •   • • •
    •   • •   • • •
    1    2      3
    ```

3. The moon goes through four phases. Describe the visual pattern of the phases and express the pattern with fractions.

4. Describe the visual pattern in a honeycomb. Name the type of polygon which makes up this pattern.

5. Dave is training for a track and field event. On his first day of practice, he runs 2 mi. If he adds 1.5 mi to the workout each week, how far will Dave run daily during his fifth week of practice? Explain your answer.

6. Sketch and explain the next figure for the pattern shown below.

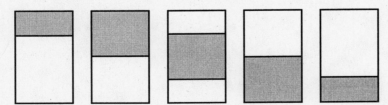

CHAPTER 7

7. A series of jars containing marbles has the following pattern:

    Jar #1 2 green, 1 red, 3 yellow
    Jar #2 4 green, 1 red, 6 yellow
    Jar #3 8 green, 1 red, 9 yellow
    Jar #5 32 green, 1 red, 15 yellow

    How many marbles would be in Jar #4?

    [A] 29   [B] 33   [C] 25   [D] 16

8. What would be the next figure for the pattern shown below?

    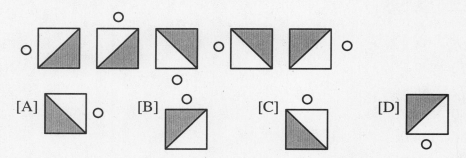

    [A]   [B]   [C]   [D]

9. Sketch the sixth and eighth figures for the pattern shown below.

    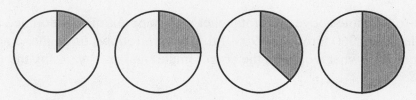

10. Figure 1 in a series is a square having sides of 1 cm each. Figure 2 in the
    series is a rectangle having adjacent sides of 1 cm and 2 cm. Figure 3, also
    a rectangle, has adjacent sides of 1 cm and 3 cm. What is the perimeter of
    Figure 5 in this series?

11. Draw the next two figures for the pattern shown below.

    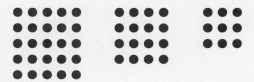

CHAPTER 7

CHAPTER 7

12. Draw the next two figures for the pattern shown below.

Total Worldwide Electrical Use (Quadrillion Btu)	
Year	Total
1960	23.0
1965	34.2
1970	49.2
1972	55.8
1980	91.0
1985	124.0
1990	170.0

13. Refer to the table above. The total energy use approximately doubled each decade from 1960 through 1990. If this pattern follows through the next twenty years, what would be the approximate total energy use by the year 2010?

14. Refer to the data in the table above. If you had only had data through 1970, what estimate would you give of total energy use for the year 2010? Read your answer to the nearest 10 quadrillion BTU.

Lesson 7-2   Objective 1: Measure and classify angles.

Dynamic Item

15. Estimate the measure of the angle:

     [A] 90°   [B] 160°   [C] 80°   [D] 180°

Dynamic Item

16. Classify the angle below.

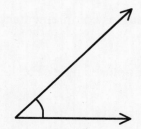

17. Consider a clock having a line drawn through the 12 and 6 o'clock points.
     As the minute hand progresses from the hour mark to 5 minutes past, how
     would you determine the angle formed at this point?

18. The hands of a clock form an angle. Name two separate times whose angle
     measure is 60°.

19. Suppose the hour hand on a clock rests on 12. Determine the measure of
     and classify the angle produced when the minute hand rests on 2.

CHAPTER 7

Lesson 7-2   Objective 2: Work with pairs of angles.

Dynamic Item
20. Find the measure of the supplement of ∠AOC.

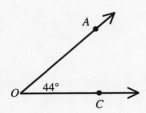

[A] 136°   [B] 46°   [C] 92°   [D] 88°

Dynamic Item
21. The complement of an angle is 29°. What is the measure of the angle?

22. Explain how to determine the measure of angles complementary and supplementary to an 80° angle.

23. Can an obtuse angle be adjacent to another obtuse angle? Explain your answer.

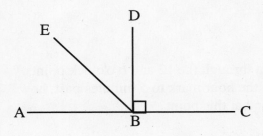

24. Use the figure above. What is the maximum number of adjacent 20° angles that can be drawn inside ∠DBC?

[A] 2   [B] 4   [C] 3   [D] 5

25. Use the figure above. What is the maximum number of adjacent 15° angles that can be drawn inside ∠DBC?

[A] 3   [B] 6   [C] 12   [D] 9

26. Is it possible to draw a pair of supplementary angles so that neither of the angles is obtuse? Explain.

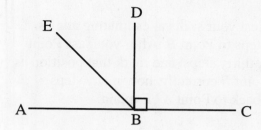

27. Name the two complementary angles in the figure above.

28. Name the two supplementary angles in the figure above.

29. Classify and determine the angle that is complementary to a 70° angle.

30. Classify and determine the angle that is supplementary to a 70° angle.

Lesson 7-3   Objective 1: Classify triangles by sides and by angles.

Dynamic Item
31. Classify the triangle with angles 68°, 22°, and 90°.

    [A] equilateral   [B] right   [C] obtuse   [D] acute

Dynamic Item
32. Classify △DEF as equilateral, isosceles, or scalene.

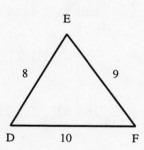

33. One angle of a right triangle is 90°. Is it possible to classify the other two angles? Explain why.

34. Can a triangle contain two obtuse angles? Explain.

35. You just told a classmate that you drew an isosceles triangle labelled *ABC* and that Angle *B* measures 40°. She replied that this must also be an acute triangle. Do you agree or disagree with her? Explain.

36. You are in a park and you decide to test your skills at estimating angles. Starting at Point *A*, you walk thirty steps to Point *B*. After you pass Point *B*, you turn 120° clockwise and walk thirty steps, and mark that position as Point *C*. If you guess your angle at Point *B* correctly, how many steps should you take to get from Point *C* back to Point *A*? Explain.

37. Classify the three triangles having the following sets of angles.
    1) 30°, 60°, 90°
    2) 55°, 30°, 95°
    3) 55°, 55°, 70°

    [A] Equilateral, Obtuse, Right   [B] Obtuse, Acute, Equilateral

    [C] Right, Obtuse, Acute   [D] Isosceles, Acute, Right

38. The measures of two angles of a triangle are multiples of 20. Classify this triangle.

    [A] Obtuse   [B] Cannot be determined   [C] Acute   [D] Right

39. A player hits a ball to second base and the second baseman throws the ball to first base. Classify the angle formed by the path of the ball.

Lesson 7-3   Objective 2: Find the measure of one angle of a triangle, given the other two measures.

Dynamic Item
40. The measures of two angles of a triangle are 68° and 54°. Find the measure of the third angle.

    [A] 122°   [B] 238°   [C] 58°   [D] 22°

Dynamic Item
41. The measures of two angles of a triangle are 42° and 52°. Find the measure of the third angle.

42.

In △*ABC* above ∠*A* is five times greater than ∠*C*. What are the measures of ∠*A* and ∠*C*?

43. If one angle of an isosceles triangle measures 80°, what are the measures of its other two angles?

44. If an isosceles triangle has an angle measuring 120°, what are the measures of its other angles?

45. Find the measure of the missing angle in each of the following triangles.

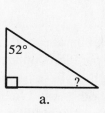 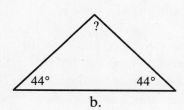 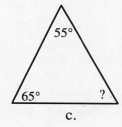

       a.   b.   c.

46. Draw a baseball diamond. Classify the two triangles that are formed by a segment drawn from first base to third base.

Lesson 7-4   Objective: Solve a problem by drawing a diagram.

Dynamic Item
47. It is known that a cyclist can travel 71.4 mi in 3 hr. How far can the same cyclist travel in 6 hr?

     [A] $144\frac{1}{5}$ mi   [B] none of these   [C] $142\frac{4}{5}$ mi   [D] $141\frac{3}{5}$ mi

Dynamic Item
48. There are sixteen teams in a soccer tournament. Each team plays until it loses 1 game. There are no ties. How many games are played?

49. Suppose you are building a tree house. Why might it be necessary to draw a diagram before building it?

50. Suppose you needed to explain the difference between a right angle and an obtuse angle to a first-grade student. You probably would show the child examples of each type of angle. Name two items in the classroom that you could use to model these angles.

51. Julie has only one- and five-dollar bills. If she has at least 2 five-dollar bills and her total is twenty-two dollars, determine the least and most number of bills Julie can have.

    [A] 6 and 20   [B] 6 and 14   [C] 8 and 20   [D] 4 and 14

52. A school band has a brass section of trumpet, trombone, and tuba players. There are twice as many trombones as tubas, and half as many trombones as trumpets. If there are two tubas in the band, what is the total number of players in the brass section?

    [A] 8   [B] 12   [C] 14   [D] 10

53. Garcia has only pennies, nickels, and dimes. His coins total 38¢. What is the lowest number of coins he can have?

54. The school band was scheduled to march in the annual parade, and the band's starting point was changed the day before the parade. You are the band director and must call three band members. Each of these band members must call three other band members. These other band members must also call three members. How many band members, including the band director, are notified of the new starting point?

55. A triangle has an angle of 100°, which is twice the measurement of another angle in the triangle. Draw the triangle and indicate its angle measures.

56. If you walk one mile on Monday and increase your distance each day by one-half mile, how many miles would you be walking on Friday?

57. Draw a rectangle having dimensions of 4 cm × 8 cm. Connect two opposite vertices to form two triangles within the rectangle. How would you classify the two triangles? Explain your reasoning.

CHAPTER 7

58. How many angles are shown below? How many of them are acute?

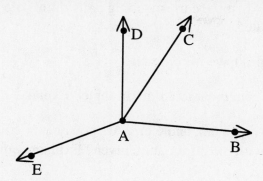

Lesson 7-5   Objective: Identify and work with congruent figures.

Dynamic Item
59. Look at the figure in the box.

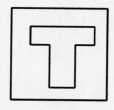

Which figure is congruent to the figure in the box?

[A]

[B]

[C]

[D]

CHAPTER 7

Dynamic Item

60. △JKL is congruent to △CDE. List the corresponding parts of the two triangles and how they are related.

61. What do two congruent triangles have in common?

62. Can an equilateral triangle be congruent to a right triangle? Explain.

63. △ABC has sides measuring 9 cm, 8 cm, and 6 cm. Are you able to create a triangle congruent to △ABC with the information given? Explain your answer.

64. Use the figure below. Is △XYZ congruent to △DEF? Why or why not?

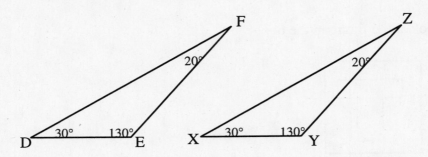

65. A triangle which is congruent to the one shown below must have which of the following angles?

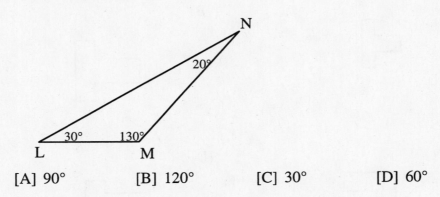

[A] 90°   [B] 120°   [C] 30°   [D] 60°

66. A triangle which is congruent to the one shown below must have which of the following total side lengths?

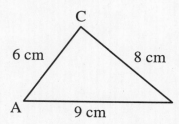

[A] 18 cm   [B] 28 cm   [C] 15 cm   [D] 23 cm

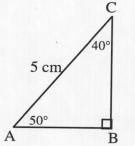 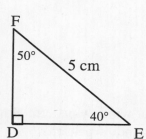

67. Use the triangles above. $\triangle ABC \cong \triangle$ _____

68. Use the triangles above. $\triangle BCA \cong \triangle$ _____

69. Use the triangles above. $\triangle CAB \cong \triangle$ _____

70. Use the triangles below. $\triangle MNO \cong \triangle QRP$

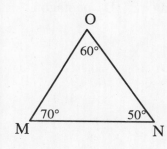 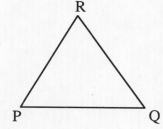

a. $\angle N \cong \angle$ _____

b. $\angle O \cong \angle$ _____

CHAPTER 7

71. The figure above shows a popular window pattern. How many congruent obtuse triangles are there in the window pattern?

72. The window pattern above is made up of triangles and quadrilaterals. How many of the acute triangles fit into one of the small quadrilaterals in the pattern?

Lesson 7-6   Objective 1: Classify polygons and identify regular polygons.

Dynamic Item
73. Name a polygon with 5 sides.

[A] hexagon   [B] quadrilateral   [C] triangle   [D] pentagon

Dynamic Item

74. Name the regular polygon.

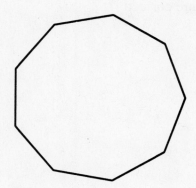

75. Name and describe four types of quadrilaterals.

76. Can a trapezoid also be a square? Why or why not?

77. One angle of a parallelogram is 90°. What is another name for this quadrilateral?

78. Explain how you would determine the measure of ∠A in quadrilateral ABCD if you know the measurements of ∠B, ∠C, and ∠D.

79. Polygon A is a square. Polygon B has four more sides than polygon A. What type of polygon is B?

80. What other types of quadrilaterals could be used to describe a square?

Lesson 7-6   Objective 2: Work with special quadrilaterals.

Dynamic Item
81. Which does NOT describe the figure correctly?

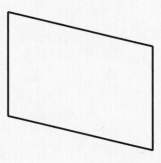

[A] rhombus   [B] polygon   [C] parallelogram   [D] quadrilateral

Dynamic Item
82. Describe the figure using as many of these words as possible: rectangle, trapezoid, square, quadrilateral, parallelogram, rhombus

83. Which set of angle measures are possible for a parallelogram?

   [A] 120°, 120°, 60°, 60°   [B] 40°, 40°, 140°, 160°

   [C] 80°, 80°, 90°, 90°   [D] 90°, 90°, 100°, 100°

84. What set of angle measures are possible for a quadrilateral?

   [A] All of these   [B] 39°, 161°, 118°, 42°

   [C] 64°, 79°, 106°, 111°   [D] 93°, 100°, 93°, 74°

85. Determine the measures of ∠A and ∠B in parallelogram *ABCD* below.

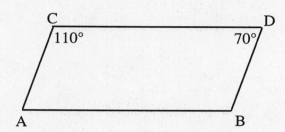

86. What type of polygons are formed by connecting one pair of opposite vertices in a hexagon?

87. A baseball field has four bases that form the shape of a quadrilateral. If someone devised a new game similar to baseball that had an extra base in the field, what type of polygon would be formed?

88. Two angles of a trapezoid measure 90° each. What can be determined of the remaining two angles?

Lesson 7-7   Objective 1: Identify parts of circles.

Dynamic Item
89. Name a diameter for circle *O* below.

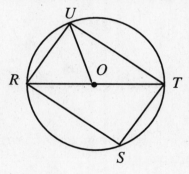

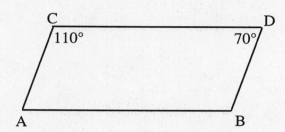

CHAPTER 7

Dynamic Item

90. Identify the dotted line.

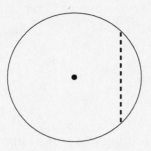

       [A] circumference   [B] radius   [C] chord   [D] center point

91. Describe segment *CD* if you are told that $\overline{CD}$ is a diameter of Circle *A*.

92. Describe segment *AB* if you are told that $\overline{AB}$ is a radius of Circle *A*.

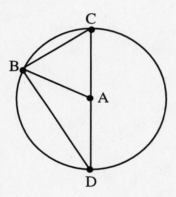

93. Use the circle above. If segment *BC* is congruent to segment *AC*, what is the measure of ∠*BCA*? Explain your answer.

94. Use the circle above. If $\overline{BC}=\overline{AC}$, is *BC* a radius of Circle *A*? Explain.

95. Describe a bicycle wheel using the parts of a circle.

96.

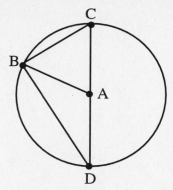

Use the circle above. Name all the radii labeled in Circle *A*.

97. Measure the width of a quarter. What part of a circle did you just measure?

Lesson 7-7   Objective 2: Work with inscribed quadrilaterals.

Dynamic Item

98. Name the polygon inscribed in the circle below.

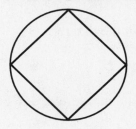

[A] pentagon   [B] quadrilateral   [C] cube   [D] octagon

Dynamic Item

99. Name the polygon inscribed in the circle below.

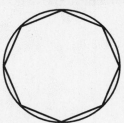

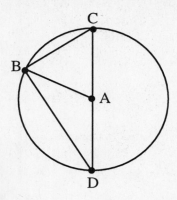

100. Use the circle above. Classify △BAD.

   [A] scalene   [B] isosceles   [C] right   [D] none of these

101. Use the circle above. $\overline{BC} = \overline{AB}$. Classify △BAC.

   [A] equilateral   [B] right   [C] isosceles   [D] scalene

102. Use the circle above. Find an isosceles triangle in the diagram.

103. Use the circle above. ∠BAD is 120°. Determine ∠D.

104. Use the circle above. If ∠BAD is 120°, what is the measure of ∠CBD?

Lesson 7-8   Objective 1: Analyze circle graphs.

Dynamic Item

105. The number of hours required in each subject of a college core curriculum is represented by the circle graph below. What percent of these hours is in math and history combined?

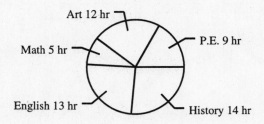

   [A] 33.8%   [B] 26.4%   [C] 35.8%   [D] 50.9%

Dynamic Item

106. The circle graph below represents a family's monthly budget. If the total monthly budget is $1700, how much is spent on housing?

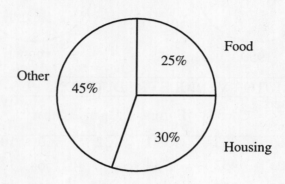

107.

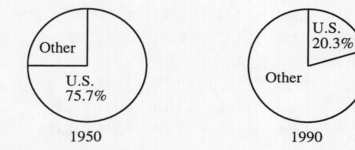

1950   1990

What can you determine about U.S. vehicle production from the two graphs?

108.

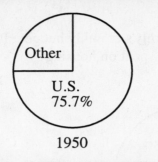

1950

1990

| WORLD MOTOR VEHICLE PRODUCTION, 1950-90 (in thousands) | | | | | | |
Year	United States	Canada	Europe	Japan	Other	World Total	U.S. share of total
1950	8,009	388	1,991	32	160	10,577	75.7%
1955	9,204	452	3,738	68	166	13,628	67.5
1960	7,905	398	6,830	482	873	16,488	47.9
1965	11,138	847	9,571	1,876	835	24,267	45.9
1970	8,284	1,160	13,243	5,289	1,427	29,403	28.2
1975	8,987	1,424	13,473	6,942	2,172	32,998	27.2
1980	8,010	1,374	15,446	11,043	2,641	38,514	20.8
1985	11,653	1,933	15,959	12,271	2,995	44,811	26.0
1989	10,874	1,934	18,946	13,026	4,216	48,996	22.2
1990	9,780	1,896	18,614	13,487	4,336	48,113	20.3

Source: The Universal Almanac

Use the information in the table to add a portion to the circle graphs to represent vehicle production in Europe for 1950 and 1990. What observation can you make comparing U.S. and Europe for the two years?

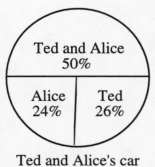

Ted and Alice's car

109. What percent of the time the car is in use is Alice occupying it?

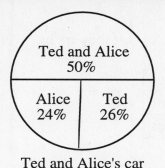

Ted and Alice's car

110. What is the least possible percent of the car's use that Ted is doing the driving?

111. What is the highest possible percent of the car's use that Ted is doing the driving?

112. What percent of the time that Alice is occupying the car is Ted with her?

113. A year later, Ted and Alice constructed a new circle graph and it was determined that Ted occupied the car 88% of the time it was used and that Alice occupied it 60% of the time. If only Ted and Alice use the car, for what percent of the time that the car was being used was it occupied by both Ted and Alice?

114. During one period of time, it was determined that Alice occupied the car 40% of its total use and Ted occupied it 52%. What can be determined by this information?

Lesson 7-8   Objective 2: Construct circle graphs.

Dynamic Item
115. The table below shows a family's monthly budget of $2,350.

Food	$400
Housing	$750
Other	$1200

If you are making a circle graph to display this information, what would be the measure (to the nearest degree) for the selection representing Other?

[A] 77°   [B] 115°   [C] 61°   [D] 184°

CHAPTER 7

Dynamic Item

116. Students at an amusement park were asked which grade they are in. Organize the results below with a circle graph.

4th Grade: 32 students	5th Grade: 32 students
6th Grade: 16 students	7th Grade: 16 students
8th Grade: 16 students	9th Grade: 16 students

WORLD MOTOR VEHICLE PRODUCTION, 1950-90 (in thousands)

Year	United States	Canada	Europe	Japan	Other	World Total	U.S. share of total
1950	8,009	388	1,991	32	160	10,577	75.7%
1955	9,204	452	3,738	68	166	13,628	67.5
1960	7,905	398	6,830	482	873	16,488	47.9
1965	11,138	847	9,571	1,876	835	24,267	45.9
1970	8,284	1,160	13,243	5,289	1,427	29,403	28.2
1975	8,987	1,424	13,473	6,942	2,172	32,998	27.2
1980	8,010	1,374	15,446	11,043	2,641	38,514	20.8
1985	11,653	1,933	15,959	12,271	2,995	44,811	26.0
1989	10,874	1,934	18,946	13,026	4,216	48,996	22.2
1990	9,780	1,896	18,614	13,487	4,336	48,113	20.3

Source: The Universal Almanac

117. Draw a circle graph using data from the chart for the year 1970. Do not display Canada separately as part of the graph. Explain what you must do to create a circle graph as directed.

118. Draw a circle graph using historical data from the chart to estimate the percentages of world total vehicle production for U.S., Europe, Japan and others for 1994. Also include your estimate of total vehicles produced.

Lesson 7-9   Objective 1: Construct a perpendicular bisector of a segment.

Dynamic Item

119.   Construct a perpendicular to the given segment through the given point.

120.   When can a perpendicular bisector of a segment also be an angle bisector?

121.   How would you define the midpoint of a segment?

122. $\overline{JK}$ bisects $\overline{LM}$ at point D. What can you say about D?

     [A] D is both the midpoint of $\overline{JK}$ and the midpoint of $\overline{LM}$

     [B] D is the midpoint of $\overline{JK}$

     [C] none of these   [D] D is the midpoint of $\overline{LM}$

CHAPTER 7

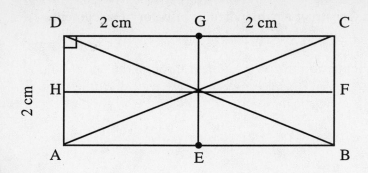

123. Use the figure above. What two polygons are formed by drawing the diagonal $\overline{DB}$ in rectangle *ABCD*?

    [A] trapezoids   [B] right triangles

    [C] squares   [D] isosceles triangles

124. Use the figure above. Name the three segment bisectors of $\overline{HF}$.

125. Use the figure above. What are the dimensions of rectangle *HFCD*?

126. Sketch rectangle *ABCD* with each of its right angles bisected.

Lesson 7-9   Objective 2: Construct the bisector of an angle.

Dynamic Item
127. Construct the angle bisector of the given angle.

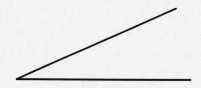

Dynamic Item

128.   Given: $\vec{SQ}$ bisects $\angle RST$. Find the measure of $\angle RST$ if $\angle RSQ = 25°$.

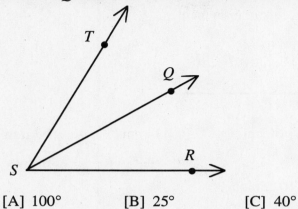

[A] 100°   [B] 25°   [C] 40°   [D] 50°

129.   How would you classify two new angles produced by bisecting an acute angle?

130.   How would you classify two new angles produced by bisecting an obtuse angle? Explain.

131.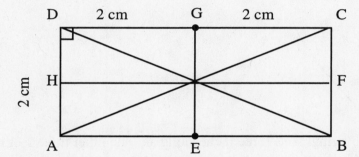

Use the figure above. What point would the bisector of $\angle DAE$ pass through?

Lesson 8-1   Objective 1: Estimate lengths and perimeter.

Dynamic Item
1. Estimate the length of this line segment.

V ——————————————— W

   [A] 70 mm   [B] 50 cm   [C] 14 cm   [D] 7 mm

Dynamic Item
2. Draw a line segment 10 cm long.

3. Could a rubber band be used as efficiently as a string to estimate the length of the perimeter of the figure below? Explain.

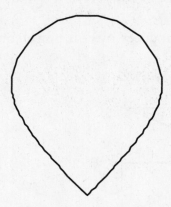

4. You have two strings, one three inches long and the other three feet long. Which would be better to use in estimating the perimeter of your bedroom floor at home? Why?

5. You are asked to quickly estimate the perimeter of your classroom. Explain the advantages and disadvantages of rounding your estimate to (1) the nearest foot and (2) the nearest inch.

6. Which unit of measure would you use to estimate the perimeter of your classroom doorway?

   [A] mi   [B] ft   [C] none of these   [D] in.

7.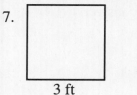

3 ft

The perimeter of the larger square is 12 ft. Estimate the perimeter of the smaller square.

8.

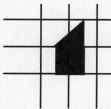

Each square in the diagram above is 5 cm by 5 cm. Estimate the shaded area's perimeter. Round to the nearest cm.

Lesson 8-1   Objective 2: Estimate areas.

Dynamic Item

9. Find the area of the figure. The area of each square is 1 cm^2.

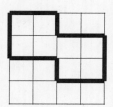

[A] 8.5 cm^2 [B] 12 cm^2 [C] 16 cm^2 [D] 8 cm^2

Dynamic Item

10. Find the area of the figure. The area of each square is 1 cm^2.

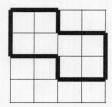

11. Estimate the area of the figure below. Explain your answer.

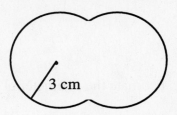

3 cm

12. Which unit of measure would you use to estimate the area of the state you live in?

   [A] mi^2 [B] yd^2 [C] ft^2 [D] in.^{2}

13.

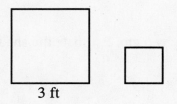

3 ft

   The area of the larger square in the figure above is 9 ft^2. Estimate the area of the smaller square.

14.

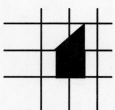

   The area of each square in the diagram above is 25 cm^2. Estimate the area of the shaded part.

CHAPTER 8

Lesson 8-2 Objective: Find the area and perimeter of parallelograms.

Dynamic Item

15. Find the area:

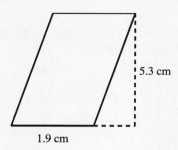

5.3 cm

1.9 cm

[A] 10.64 cm^2 [B] 5.035 cm^2 [C] 29.68 cm^2 [D] 10.07 cm^2

Dynamic Item

16. One side of a parallelogram has a length of 2.1 kilometers while another side has a length of 65.1 kilometers. What is the perimeter of the parallelogram?

17. The formula for the perimeter of a square is $P = 4S$. Can you use this formula to determine the perimeter of all rectangles? Explain.

18. The formula for the perimeter of a rectangle is $P = 2(L + W)$. Can you use this formula to determine the perimeter of all squares? Explain.

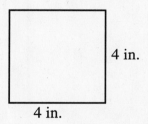

4 in.

4 in.

19. The square in the figure above has an area of 16 in.^{2} . How does the figure's area change when the length is doubled and the width is halved?

[A] cannot tell   [B] no change   [C] decreases   [D] increases

20. Use the figure above. How does the figure's area change when the length is increased by one inch and the width is decreased by one inch?

[A] decreases   [B] no change   [C] increases   [D] cannot tell

21. A parallelogram has an area of 36 cm^2. What can you conclude about this figure if the base = 6 cm?

22. What is the perimeter of a square having an area of 121 in.^{2} ? Explain how you would determine this.

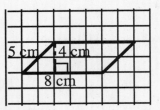

23. What is the area of the parallelogram in the figure above?

24. What is the perimeter of the parallelogram in the figure above?

25. What is the area of a square having a perimeter of 24 in.?

26. What is the width of a rectangle that has an area of 13 m^2 and a length of 26 m?

CHAPTER 8

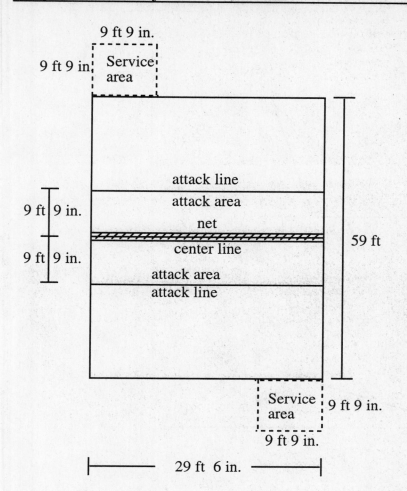

27. The figure above represents the layout of a volleyball court. What is the total playing area of a volleyball court in ft^2, not including the service area?

28. The figure above represents the layout of a volleyball court. What is the perimeter of the attack area on one side of the court?

CHAPTER 8

Lesson 8-3   Objective 1: Find the area of triangles.

Dynamic Item
29. Find the area:

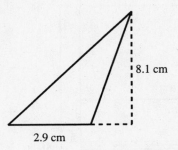

8.1 cm

2.9 cm

[A] 11 cm^2 [B] 22 cm^2 [C] 23.49 cm^2 [D] 11.745 cm^2

Dynamic Item
30. Find the area:

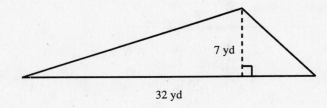

7 yd

32 yd

31. A rectangle's dimensions are 12 in. by 6 in. Explain how you would determine the area of each of the two triangles formed by drawing a diagonal connecting two opposite corners of the rectangle.

32. The area of $\triangle ABC$ in the figure below is which of the following?

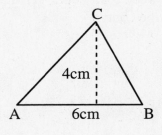

C

4cm

A   6cm   B

[A] 10 cm^2 [B] 12 cm^2 [C] 24 cm^2 [D] 18 cm^2

33. What is the area of triangle *LMN* below? Draw a triangle having the same height as △*LMN*, but twice the area.

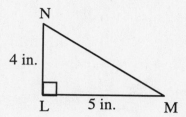

34. What is the area of △*JKL*?

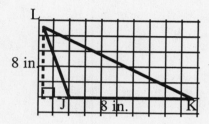

35. Draw two triangles having areas of three units, using whole numbers as base and height.

36. What is the area of a triangle with a base of 0.5 ft and a height of 1 ft?

Lesson 8-3   Objective 2: Find the area of trapezoids.

Dynamic Item
37. Find the area:

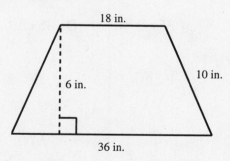

[A] 162 in.² [B] 540 in.² [C] 324 in.² [D] 270 in.²

CHAPTER 8

Dynamic Item

38. Find the area:

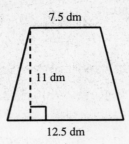

7.5 dm

11 dm

12.5 dm

39. Draw a trapezoid having the same area and height as △*LMN* below, and whole number values for the bases.

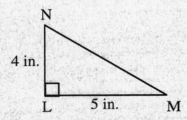

N

4 in.

L   5 in.   M

40. What is the area of trapezoid *DEFG* in the figure below?

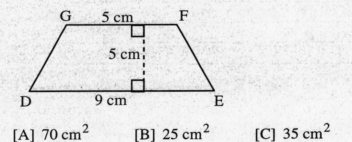

G   5 cm   F

5 cm

D   9 cm   E

[A] 70 cm²   [B] 25 cm²   [C] 35 cm²   [D] 45 cm²

41. What is the area of trapezoid *MNOP*?

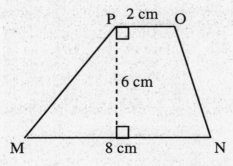

P   2 cm   O

6 cm

M   8 cm   N

CHAPTER 8

42. A trapezoid has an area of 25 units. Its height is 10 units and one base is 1.5 units. What is the length of the other base?

43. What is the area of a trapezoid with bases of 8 cm and 11 cm and a height of 20 cm?

Lesson 8-4 Objective 1: Find the circumference of a circle.

Dynamic Item
44. If a circle has a radius of 9 inches, what is the circumference rounded to the nearest whole number? (Use $\pi = 3.14$)

    [A] 254 in.   [B] 57 in.   [C] 29 in.   [D] 114 in.

Dynamic Item
45. Calculate the circumference of the circle. (Use $\pi \approx 3.14$)

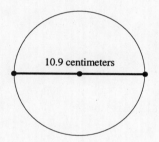

10.9 centimeters

    [A] 34.226 centimeters   [B] 17.113 centimeters
    [C] 93.2659 centimeters   [D] 14.04 centimeters

46. Explain how to determine the diameter of a circle if you know the measure of its circumference.

47. You know that three circles have circumferences of 200 in., 400 in. and 600 in. The diameter of the smallest circle is 63.7 in. How would you determine the diameters of the other two circles without using π?

48. Which of the following most closely represents the circumference of the circle *J* in the figure below?

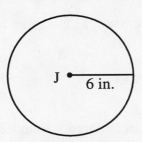

   [A] 38 in.   [B] 19 in.   [C] 12 in.   [D] 24 in.

49. What is the approximate length of the diameter of a circle that has a circumference of 100 cm? Round to the nearest cm.

50.

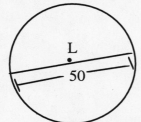

   Complete the equation for the circle *L* in the figure above: Circumference = π_____

Lesson 8-4   Objective 2: Find the area of a circle.

Dynamic Item
51. Find the area:

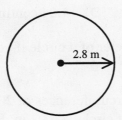

   [A] 24.6176 m^2 [B] 98.4704 m^2 [C] 6.1544 m^2 [D] 17.584 m^2

Dynamic Item
52. Find the area of a circle with a diameter of 32 feet. Use 3.14 for π.

CHAPTER 8

53. Which of the following most closely represents the area of the circle *J* in the figure below?

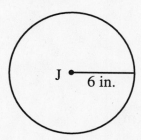

    [A] 226 in.²   [B] 38 in.²   [C] 19 in.²   [D] 113 in.²

54. Jamey's dog Mojo has his exercise area in the back yard. A stake in the ground has a thirty foot rope tied to it. The other end of the rope is fastened to Mojo's collar to keep him from wandering away. Explain how you would determine the total exercise area for the dog. Round your answer to the nearest ft².

55. What is the ratio of the radius of circle *A* to the radius of circle *B* below? What is the ratio of the area of circle *A* to the area of circle *B*? What do you think is the ratio of the areas of two circles whose radii are in a ratio of 1 to 3?

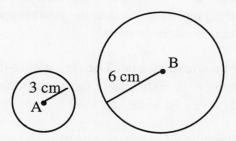

56. What is the approximate length of the radius of a circle that has an area of 78.5 in.² ?

57.

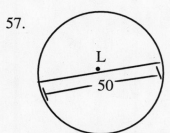

    Complete the equation for the circle *L* in the figure above: Area = π____²

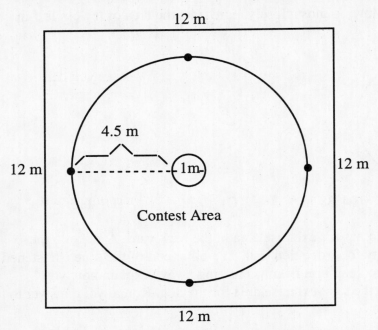

(Source: Rules of the Game 1990 St. Martin's Press)

58. The figure above shows the area of a wrestling mat. The area within the large circle is the in-bounds wrestling area. Estimate to the nearest tenth the total in-bounds area of a wrestling mat. Estimate to the nearest tenth the area of the section of the mat that is not in-bounds.

59. The figure above shows the area of a wrestling mat. The area within the large circle is the in-bounds wrestling area. Estimate to the nearest tenth the circumference of the in-bounds area of a wrestling mat.

Lesson 8-5   Objective 1: Find perfect squares and square roots of perfect squares.

Dynamic Item

60. Evaluate the expression: 4^2

   [A] 4   [B] 6   [C] 8   [D] 16

Dynamic Item

61. Simplify: $\sqrt{49}$

62. Is the square of any whole number also a whole number? Explain.

63. A square measuring 1 ft by 1 ft can be described as one square foot. How can this same square by described in inches?

64. Write the squares of the numbers one through ten. What can you determine about the differences between the square of one number to the next?

65. Solve for l and m:

    a. $4^2 - (4 \cdot 4) + \sqrt{1} = l$

    b. $11^2 - (11 \cdot 11) + \sqrt{16} = m$

    What can you conclude from the two equations? Use this conclusion to solve for n:

    c. $1{,}263^2 - (1{,}263 \cdot 1{,}263) + \sqrt{81} = n$

66. Give an example of three whole numbers with the following characteristics: (a) number A is the square root of number B; (b) number B is the square root of number C; (c) number C is less than 100. Explain your answer.

67. A checkerboard is made up of equal amounts of red and black squares. There are eight squares to a side. How many black squares are in a checkerboard?

    [A] 32   [B] 16   [C] 64   [D] 8

68. What is the area of a square having a perimeter of 32 in.?

69. The area of one square room in Chelsey's house is 100 feet^2 and the area of her square bedroom is 64 feet^2. What is the sum of the perimeters of both rooms?

70. Find A, B, C and D in the table below.

$\sqrt{25}$	+	$\sqrt{36}$	-	$\sqrt{9}$	=	A
$\sqrt{49}$	+	B	-	$\sqrt{1}$	=	8
C^2	+	$\sqrt{121}$	-	$\sqrt{81}$	=	38
$\sqrt{16}$	+	$\sqrt{144}$	-	D^2	=	7

CHAPTER 8

Lesson 8-5   Objective 2: Estimate square roots.

Dynamic Item

71. $\sqrt{46}$ is approximately equal to ___.

   [A] 7   [B] 4.6   [C] 70   [D] 9

Dynamic Item

72. Between which two consecutive whole numbers is $\sqrt{10}$?

73. The legs of a right triangle have unit measurements of 1 and 20. What is the unit length of the hypotenuse?

   [A] $\sqrt{401}$ [B] $\sqrt{420}$ [C] $\sqrt{410}$ [D] $\sqrt{400}$

74. What is the length of a diagonal of a square having a perimeter of 26 mm? Round to the nearest mm.

75. Write three whole numbers whose square roots are between 14 and 15.

Lesson 8-6   Objective 1: Use the Pythagorean theorem.

Dynamic Item

76. Find the unknown length.

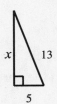

   [A] 9   [B] 18   [C] 8   [D] 12

Dynamic Item

77. The length of the legs of a right triangle are $a = 14$ and $b = 6$. Find the length of the hypotenuse.

78. What do you know about the legs and hypotenuse of a right triangle with two congruent sides? Explain.

79. Explain how to find the length of a side of a rectangle when you know the length of its diagonal and another side.

80. Two sides of a right triangle measure 15 in. and 25 in. Explain how you can find the third side if the lengths of all three sides are whole numbers.

81. The hypotenuse of a right triangle is 125% the length of the longer leg. Give an example of a triangle with this characteristic by listing the length of all three sides.

82. A right triangle has a leg with a length of 6 in. and a hypotenuse of 10 in. What is the length of the third side?

    [A] 9 in.   [B] 6 in.   [C] 8 in.   [D] 7 in.

83. What is the perimeter of a right triangle with legs measuring 9 ft and 12 ft?

    [A] 36 ft.   [B] 15 ft.   [C] 25 ft.   [D] 42 ft.

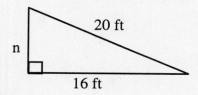

84. What is the value *n* in the figure above?

85. What is the area of the figure above?

86. What is the perimeter of the figure above?

87. A right triangle has a leg measuring 15 cm and a hypotenuse of 25 cm. How long is the third side of the triangle?

88. The western border of Utah stretches approximately 350 miles and the southern border is about 280 miles. If the intersection of these two borders represents a right angle, what is your estimate of the distance from the state's northwest corner to its southeast corner? Use the Pythagorean Theorem to assist you in your answer.

Lesson 8-6   Objective 2: Determine whether a triangle is a right triangle.

Dynamic Item
   89. Which set of side lengths cannot form a right triangle?

       [A] 10 mm, 24 mm, 26 mm   [B] 20 mm, 48 mm, 52 mm

       [C] 5 mm, 12 mm, 13 mm   [D] 11 mm, 24 mm, 26 mm

Dynamic Item
   90. Is a triangle with sides of length 12 cm, 16 cm, and 20 cm a right triangle?

   91. Is a triangle with sides 6 cm,10 cm, and 15 cm a right triangle? Explain your answer.

Lesson 8-7   Objective: Use a calculator to apply the Pythagorean theorem.

Dynamic Item
   92. Find the length of the leg of this right triangle to 3 decimal places.

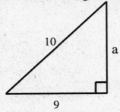

       [A] 13.454   [B] 4.359   [C] 3   [D] 4.680

Dynamic Item
   93. How long is a string reaching from the top of a 7-ft pole to a point 5 ft from the pole? Give an exact answer and an answer to 3 decimal places.

   94. A rectangular swimming pool has dimensions of 40 ft × 20 ft. Explain how you would determine the longest distance you could swim in a straight line in this pool. Round your answer to the nearest foot.

   95. Explain how you would use the Pythagorean Theorem to find the length of a catcher's throw to second base in a baseball diamond. (Hint: The distance between each base is 90 ft.)

96. Explain how you would determine the perimeter of the rectangle. Round your answer to the nearest cm.

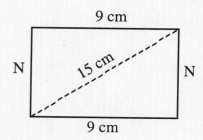

97. The hypotenuse of a right triangle is 10 in. Find two different pairs of sides that would form a right triangle with this hypotenuse. Round your answers to the nearest $\frac{1}{2}$ inch.

98. A triangle has legs a and b and hypotenuse h. Which of the following is true?

 [A] $a > h$ [B] $a + b = h$ [C] $a + b > h$ [D] $h > a + b$

99. What is the area of a right triangle with a hypotenuse of 30 cm and one leg of 18 cm?

100. The two legs of a right triangle are 20 in. and 24 in. What is the perimeter of the triangle? Round to the nearest in.

101. What is the area of a right triangle with a leg of 1 ft and a hypotenuse of $\sqrt{2}$ ft?

Free Skating Arena

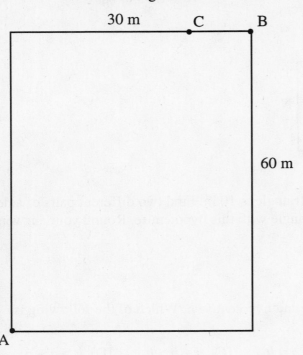

30 m   C   B

60 m

A

102.

The figure above shows the dimensions of a rectangular figure skating rink. What is the distance from Point A to Point B?

103. The figure above shows the dimensions of a rectangular figure skating rink. If a figure skater travelled 65 meters from Point A to Point C, how far would Point C be from Point B?

Lesson 8-8   Objective 1: Identify prisms.

Dynamic Item
104. Identify the figure.

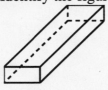

[A] squared prism   [B] cube

[C] triangular prism   [D] rectangular prism

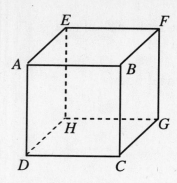

105. Name three faces of the cube above that intersect at point *G*.

106. In the cube above, $\overline{AB}$ is parallel to $\overline{DC}$ and $\overline{EF}$. Is $\overline{AB}$ parallel to any other line segments in the cube? Explain.

107. Use the figure above. $\overline{BF}$ is parallel to:

    [A] $\overline{HG}$ [B] $\overline{BA}$ [C] none of these   [D] $\overline{EH}$

108. How many faces does a cube have?

    [A] 4   [B] 1   [C] 6   [D] 8

109. Which figure below is not a prism?

[A]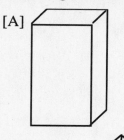

[B]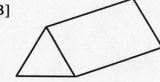

[C]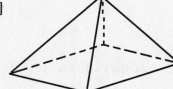

[D]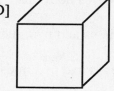

110. Name three things you see every day that are prisms.

Dynamic Item

111. State the number and shape of the faces needed to make a shell of a hexagonal prism.

Lesson 8-8   Objective 2: Identify other three-dimensional figures.

Dynamic Item

112. The party hat has the shape of a _____.

[A] cone   [B] cylinder   [C] circle   [D] sphere

113. Is a circle a three-dimensional figure?

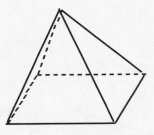

114. Describe the faces of the figure above.

115. How many faces does this figure have?

116. How are prisms and pyramids alike? How are they different?

117. How are cones and pyramids alike? How are they different?

Dynamic Item

118. Draw a picture of a triangular pyramid.

Lesson 8-9   Objective 1: Find surface area of prisms.

Dynamic Item

119. Calculate the surface area of a rectangular solid that is 16 inches long, 9 inches wide, and 15 inches high.

[A] 1013 in.^{2} [B] 2160 in.^{2} [C] 1038 in.^{2} [D] 988 in.^{2}

Dynamic Item

120. Find the surface area of the triangular prism.

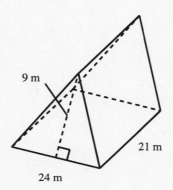

121. Explain how you can estimate the amount of paper needed to wrap a large box which is 2.5 × 3.5 × 4 ft. The wrapping paper comes in rolls of 60 square feet. How many rolls will you need?

122. What is another name for a rectangular prism with all edges having congruent lengths? Explain your answer.

123. What is the smallest number of faces necessary to make a prism? Explain your answer.

124. Draw a rectangular prism having a surface area of 150 cm^2. Mark the sides of the prism to show the area.

125. What is the maximum number of different sized faces that a rectangular prism can have?

[A] 4   [B] 6   [C] 3   [D] 5

126. What is the surface area of a rectangular prism with dimensions of 3 ft by 2 ft by 12 ft?

127. What is the surface area of a rectangular prism with dimensions of 8 cm by 6 cm by 0.5 cm?

Lesson 8-9   Objective 2: Find the surface area of cyliders.

Dynamic Item
128. Find the surface area of the cylinder to the nearest square unit. (Use $\pi = 3.14$)

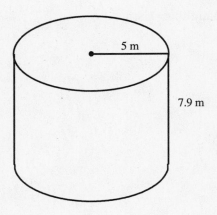

[A] 65 m^2 [B] 203 m^2 [C] 40 m^2 [D] 405 m^2

Dynamic Item
129. Calculate the surface area of a cylindrical water tank that is 11 m high and has a diameter of 6 m. Use $\pi = 3.14$.

130. Your little sister is making a pencil holder out of a juice can. The can is 8.8 cm high.and has a diameter of 5.5 cm. How much paper will she need to cover the outside of the can (not the bottom or the top)?

131. Draw a net for the cylinder. Find its surface area.

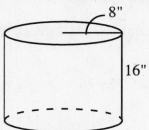

132. Which has a greater surface area: a cylinder with height 8 cm and radius 6 cm, or a cylinder with height 6 cm and radius 8 cm? Explain how you figured it out.

Lesson 8-10   Objective 1: Find the volume of a prism.

Dynamic Item

133. Find the volume of a rectangular prism that is 8 inches long, 6 inches wide, and 5 inches high.

    [A] 236 in.^{3} [B] 340 in.^{3} [C] 19 in.^{3} [D] 240 in.^{3}

Dynamic Item

134. Find the volume of the triangular prism.

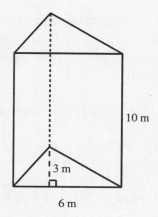

10 m

3 m

6 m

135. A rectangular prism has dimensions of 3 in. × 6 in. × 7 in. Another rectangular prism has dimensions of 2 in. × 7 in. × 9 in. Are the volumes of the two prisms the same? If not, which one has the greater volume? Explain your answer.

136. A three-dimensional tic-tac-toe game has three layers. Each layer is a plastic square with a side of 20 cm and a thickness of 0.5 cm. The space between each layer is 8 cm high. Explain how you can find the dimensions of the smallest box needed to package the game. Find the volume of this box.

137. Draw a rectangular prism with a volume of 300 cm^3.

138. Draw two different rectangular prisms having a volume of 150 in.^{3}. Give the dimensions of each prism.

139. A cube has a side of 4 in. If you double the length of each side, the volume of the cube is multiplied by what number?

   [A] 2   [B] 4   [C] 16   [D] 8

140. A rectangular prism has length of 6 cm, a width of 4 cm and a height of 8 cm. If the length is doubled, the volume will be multiplied by what number?

   [A] 8   [B] 16   [C] 2   [D] 4

141. A cube has a volume of 27 in.^{3}. What is the length of each side?

142. A cube has a volume of 64 mm^3. What is the area of each face?

143. A rectangular prism has a volume of 72 cm^3. Its length is 3 cm and its width is 4 cm. What is the prism's height?

144. A rectangular prism is 6 in. by 2 in. by 18 in. What is its volume?

Lesson 8-10   Objective 2: Find the volume of cylinders.

Dynamic Item
145. Find the volume of the cylinder that has a diameter of 14 feet and a height of 12 feet. (Use $\pi \approx 3.14$.)

   [A] 527.5 cu ft   [B] 1846.3 cu ft   [C] 615.4 cu ft   [D] 2461.8 cu ft

Dynamic Item
146. Find the volume of the cylinder. Use 3.14 for π.

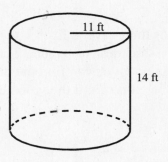

147. A cylinder has a volume of approximately 615 in.^{3}. If the radius is 7 in, what is the height? Round to the nearest in.

148. A cylinder has a diameter of 14 m and a height of 11 m. What is its volume? Round to the nearest meter.

Lesson 8-11   Objective: Solve by using Guess and Test.

Dynamic Item
149. The sum of three consecutive odd numbers is 75. Find the numbers.

    [A] 23, 24, 25   [B] 24, 25, 26   [C] 23, 25, 27   [D] 21, 25, 29

Dynamic Item
150. When Stephanie opened her book she found that the product of the page numbers was 26,406. What were the page numbers?

151. Most calculators can determine n if you are given the square of the number, n^2, but cannot determine n if you are given the cubed value n^3. Can you determine n^2 with a calculator if you are given n^4? Explain.

152. A classmate states that she can determine by mental math that the sides of a cube with a volume of 54,872 cm^3 must measure between 40 cm and 50 cm. Is she correct? Explain.

153. A rectangular prism has a volume of 70 cm^3, a height of 2 cm, and a base width of 5 cm. A second rectangular prism has a volume of 64 cm^3, a height of 2 cm, and a base width of 4 cm. Which prism's base has the greater length? Explain.

154. What is the approximate length of each edge of a cube with a volume of 150 cm^3?

    [A] 12.2 cm   [B] 5.3 cm^2 [C] 12.2 cm^2 [D] 5.3 cm

155. The volume of a cube is 1,331 in.^{3}. What is the area of each face?

    [A] 11 in.^{2} [B] 121 in.^{2} [C] 36.5 in.^{2} [D] 222 in.^{2}

156. David is thinking of a number between one and ten. After each guess you make, he tells you whether his number is higher or lower than your guess. Explain how you would determine the lowest number of guesses you must make to be certain of getting David's number.

157. Brad has eight marbles and gives Rhea half of them. Rhea adds the marbles to her collection and then gives Brad half of her marbles. Brad has twelve marbles now. How many marbles did Rhea have originally?

158. A rectangular prism has a volume of 81 in.^{3}. The length of its base is three times the width. The height of the prism is equal to the width. What are the dimensions of the prism?

159. What is the area of the smallest face of a rectangular prism with a volume of 48 cm^3, a height of 4 cm and a length of 12 cm?

160. A tree cutter's method of tree removal is by repeated cuts of half of the remaining tree height until it reaches close to ground level. After seven cuts of one tree, it is reduced to a height of 3 in. What was the original height of the tree?

Lesson 9-1   Objective 1: Find the experimental probability of an event.

Dynamic Item

1. After the introduction of a new soft drink, a taste test is conducted to see how it is being received. Of those who participated, 64 said they preferred the new soft drink, 112 preferred the old soft drink, and 24 could not tell any difference. What is the probability that a person in this survey preferred the new soft drink?

    [A] $\dfrac{8}{25}$ [B] $\dfrac{8}{17}$ [C] $\dfrac{4}{7}$ [D] $\dfrac{4}{11}$

Dynamic Item

2. In your last 15 basketball games, you attempted 75 free throws and made 45. What is the experimental probability of you making a free throw in your next game?

3. Jamal is considering joining the school basketball team and he devised an experiment based on the number of free throws made per twenty attempts. As he repeated this experiment four times one day, he noticed that P(make a basket) increased in each successive experiment. What would be a reasonable explanation for this?

4. Isiah is the star player on his school's basketball team. One afternoon he devised an experiment based on the number of free throws made per twenty attempts to determine what his P(make a basket) was. During the afternoon, he conducted the experiment five times and discovered that in the fourth and fifth experiment the P(make a basket) decreased. What would be a reasonable explanation for this?

CHAPTER 9

5. In a game using the chart below, you earn points if you toss heads in accordance with choice A, B or C. If you choose A and you toss two heads, you earn four points. If you choose B and toss two heads and a tail, you earn zero points. Each choice you make counts as one turn. How would you use the probability of tossing continuous heads to determine the choice of A, B or C to earn points, while taking the lowest number of turns?

Choice	All Heads Points Given
(A) 2 tosses	4
(B) 3 tosses	6
(C) 4 tosses	10

6. You toss a coin 30 times and get 12 heads. The experimental probability of getting heads is:

   [A] $\frac{1}{2}$ [B] $\frac{2}{5}$ [C] $\frac{3}{5}$ [D] $\frac{2}{3}$

7. You toss a coin 80 times and get 45 heads. The experimental probability of getting tails is:

   [A] $\frac{9}{16}$ [B] $\frac{15}{16}$ [C] $\frac{1}{2}$ [D] $\frac{7}{16}$

8. Eric tossed a coin ten times. The first six tosses resulted in five heads and one tail. What is the probability that the final four tosses will be all tails? Explain your answer.

Lesson 9-1   Objective 2: Use simulations to find experimental probability.

Dynamic Item

9. You work at a T-shirt printing business. 564 of 4,700 T-shirts shipped are printed improperly. What is the experimental probability that a T-shirt is printed improperly?

   [A] 5.64%   [B] 47%   [C] 12%   [D] 11%

Dynamic Item

10. A company manufactures disposable 35 mm cameras. On the average there are 22 defective cameras per 500.   What is the probability that a camera will be defective?

	# Heads	# Tails	# Tosses	P(heads)
A	1	1	2	50%
B	3	2	5	60%
C	6	4	10	60%
D	24	26	50	48%

11. Use the table above. For 50 tosses, what was the experimental probability of heads?

12. Use the table above. For five tosses, what was the experimental probability of tails?

13. Use the table above. Compare the experimental probabilities of heads in trials B and C.

14. A cereal company is putting one of five different hockey cards in its boxes of cereal. Explain how to use a number cube to estimate the probability of getting all the cards if you buy 10 boxes. Hint: ignore the side 6 on the cube.

15. The frequency table shows the results of spinning a spinner with the numbers 0–9. There were 5 sets of 10 spins. Use the table to estimate the probability of spinning the number 8 exactly twice in 10 spins.

Trial	0	1	2	3	4	5	6	7	8	9
1	II		I	I	I	I	I		II	I
2	I	II	I	I	I	I	I	I		I
3		I	II	II	I	I			I	I
4	I		I		II	I	II	II		II
5	I	I	I	I	I	I	I	I	I	I

Do you think that the results would be different if you had more trials?

Lesson 9-2   Objective 1: Simulate a problem.

Dynamic Item

16. Describe a simulated experiment that would test the following: Your newspaper arrives before 7:00 a.m. five-sixths of the time and after 7:00 a.m. one-sixth of the time. How many days would you expect to pass before your paper has arrived before 7:00 a.m. 3 days in a row?

[A] Toss a six-sided number cube until you get 2 numbers greater than one in a row, and record the number of tosses needed. Repeat the experiment several times and divide the sum of the tosses needed by the number of trials.

[B] Toss a coin until you get 2 heads in a row, and record the number of tosses needed. Repeat the experiment several times and divide the sum of the tosses needed by the number of trials.

[C] Toss a six-sided number cube until you get 3 numbers greater than one in a row, and record the number of tosses needed. Repeat the experiment several times and divide the sum of the tosses needed by the number of trials.

[D] Toss a coin until you get 3 heads in a row, and record the number of tosses needed. Repeat the experiment several times and divide the sum of the tosses needed by the number of trials.

Dynamic Item

17. Describe a simulated experiment that would test the following: Your newspaper arrives before 7:00 am. half of the time and after 7:00 am. half of the time. How many days would you expect to pass before your paper has arrived before 7:00 am. 5 days in a row?

18. There are thirty-six possible combinations from the roll of two number cubes. Explain what you believe the probability would be of rolling all of these combinations in thirty-six rolls of the cubes.

19. What is a simulation?

20. Which ratio shows the probability of getting four consecutive twos from tossing a fair number cube?

[A] $\dfrac{1}{24}$ [B] $\dfrac{1}{1,296}$ [C] $\dfrac{1}{36}$ [D] $\dfrac{2}{3}$

CHAPTER 9

21. Which ratio below shows the probability of rolling a twelve with two number cubes?

    [A] $\dfrac{1}{36}$ [B] $\dfrac{1}{6}$ [C] $\dfrac{1}{2}$ [D] $\dfrac{1}{12}$

22. Which ratio shows the probability of getting three consecutive heads from coin tossing?

    [A] $\dfrac{1}{16}$ [B] $\dfrac{1}{4}$ [C] $\dfrac{1}{8}$ [D] $\dfrac{1}{2}$

23. You are given a deck of shuffled playing cards. How many cards must you draw to be absolutely certain of obtaining a non-spade? Explain your answer.

Lesson 9-2   Objective 2: Solve problems using any strategy.

24. Adam's soccer team needs new uniforms for next year's season. In order to finance the purchase of sixteen new uniforms, the players are asked to sell packages of popcorn for $1.00 each. If each uniform costs thirty dollars and the profit from each package sold is $0.25, how many packages must be sold to pay for the uniforms?

25. Adam's soccer team needs new uniforms for next year's season. In order to finance the purchase of sixteen new uniforms, the players are asked to sell packages of popcorn at $1.00 each. Each uniform costs twenty-five dollars. If the profit from each package sold is $0.40, and the team sells 2,000 packages, how much money would be available to purchase other team supplies after the uniforms are paid for?

26. Adam's soccer team needs new uniforms for next year's season. In order to finance the purchase of sixteen new uniforms, the players are asked to sell packages of popcorn for $1.00 each. Each uniform costs thirty-three dollars. If the team sells 1,760 packages and earns just enough to pay for the uniforms, what must the profit be for each package sold?

27. Adam's soccer team needs new uniforms for next year's season. In order to finance the purchase of sixteen new uniforms, the players are asked to sell packages of popcorn for $1.00 each. If the team sells 992 packages at a profit of $0.50 per package and earns just enough to pay for the uniforms, how much does each uniform cost?

Lesson 9-3   Objective 1: Find the theoretical probability of an event.

Dynamic Item

28. What is the probability of drawing a ten from a deck of 52 playing cards?

    [A] $\dfrac{1}{13}$ [B] $\dfrac{2}{13}$ [C] $\dfrac{1}{25}$ [D] $\dfrac{4}{39}$

Dynamic Item

29. A number cube is rolled 330 times. The number three comes up 53 times.
    a) What is the theoretical probability of rolling a three?
    b) What is the experimental probability of rolling a three?

30. Describe a situation where only two outcomes are possible and a situation where more than two outcomes are possible.

31. You toss a quarter twenty times, resulting in 12 heads and 8 tails. What is the probability that your next toss will be a heads? Explain.

32. Your first roll of a six-sided number cube is a four. What is the probability that the outcome of the second roll will be higher than the first roll?

    [A] $\dfrac{2}{4}$ [B] $\dfrac{4}{6}$ [C] $\dfrac{2}{6}$ [D] $\dfrac{3}{3}$

33. In order to determine who goes first in a board game, you and your opponent, Sara, must roll a number cube. Whoever rolls the higher number goes first. You roll a three. Explain the probabilities of the outcomes of Sara's roll.

CHAPTER 9

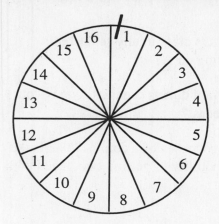

34. Use the figure above. What is the probability of the spinning wheel stopping on a single digit number?

35. Use the figure above. What is the probability of the spinning wheel stopping on the number twelve?

36.

Number of Students Who Play on More Than One Sports Team	
1985	17%
1986	21%
1987	19%
1988	28%
1989	25%
1990	24%

Using the information in the table above, what is the probability that a given student in 1988 played less than one sport?

Lesson 9-3   Objective 2: Find the probability of a complement.

Dynamic Item

37. Six balls numbered from 1 to 6 are placed in an urn. One ball is selected at random. Find the probability that it is NOT number 2.

[A] $\frac{1}{6}$ [B] $\frac{2}{3}$ [C] $\frac{1}{2}$ [D] $\frac{5}{6}$

CHAPTER 9

Dynamic Item

38. The probability of getting an A in Mrs. Ford's class in any semester is 17%. What is the probability of NOT getting an A?

39. The weatherman reports a 60% chance of rain during the next twenty-four hours. What is the complement of this forecast?

40. The probability of getting two tails with two tosses of a coin is 25%. Is the complement of this event equal to the probability of getting two heads with two tosses? Explain your answer.

41. When rolling a number cube, the probability of rolling a 3 is $\frac{1}{6}$. What is the probability of the complement of P(3)?

[A] $\frac{1}{3}$ [B] $\frac{5}{6}$ [C] $\frac{1}{6}$ [D] $\frac{1}{2}$

Lesson 9-4 Objective 1: Find a sample space.

Dynamic Item

42. A spinner that has 4 sections of equal area, numbered from 1 to 4, is spun two times in succession. Which of the following is/are not part of the list of ordered pairs that represent all the equally likely events?
I. (0, 1) II. (4, 4) III. (2, 4) IV. (4, 2)

[A] I only   [B] I and II only

[C] II only   [D] All of the outcomes are possible.

Dynamic Item

43. A spinner that has 4 sections of equal area, numbered from 1 to 4, is spun two times in succession. Find the sample space composed of equally likely events.

44. What does each stage in a tree diagram represent?

45. How does the appearance of a sample space in a grid differ from that in a tree diagram?

46. What would be the easier sample space to make for the rolling of two number cubes, a grid or a tree diagram? Make both diagrams as part of your explanation.

47. Which of the following does not show each possible outcome in a given situation?

   [A] a grid   [B] both a grid and a tree diagram

   [C] the counting principle   [D] a tree diagram

48. In a sample space for tossing three coins, Millie states that there is only one possible outcome for two heads and a tail if the first two coins tossed are heads. Do you agree with her? Explain why or why not.

Lesson 9-4   Objective 2: Use the counting principle.

Dynamic Item
49. Stanwood Builders has a development of new homes. There are four different floor plans, four exterior colors, and an option of either a two- or a three-car garage. How many choices are there for one home?

   [A] 32   [B] 18   [C] 40   [D] 48

Dynamic Item
50. Account numbers for Century Oil Company consist of eight digits. If the first digit cannot be a 0, how many account numbers are possible?

51. How many possible outcomes are there in a sample space for tossing four coins?

   [A] 12   [B] 16   [C] 8   [D] 4

52. What is the number of possible outcomes in a sample space for two number cubes and one coin?

53. In a sample space for rolling two number cubes and tossing one coin, how many possible outcomes include the coin being a heads?

54. How many possible outcomes are there in a sample space for the rolling of:
   a. one number cube?
   b. two number cubes?
   c. three number cubes?

55. In a sample space for rolling two number cubes, what is the probability of rolling two different numbers?

56. In a sample space for rolling two number cubes, what is the probability of rolling two of the same number?

CHAPTER 9

57. In a sample space for rolling two number cubes, what is the probability of rolling two 3's?

Lesson 9-5   Objective 1: Find the probability of independent events.

Dynamic Item
58. Two urns each contain blue balls and red balls. Urn I contains two blue balls and three red balls and Urn II contains four blue balls and four red balls. A ball is drawn from each urn. What is the probability that both balls are blue?

[A] $\dfrac{3}{20}$ [B] $\dfrac{1}{5}$ [C] $\dfrac{3}{10}$ [D] $\dfrac{7}{40}$

Dynamic Item
59. A drawer contains 6 red socks, 8 white socks, and 2 blue socks. Without looking, you draw out a sock, return it, and draw out a second sock. What is the probability that the first sock is blue and the second sock is red?

60. Are the events in a series of coin tosses dependent? Explain your answers.

61. Suppose you were given a bag containing five red and five blue marbles. Explain what would make events dependent and independent if you were asked to determine the probabilities of choosing red marbles in succeeding events.

62. What is the most common sum of numbers rolled by two number cubes? What is the probability of this sum being rolled? Explain your answer.

63. Which two events are independent?

   [A] go sledding, snow   [B] sleep, dream

   [C] do chores, earn allowance   [D] count to 100, fix a bike

CHAPTER 9

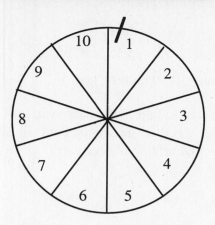

64. Refer to the spinning wheel figure above. What is the probability of spinning the same number three times consecutively?

65. Refer to the spinning wheel figure above. What is the probability that three nines will be spun consecutively?

66. Refer to the spinning wheel figure above. What is the probability that three different numbers will be spun consecutively?

67. Refer to the spinning wheel figure above. What is the probability that an even number will be spun followed by an odd number?

68. Suppose you toss a coin and roll a number cube. Find the probability that you toss heads and roll a number greater than 4.

Lesson 9-5 Objective 2: Find the probability of dependent events.

Dynamic Item
69. A bag contains 3 green marbles and 5 blue marbles. Two marbles are drawn at random. One marble is drawn and not replaced. Then a second marble is drawn. What is the probability that the first marble is blue and the second one is green?

[A] $\dfrac{5}{56}$ [B] $\dfrac{5}{3}$ [C] $\dfrac{15}{56}$ [D] $\dfrac{1}{5}$

Dynamic Item
70. A drawer contains 7 red socks, 4 white socks, and 3 blue socks. Without looking, you draw out a sock and then draw out a second sock without returning the first sock. What is the probability that the first sock and the second sock are both white?

CHAPTER 9

71. Which two events are dependent?

    [A] toss a heads, toss a tails   [B] wear brown socks, eat lunch

    [C] talk to a friend, feed your dog   [D] study, do well on a test

72. You are given a deck of playing cards and asked to take two cards from the deck. If you are then asked what the probability is that the second card picked is a club, how would the first card picked affect your answer? Indicate the probabilities in your answers.

73.

Home-Game Win Streaks	
Team	# Games
Auburn	59
Stanford	37
Louisiana Tech	29
Penn State	20

    The chart above shows the longest home-game win streaks among Division I women's basketball teams. The extension of the win streaks shown in the chart is dependent on which two events?

Lesson 9-6   Objective: Find permutations.

Dynamic Item
74. How many different ways can you arrange seven books on a shelf?

    [A] 28   [B] 49   [C] 5,040   [D] 14

Dynamic Item
75. How many different ways can 7 different runners finish in first, second, and third places in a race?

76. You are charged $0.59 for an item at a convenience store. You give the clerk a one dollar bill and you are given back $0.41 in change; a quarter, dime, nickel and penny. For what reason might you prefer to be given your change in a particular permutation?

77. What is the number of permutations that can be made using the letters PEN?

    [A] 1   [B] 3   [C] 8   [D] 6

78. There are four children in Maria's family. How many permutations are there listing the children in all possible age orders?

79. List all the permutations of the numerals 3, 5, and 7. How many numbers are in your list?

80. How many permutations are there, using all of the following five letters at one time: A, B, C, D and E?

81. How many permutations are there, using any of the following five letters at one time: A, B, C, D and E?

82. Suppose that a car is manufactured in 4 models, 12 colors, 3 engine sizes, and 2 transmissions. How many different cars are available?

83. Five class officers are going to be photographed. If the class president sits in the middle, how many ways can they line up?

84. Give an example of when you have used permutations in your everyday life.

85. You want to arrange five books on a shelf. How many ways can you arrange them?

Lesson 9-7   Objective: Find combinations.

Dynamic Item
86. A panel of judges is to consist of four women and three men. A list of potential judges has five women and five men on it. How many different panels could be created from this list?

    [A] 50   [B] 11   [C] 100   [D] 10

Dynamic Item
87. Heidi owns 6 cassettes and is taking 4 of them on vacation. In how many ways can she choose 4 cassettes from the 6?

88. What is the difference between a permutation and a combination?

89. Andy was given five pictures and asked to present four different combinations of any four of the pictures. Is this possible? Explain.

90. Arlene was given four pictures and asked to present four different combinations of all four pictures. Is this possible? Explain.

91. What is the number of combinations that can be made using the letters OFF?

    [A] 1   [B] 6   [C] 8   [D] 3

92. Mr. and Mrs. Hong have five children. How many combinations of boys and girls are possible in the Hong's family?

93. Tim is thinking of two numbers from one to ten. If you are asked to guess the two numbers, how many different combinations would you have to choose from?

94. The Burger Diner offers hamburgers with or without any or all of the following: catsup, lettuce, and mayonnaise. How many ways can you get a burger?

    [A] 3 ways   [B] 12 ways   [C] 10 ways   [D] 8 ways

95. Four students are waiting in line. Two of them are called at once. How many ways could they be called?

96. Five people at a party all shake hands with each other. How many handshakes are there? Is this a permutation or a combination? Explain.

97. You have 5 books to put on a shelf that only holds 4. How many different sets of 4 books can you put on the shelf?

Lesson 9-8 Objective: Estimate the size of a population using the capture/recapture method.

Dynamic Item
98. Game wardens use experiments to help determine the number of fish in a lake. Suppose 100 fish are caught, tagged, and released back into the lake. Two weeks later 80 fish are caught, of which 4 are found to have tags. Using this information, estimate the number of fish in the lake.

    [A] 2,000   [B] 8,000   [C] 96   [D] 176

Dynamic Item
99. Game wardens use experiments to help determine the number of fish in a lake. Suppose 80 fish are caught, tagged, and released back into the lake. Two weeks later 40 fish are caught, of which 4 are found to have tags. Using this information, estimate the number of fish in the lake.

Data collected in one area of the Bridger Mountains by the Montana Department of Fish, Wildlife and Parks are given below.

Date	Conditions	Number of Deer Marked in February of Given Year	Total Deer Counted	Marked Deer Counted
3/79	Patchy snow, -7°C	101	1173	65
3/80	Patchy snow, -4°C; deer scattered	83	1017	42
3/81	Mostly bare, dry, 1°C; deer scattered	60	1212	32
3/82	Light snow cover, 1°C; deer at low elevation	36	1707	30
3/83	Mostly bare, -4°C; deer at low elevation	89	1612	68
3/84	Bare, dry, 6°C; large deer groups at low elevation	59	1590	37
3/85	Mostly bare, dry; deer at low elevation	54	1417	42
3/86	Mostly bare, dry; deer at low elevation	110	1608	85
3/87	2 cm snow cover; deer normally distributed	83	1469	52

100. Would a prediction for any of the dates in the chart above be more accurate if there were more "total deer counted"? Explain.

101. Could conditions be a factor in determining the prediction of total deer on a given date in the chart above? Explain your answer.

102. Using the chart above, calculate the estimate of deer populations for the years 1984 and 1985. What factors could be attributed to the change from one year to the next?

103. Use the chart above. The highest percentage of marked deer counted, out of the number of deer marked, occurred in which of the following periods?

[A] 3/86　　[B] 3/83　　[C] none of these　　[D] 3/82

104. Use the chart above. The lowest percentage of marked deer counted, out of the number of deer marked, occurred in which of the following periods?

[A] none of these　　[B] 3/82　　[C] 3/85　　[D] 3/80

105. If at the end of the observation during the 3/87 period in the chart above four extra marked deer were counted, how would this affect the data sheet and the estimate of deer population for the period in comparison to estimate calculated by the data on the chart?

Data collected in one area of the Bridger Mountains by the Montana Department of Fish, Wildlife and Parks are given below.

Date	Conditions	Number of Deer Marked in February of Given Year	Total Deer Counted	Marked Deer Counted
3/79	Patchy snow, -7°C	101	1173	65
3/80	Patchy snow, -4°C; deer scattered	83	1017	42
3/81	Mostly bare, dry, 1°C; deer scattered	60	1212	32
3/82	Light snow cover, 1°C; deer at low elevation	36	1707	30
3/83	Mostly bare, -4°C; deer at low elevation	89	1612	68
3/84	Bare, dry, 6°C; large deer groups at low elevation	59	1590	37
3/85	Mostly bare, dry; deer at low elevation	54	1417	42
3/86	Mostly bare, dry; deer at low elevation	110	1608	85
3/87	2 cm snow cover; deer normally distributed	83	1469	52

106. Using the chart above, what is the average temperature recorded for the years 1979-1984? Round to the nearest tenth.

107. Refer to the chart above. Suppose researchers counted all 101 marked deer in 3/79. What would be the estimate of deer population?

108. Refer to the chart above. What is the estimate of deer population for the period 3/81? What would the estimate be if the number of deer marked that February was doubled?

109. Refer to the chart above. What is the estimate of deer population for the period 3/86? What would the estimate be if the number of marked deer counted was halved?

Top Participating Sports	
Sport	Millions of People
Swimming	71
Exercise walking	67
Bicycle riding	57
Fishing	47
Camping	47

110. The chart above shows the sports with the greatest participation during 1989. The survey was made up of 20,000 men and women in the U.S. What must be true about the people surveyed to make these fair statistics?

111. Refer to the chart above. Give an example of what could make these statistics unreliable.

CHAPTER 9

Lesson 10-1   Objective 1: Identify and continue arithmetic sequences.

Dynamic Item
1. Start with 3 and add 9 repeatedly. What are the first five numbers in the number pattern?

    [A] 3, 12, 21, 30, 39   [B] 3, 21, 30, 39, 48

    [C] 9, 12, 15, 18, 21   [D] 3, 27, 54, 81, 108

Dynamic Item
2. Write a rule to describe the number pattern.
    5, 7, 9, 11, 13

3. Write a rule to describe a sequence that starts with 1 and shows 10 as its fourth term.

4. What number is missing in this sequence? 1, 2, 6, 24, _____, 720

    [A] 120   [B] 525   [C] 618   [D] 96

5. Which term in the following sequence will be the same as the fourth term in the sequence?
    1, 15, 8, 22

    [A] fifth term   [B] seventh term   [C] ninth term   [D] sixth term

6. Examine the numbers below and look for patterns.

    Row 1   1
    Row 2   1 2
    Row 3   1 2 4
    Row 4   1 2 4 8
    Row 5   1 2 4 8 16

    What is the last number in the 8th row?

Lesson 10-1   Objective 2: Identify and continue geometric and other sequences.

Dynamic Item

7. A grocery clerk sets up a display of oranges in the form of a triangle using 7 oranges at the base and 1 at the top. (Only part of the display is shown below.)

    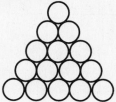

    How many oranges were used by the clerk to make the arrangement?

    [A] 21   [B] 42   [C] 28   [D] 35

Dynamic Item

8. Which of the following rules describes the number pattern?
    4, 20, 100, 500

    [A] Start with 4 and add 5 repeatedly.

    [B] Start with 4 and add 20 repeatedly.

    [C] Start with 5 and multiply by 4 repeatedly.

    [D] Start with 4 and multiply by 5 repeatedly.

Dynamic Item

9. Identify the next three terms in the sequence. 2, 6, 18, 54, ...

10. How are an arithmetic sequence and a geometric sequence alike? How are they different?

11. Describe two traits of sequences that are neither arithmetic nor geometric.

12. Write a rule to describe a geometric sequence and another rule to describe an arithmetic sequence so that the fifth term in each sequence is the same number.

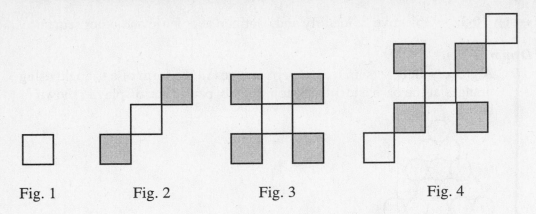

Fig. 1   Fig. 2   Fig. 3   Fig. 4

13. The first four figures in a pattern of algebra tiles are shown above. How many shaded tiles would be in the seventh figure?

14. Identify the sequence modeled by the algebra tiles shown above as arithmetic, geometric, or neither. Write a rule to describe the sequence.

15. Suppose October 1 is a Tuesday. Write a rule to identify the second Wednesday, third Thursday, and fourth Friday of the month. Use the rule to identify the dates of these special days.

Year Employed	Hourly Rate
1	$4.50
2	$5.00
3	$5.75
4	$6.75

16. Employees of <u>Hometown Groceries</u> are paid according to the scale shown above. Write a rule to describe this sequence.

17. According to the table above, how many years must you work at <u>Hometown Groceries</u> in order to be paid at an hourly rate that is more than double the rate you received during your first year of employment? What will your hourly rate of pay be?

Lesson 10-2   Objective 1: Write numbers in scientific form.

Dynamic Item
18. What is 26,000 in scientific notation?

[A] 2.6×10^{-4} [B] 2.6×10^{4} [C] 2.6×10^{5} [D] 2.6×10^{-3}

Dynamic Item
19. Write 3,030 in scientific notation.

20. Explain why scientific notation is particularly helpful to astronomers who study distances between objects in space.

21. Write a letter to a classmate explaining how to write 62,000,000 in scientific notation.

22. In comparing two numbers expressed in scientific notation, can one assume that the number with the greater exponent is automatically the larger number? Provide evidence for your answer.

23. Which of the following numbers has the greatest value?

[A] 6.5×10^{4} [B] 9.9×10^{4} [C] 8.12×10^{3} [D] 1.111×10^{5}

24. The diameter of Mercury, the smallest planet of the solar system, is about 3.1×10^{3} miles. The largest planet's diameter, that of Jupiter, is about 8.8×10^{4} miles. What is the difference between the diameters of these planets expressed in scientific notation?

25. The Pacific Ocean covers approximately 64,186,300 square miles of Earth's surface while the Atlantic Ocean stretches for about 33,420,000 square miles. Express both of these areas in scientific notation.

26. Mount McKinley in Alaska rises 20,320 feet in the air while Mount Kosciusko in Australia stretches a mere 7,310 feet. What is the difference in the height of these mountains expressed in scientific notation?

27. The largest of the Great Lakes, Lake Superior, covers a total area of about $31,700 \text{ mi}^{2}$ while the smallest Great Lake, Lake Erie, covers only $9,910 \text{ mi}^{2}$. What is the total area covered by these two lakes expressed in scientific notation?

CHAPTER 10

Lesson 10-2   Objective 2: Write numbers in standard form.

Dynamic Item

28. Write in standard notation: 3.43×10^6

[A] 3,430,000   [B] 34,300,000   [C] 0.00000343   [D] 343,000

Dynamic Item

29. Express in standard form without exponents: 4.19×10^5

30. A classmate tells you that the exponent of any number written in scientific notation is always the number of zeros that appear in the number when written in standard form. For example, 5,000,000 becomes 5×10^6. How would you respond to your friend?

31. Which of the following numbers expressed in scientific notation is 3.174×10^5 ?

[A] 317,400,000   [B] 317,400   [C] 31,740,000   [D] 3,174,000

Lesson 10-3   Objective 1: Solve a problem by solving a simpler problem.

Dynamic Item

32. If 13 points are arranged in a circle, how many lines are needed to join every point to every other point once?

[A] 78   [B] 91   [C] 85   [D] 72

Dynamic Item

33. If 23 points are arranged in a circle, how many lines are needed to join every point to every other point once?

34. The grid below shows a 2 × 2 square. You can mark off many such squares in the whole grid. How many 2 × 2 squares are there?

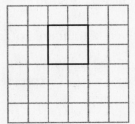

35. Your school is playing in a soccer tournament. The loser of each game is eliminated. How many games will be played, if there are 32 teams competing?

Lesson 10-3   Objective 2: Solve problems using any method.

36. William produces 35 items in 20 min. Bob produces 33 items in 18 min. Which worker is more productive? Explain.

37. Joshua opens his math book. The product of the two facing pages is 342. What are the two page numbers?

38. The school cafeteria offers 4 different types of beverages, 3 different types of sandwiches, and 2 different kinds of desserts. How many different lunch combinations are available?

39. Both Adam and Carol wish to purchase a $25 savings bond. Adam has $11 in his savings account and adds $3 each week. Carol has $9 in her savings account and adds $1.50 each week. How much longer will it take Carol to buy her savings bond than Adam?

40. Alissa has 3 different pairs of pants, 5 different sweaters, and 8 pairs of socks. How many different clothing combinations does she have to choose from?

41. A florist shop estimates that one worker can create an arrangement in 12 min. At 10:30 A.M., the shop receives a rush order for 64 arrangements to be picked up at 5:00 P.M. How many workers must work on this order non-stop in order to meet the deadline?

42. Four out of every seven students in a class of 91 students participate in a local fundraiser. How many students participated in the event?

43. The sum of three consecutive odd integers is 117. What are the integers?

Lesson 10-4   Objective 1: Find simple interest.

Dynamic Item
44. Sylvia bought a 6-month $700 certificate of deposit. At the end of 6 months, she received $35 simple interest. What rate of interest did the certificate pay?

    [A] 8.3%   [B] 5%   [C] 10%   [D] 12%

CHAPTER 10

Dynamic Item

45. What is the simple interest on $3,995 principal borrowed at the interest rate of 12.5 % for 1 year?

46. Write a sentence using the words "interest" and "rate."

47. Suppose you wanted to open a savings account at a local bank. You would probably investigate a number of banks to determine which offers the best investment opportunity. Make a list of questions you would ask officials of each bank you visited.

48. You deposited $700 in an account that pays at a rate of $0.06 for every dollar in the account each year. What is the amount in the account at the end of the first year?

Lesson 10-4   Objective 2: Find compound interest.

Dynamic Item

49. What amount (to the nearest dollar) will an account have after 10 years if $380 is invested at 8% interest compounded annually?

    [A] $135,678   [B] $3,420   [C] $820   [D] $34,200

Dynamic Item

50. If $330 is invested for 10 years at 6%, compounded annually, find the future value. (Round to the nearest dollar)

51. Carla invested $200 in a stock whose value doubles each year. How long will it take for her investment to be worth more than $10,000?

Three - Year Super Savings Plan	
Year	Interest Rate Dollar Per Year
1	$0.03
2	$0.05
3	$0.07

52. Daria placed $2,000 in the Super Savings Plan. What is the value of her investment at the end of the three year period?

53. Mica opened a Super Savings Plan account with $1,000. At the beginning of Year 2, he added an additional $3,000 to the account. What is the value of his investment at the end of the three year period?

54. On your sixth birthday, you deposit $100 in an account that pays 5% interest, compounded annually. How much is in the account on the day you turn 13?

55. Which of the following accounts will yield the greatest amount of interest on an initial deposit of $500.00?

    [A] Account that pays 5% interest compounded annually for 6 years

    [B] Account that pays 4% interest compounded annually for 4 years

    [C] Account that pays 3% interest compounded annually for 5 years

    [D] Account that pays 6% interest compounded annually for 3 years

56. You borrow $200 from a relative for six months. You agree to pay compound interest at the rate of 1% per month. How much interest will you pay your relative when you return the money at the end of the six months?

    [A] $210.00   [B] $201.00   [C] $12.30   [D] $11.66

57. You deposit $100 in a bank account that pays 4% interest compounded annually. How much money is in the account after 6 years?

58. Mark estimates that the cost of a used car in fairly good condition will be about $6,000 when he gets his driver's license in 5 years. A 5-year savings plan offered by his bank pays 9% interest compounded annually. About how much must Mark place in the account now to have enough for a car in 5 years?

Lesson 10-5   Objective 1: Represent functions with tables and rules.

Dynamic Item

59. The function machine below shows Molly's hourly wage. Suppose Molly works 12 hours (input). What are her wages ?

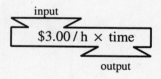

    [A] $36.00   [B] $3.00   [C] $15.00   [D] $39.00

CHAPTER 10

Dynamic Item

60. Make a table of values for the function rule: output = 7 · input + 4

61. Describe the relationship that exists between a rule and a function.

62. What are three ways you could represent a function?

63. The formula $P = 4s$ is an example of a function rule. It represents the relationship between the length of one side of a square and the perimeter of the square. Use the rule to complete the table below. If you made a graph of this data, what shape would you observe?

Length of One Side (s)	Perimeter (P)
1	4
2	8
3	
4	
5	

64. Write a rule that describes the function in the table below.

Input	1	2	3
Output	4	7	10

65. On the function machine shown below, the function rule is given as a variable expression. When the output is 99, what is the input?

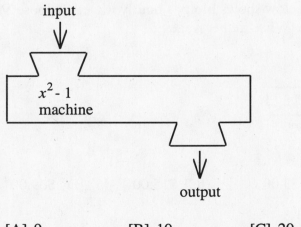

[A] 9   [B] 10   [C] 20   [D] 100

66. Select the rule that describes the function illustrated in the table below.

Input	1	2	3	4
Output	5	7	9	11

[A] $4 - x$ [B] $2x + 3$ [C] $3x - 1$ [D] $x + 4$

67. Scientists estimate the maximum speed of a cheetah to be about 70 mph. Write a rule to describe the relationship that exists between time and the distance a cheetah travels when running at maximum speed.

68. The sea turtle has been found to swim at a maximum rate of 20 mph. How far would a sea turtle travel if swimming at its maximum rate for a period of 8 hours?

69. Rico made a function table to illustrate the rate he charges for mowing lawns. Complete the table. Then write a rule for the function.

Total Hours	Total Earnings
1	
2	
3	$12.75
4	$17.00
5	$21.25

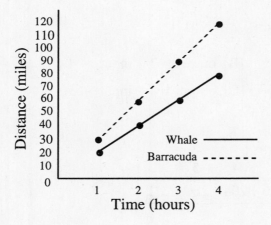

70. The graph illustrates the average speeds of whales and barracuda. Write a rule to represent distance as a function of time for each animal.

CHAPTER 10

71.

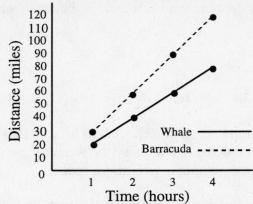

How far would a barracuda travel in 6 hours? How long would it take a whale to travel this same distance?

Lesson 10-5   Objective 2: Graph functions.

Dynamic Item

72. From the graph of values, determine the function rule.

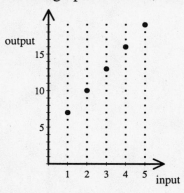

[A] output = 5 · input − 2   [B] output = 3 · input + 4

[C] output = 2 · input + 5   [D] output = 4 · input − 3

Dynamic Item

73. Graph the function for:

Input	(years)	1	2	3	4	5	6
Output	(weeks)	52	104	156	208	260	312

74. Use the table below to write a function rule. Then graph the function.

Input	Output
0	1
1	$1\frac{1}{2}$
2	2
3	$2\frac{1}{2}$
4	3

75. Which graph below shows the rule Output = 2 × Input?

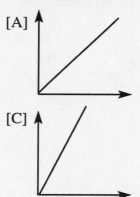

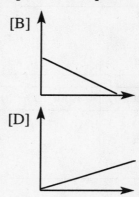

76. The graph shows the distance traveled by cars going at different speeds. Which car is going fastest? How do you know?

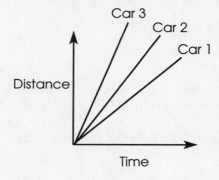

Lesson 10-6   Objective 1: Make a table given a function rule.

Dynamic Item

77. Complete the function table.

input (n)	output ($n - 5$)
3	
3	
4	

[A]

input (n)	output ($n - 5$)
3	−2
3	−2
4	−1

[B]

input (n)	output ($n - 5$)
3	13
3	13
4	14

[C]

input (n)	output ($n - 5$)
3	−8
3	−8
4	−9

[D]

input (n)	output ($n - 5$)
3	8
3	8
4	9

Dynamic Item

78. Complete the function table.

input (n)	output ($n+2$)
1	
3	
7	

79. What is the input and related output in the function rule $f(n) = 4n + 5$?

80. Make a table for the function represented by the rule $f(n) = 10 - 2n$. Find $f(1), f(2), f(3),$ and $f(4)$.

81. The distance that an object falls when dropped from a height is given by the rule $d = \dfrac{1}{2}gt^2$ where $g = 32$ ft/sec/sec, and $t =$ time. Complete the table showing the distance an object has fallen when $t = 1$ sec, 2 sec, . . . 7 sec.

Time (sec)	1	2	3	4	5	6	7
Distance (ft)	16						

82. Your older sister is working part-time at a novelty store. Some of the most-often bought items are funny noses at 29¢ each and buzzers at 79¢ each. To help her figure out how much people owe, complete the table below.

	1	2	3	4	5	6	7
Noses	29¢						
Buzzers	79¢						

Lesson 10-6   Objective 2: Find a function rule given the table.

Dynamic Item

83. Write a function rule for the table.

n	4	5	6	7
$f(n)$	16	25	36	49

   [A] $f(n) = 4n$ [B] $f(n) = 4 - n$ [C] $f(n) = n^4$ [D] $f(n) = n^2$

Dynamic Item

84. Write a rule for the following function represented by the table.

n	2	3	4	5
$f(n)$	4	9	16	25

85. Samuel wants to buy a bicycle for $121.99. He works at a local pizza shop and earns $3.80/h after taxes. How can Samuel use a function to find out how many hours he must work to pay for his bicycle?

86. Write a rule for a function in which the output is always less than the input when n is a positive number.

87. Which of the rules below describes the function represented by the table below?

n $f(n)$

1   3

2   8

3   13

   [A] $f(n) = 3n$ [B] $f(n) = 6n$ [C] $f(n) = 3n - 4$ [D] $f(n) = 5n - 2$

88. All of the following are input/output pairs for the function $f(n) = -2n + 3$ EXCEPT

[A] $f(1) = 1$ [B] $f(5) = -7$ [C] $f(2) = 1$ [D] $f(3) = -3$

89. Write a rule for the function represented in the graph below.

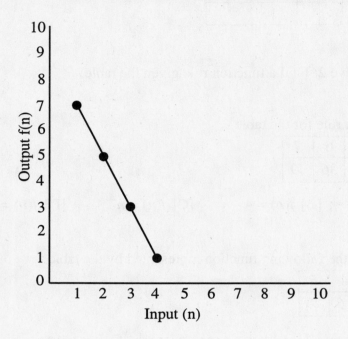

90. Carla puts the same amount of money in her piggy bank each day. Her savings plan is represented in the graph below. Write a rule for the function represented in the graph.

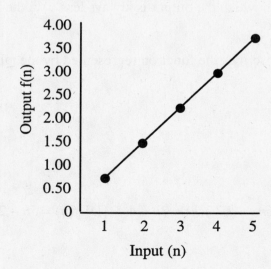

91. A video store charges $2.75 for each day a video is rented. Write a rule to represent the rental charges. Use the rule to determine how much a person owes for a video rented for 4 days.

Lesson 10-7   Objective 1: Write a description for a graph.

Dynamic Item

92. The graph below corresponds to Mrs. Jeffery's shopping trip to the mall by car.

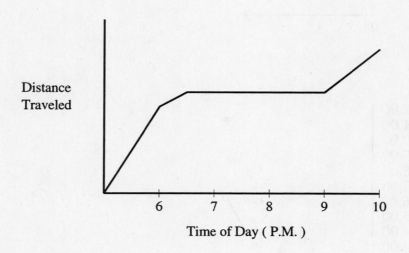

Distance Traveled

Time of Day (P.M.)

What was most likely happening between 6:45 and 9:00 P.M.?

[A] Mrs. Jeffery was at the mall shopping.

[B] Mrs. Jeffery was doing the speed limit on the highway.

[C] Mrs. Jeffery got tired and went home.

[D] Mrs. Jeffery was looking for a parking space.

CHAPTER 10

Dynamic Item

93. Describe an activity that could be represented by this graph.

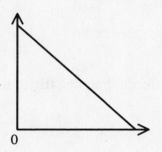

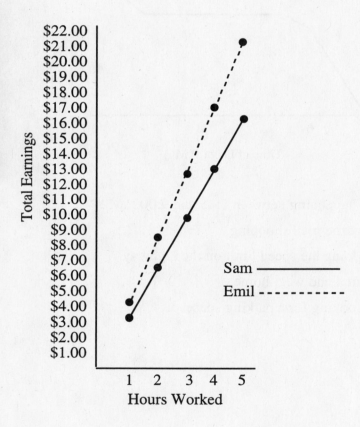

94. Write a rule for each function represented on the graph. Let *n* represent the number of hours worked.

95. Use the rules to determine the difference in wages received by the workers if they both work for 11 hours.

96. Describe a real-world situation that could be represented by the graph below.

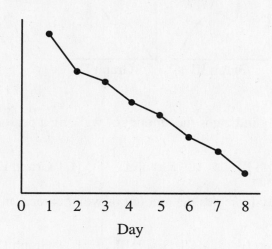

97. A student polled her classmates to determine the average amount of time spent daily watching television. She made a graph to show the results of her poll. Identify two facts you can draw from the graph.

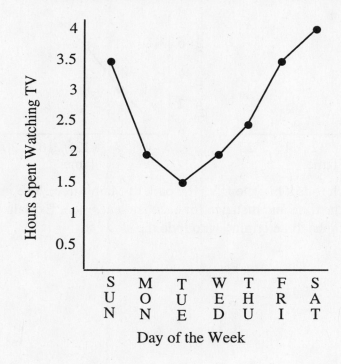

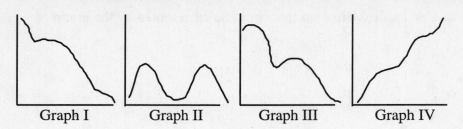

Graph I   Graph II   Graph III   Graph IV

98. Which graph above probably indicates the amount of walking a person does during a 24-hour period?

[A] Graph I   [B] Graph III   [C] Graph IV   [D] Graph II

99. Which graph above probably indicates the amount of weight a person has gained since the age of 5?

[A] Graph II   [B] Graph I   [C] Graph III   [D] Graph IV

100.   **Rita**   **Juan**

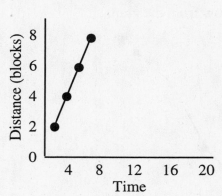
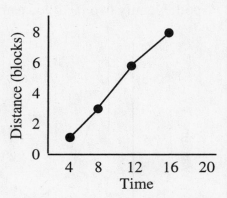

Juan and Rita each rode a bicycle from the park to Main Street. The graph above represents the time and distance for each student's ride. Explain how you can use the graphs to determine who rode the slowest.

Chapter 10: Patterns and Functions

Lesson 10-7   Objective 2: Sketch a graph from a description.

Dynamic Item
101. Draw a graph to represent the depth of liquid in the bottle shown as water
      is poured into it at a constant rate.

102. What does a straight horizontal line or "flat" segment indicate on a graph?

103. Suppose you were asked to graph variations in your height between the
      ages of 5 and 10. How would you go about completing the task?

104.   **Rita**   **Juan**

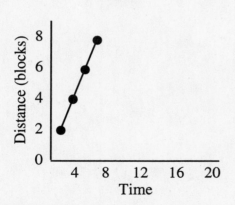   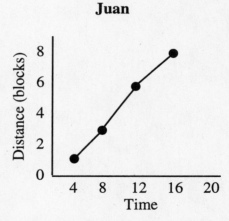

      Explain how the steepness of the graph above is related to the speed of the
      rider.

HOUR	NUMBER OF YEAST CELLS
0	0
2	28
4	76
6	120
8	0

105. A scientist observed a population of yeast cells in a glass dish every two hours for an eight hour period. Her data is shown above. Make a graph to represent the data.

106. A scientist observed a population of yeast cells in a glass dish every two hours for an eight hour period. Her data is shown above. What conclusions can you draw from your graph?

<u>**Lesson 11-1**</u>   Objective 1: Graph points on the coordinate plane.

Dynamic Item
1. Which of the following is the graph of the point $C(-1, -2)$?

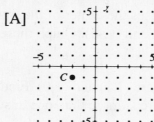

[A]

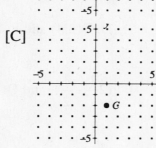

[C]

[B]

[D]

Dynamic Item
2. Name the ordered pair for point A.

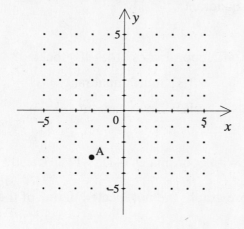

3. Use the terms x-axis, y-axis and origin in a complete sentence.

4. Describe how you would graph a point on a coordinate plane.

5. Explain the similarities between latitude and longitude and the axes of a graph.

CHAPTER 11

6. The coordinates of three vertices of a rectangle are (-4,1), (-1,3), and (-4,3). Which of these points is the fourth vertex?

    [A] (0,3)   [B] (-4,-1)   [C] (1,3)   [D] (-1,1)

7. An architect is designing a parking lot. He uses the center of the lot as the origin, and puts lights at (-3,-2), (0,5), (5,1), and (1,-5). Graph these points to show where the lights would go.

8. The coordinates of two vertices of a square are (1,2) and (1,0). Find the coordinates of the other vertices. (Hint: There is more than one answer.)

9. Graph the following points: A(-5,2), B(4,3), C(0,-1), D(2,4) and E(1,-5) on a coordinate plane.

10. Graph the following points: M($-\frac{1}{2}$,2), N(0,1$\frac{1}{2}$), P(2$\frac{1}{2}$,-$\frac{1}{2}$), and Q(-3,-1$\frac{1}{2}$) on a coordinate plane.

11. Using the origin as its center, draw a circle with a radius of 6 units. Identify three points on the circle.

Lesson 11-1   Objective 2: Identify quadrants.

Dynamic Item
12. In which quadrant is the point with coordinates (14, −13) located?

    [A] third quadrant   [B] fourth quadrant

    [C] second quadrant   [D] first quadrant

Dynamic Item
13. In which quadrant is the point with coordinates (−12, −11) located?

14. Name three ordered pairs whose graphs are not located in one of the four quadrants.

15. In which quadrant are both coordinates of a point negative?

    [A] Quadrant IV   [B] Quadrant III   [C] Quadrant I   [D] Quadrant II

16. In which quadrant is the x-coordinate negative and the y-coordinate positive?

    [A] Quadrant III   [B] Quadrant I   [C] Quadrant II   [D] Quadrant IV

Lesson 11-2   Objective 1: Find ordered pairs that are solutions to equations in two variables.

Dynamic Item

17. Which ordered pair is a solution of the equation $3x + 2y = -11$?

  [A] $(-1, -3)$ [B] $(-4, -1)$ [C] $(-3, -1)$ [D] $(-1, -4)$

Dynamic Item

18. Determine if the ordered pair $(-4, 2)$ is a solution of $4x - 3y = -10$.

19. Write a letter to a friend explaining what is meant by the term "linear equation."

20. Explain how to determine whether an ordered pair is a solution of an equation.

21. Write two different equations whose solution is $(5, 3)$.

22. Create an input/output table for the equation $y = 4x - 1$. Be sure your table includes at least three input/output values.

23. Find two solutions of $y = 2x + \dfrac{1}{2}$.

24. Create an input/output table for the equation $y = \dfrac{1}{2}x + 2$. Be sure your table includes at least three input/output values.

CHAPTER 11

25.

Average Number of Movies a Person Sees Each Year	
United States	4.5
Canada	3.0
France	2.5
Austria	1.5
Turkey	0.5

The table above shows the average number of movies a person sees each year in a variety of countries. You can make an input/output table to identify the average number of movies a person in each of these countries views over a 5-year period. Use the equation $y = x$(average for one year) where x is the number of years and y is the number of movies. Make such a table for a person residing in Canada and a person residing in Austria.

Lesson 11-2   Objective 2: Graph linear equations.

Dynamic Item

26. Which of these equations is shown on the graph?

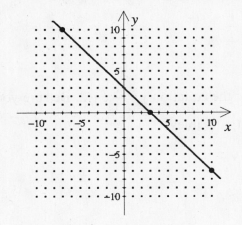

[A] $y = -x - 3$ [B] $y = 3x + 3$ [C] $y = -x + 3$ [D] $y = -x$

Dynamic Item

27. Make a table and graph $x + y = 7$.

28. All of the following points lie on the line $y = 3x - 4$ EXCEPT

[A] (0,-4)   [B] (1,-1)   [C] (-2,10)   [D] (5,11)

29. All of the following points lie on the line $y = -2x + 3$ EXCEPT

 [A] (-2,7)   [B] (5,-7)   [C] (-1,6)   [D] (0,1)

30. The coordinate plane below shows the graph of which equation?

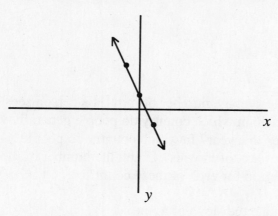

 [A] $y = x + 3$ [B] $y = 2x - 1$ [C] $y = \frac{1}{2}x + 2$ [D] $y = -2x + 1$

31. The coordinate plane below shows the graph of which equation?

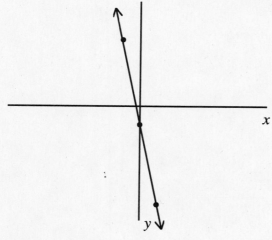

 [A] $y = 6x - 1$ [B] $y = -x + 5$ [C] $y = 3x + 2$ [D] $y = -5x - 1$

CHAPTER 11

32.

Average Number of Movies a Person Sees Each Year	
United States	4.5
Canada	3.0
France	2.5
Austria	1.5
Turkey	0.5

The table above shows the average number of movies a person sees each year in a variety of countries. In which country do people generally view the most amount of movies in a year? In which country do people generally view the least amount of movies? Graph the number of movies viewed over a five-year period for each of these countries.

Lesson 11-3   Objective: Calculate the slope of a line.

Dynamic Item
33. Find the slope of the line passing through the points $A(-7, 5)$ and $B(-4, -6)$.

[A] $-\dfrac{3}{11}$ [B] $-\dfrac{13}{11}$ [C] $-\dfrac{11}{3}$ [D] $\dfrac{1}{11}$

Dynamic Item
34. Find the slope of the line.

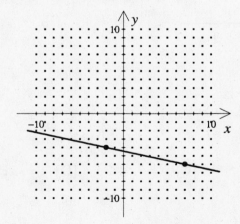

35. Explain how to determine the slope of a line which contains points $(2, 5)$ and $(-1, -4)$.

36. How can you identify the slope of the line $y = -\frac{1}{2}x$ without graphing the line on a coordinate plane?

37. Write an equation for a line that has a slope steeper than the line $y = 5x$. Explain your answer.

38. Architects use the concept of slope to draw blueprints. What determines the slope of a roof when the architect draws up the plan?

39. In the coordinate plane below, all of the following are points on line m EXCEPT

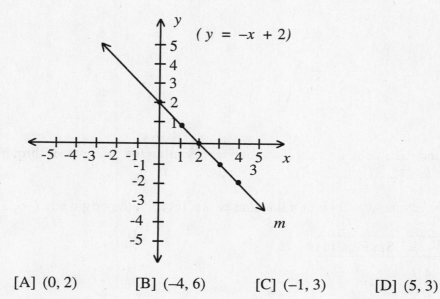

($y = -x + 2$)

m

[A] (0, 2)   [B] (–4, 6)   [C] (–1, 3)   [D] (5, 3)

40. A line contains two points with coordinates (1, 4) and (3, 12). Which expression can you use to find the slope of the line?

[A] $\dfrac{3-1}{12-4}$ [B] $\dfrac{12-1}{3-4}$ [C] $\dfrac{12-4}{3-1}$ [D] $\dfrac{12-3}{4-1}$

41. Points (2, 6) and (–1, –3) lie on Line t. Points (–1, 2) and (2, –4) lie on Line r. Which line has the steepest slope? Explain your answer.

CHAPTER 11

42. Write an equation for the line shown on the coordinate plane below. What is the slope of this line?

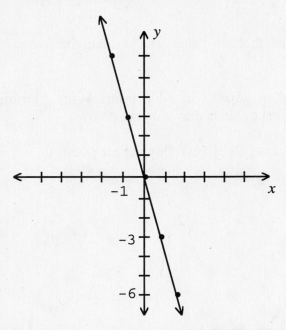

43. Find the slope of a road if the line representing the road passes through the points (5, 3) and (25, 8).

44. Determine the slope of a line that passes through the origin and (–6, 3).

45.

Week	Savings ($)
4	8
5	10
6	12
7	14

The table above shows Jeffrey's savings between the fourth and seventh weeks. Jeffrey saved at the same rate during this time. Find the rate of savings per week. Plot these points and draw the line containing them.

Week	Savings ($)
4	8
5	10
6	12
7	14

46.

The table above shows Jeffrey's savings between the fourth and seventh weeks. Jeffrey saved at the same rate during this time. Find the slope of the line passing through (7, 14) and (5, 10). How does the slope compare with the savings?

Lesson 11-4   Objective 1: Draw graphs of parabolas.

Dynamic Item

47. Graph $y = -\frac{1}{4}x^2$.

[A] 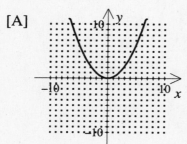   [B]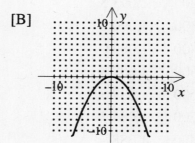

[C] 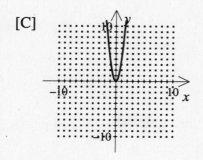   [D]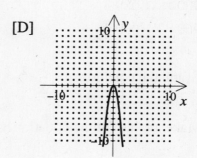

Dynamic Item

48. Sketch the graph of the equation.
$$y = 4x^2$$

49. How is a parabola similar to a linear equation? How do they differ?

50. Compare the graphs of the following equations.
    $y = x^2$; $y = |-x|^2$; $y = -(x^2)$

51. Give two examples of common objects that have the same shape as a parabola.

52. Draw a parabola. Then write a situation that the graph could represent.

53. Civil engineers use parabolas to design highways. They design transition curves to smooth out peaks and valleys. The table below shows the elevation at particular points (x) along a parabolic curve. Use the table below to draw a graph of this 960 ft curve.

x	elevation y
0	1,100.0
100	1,096.3
200	1,093.3
300	1,090.8
400	1,089.0
500	1,087.8
600	1,087.3
700	1,087.3
800	1,088.0
900	1,089.3
960	1,090.4

54. Graph the equation $y = \dfrac{1}{2}x^2$.

55. Make a table for the equation $y = -x^2$ then graph the ordered pairs.

56. Graph $y = x^2$, $y = 2x^2$, and $y = \dfrac{1}{2}x^2$ on the same coordinate plane. What can you conclude about the width of the parabolas?

57. Graph the equation $y = x^2 - 4$.

Lesson 11-4   Objective 2: Draw graphs of absolute value functions.

Dynamic Item

58. Which is the graph of the absolute value equation $y = |x - 4|$?

[A]

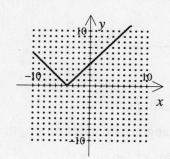

[B]

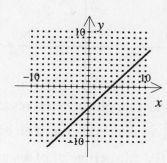

[C]

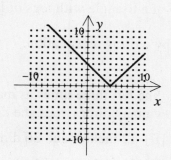

[D]

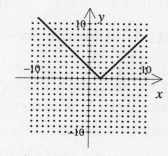

Dynamic Item

59. Graph the absolute value equation $y = |-x - 5|$.

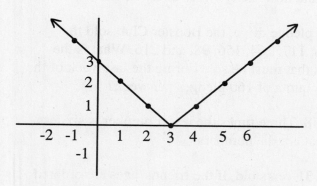

60. Which equation does the graph above represent?

[A] $y = 3x^2$ [B] $y = 3 + |x|$ [C] $y = |x - 3|$ [D] $y = \frac{1}{3}x^2$

61.

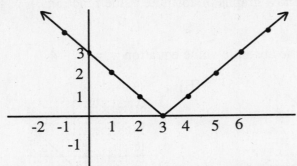

The graph above represents which relationship?

[A] the perimeter of an equilateral triangle with sides of length x

[B] the perimeter of a square with sides of length x

[C] none of these   [D] the area of a triangle with legs of length x

Lesson 11-5   Objective: Solve a problem by writing an equation.

Dynamic Item
62. Kaye has $4.90 in nickels and dimes. She has three times as many dimes as nickels. How many nickels and how many dimes does she have?

[A] 14 nickels and 42 dimes   [B] 12 nickels and 36 dimes

[C] 12 nickels and 43 dimes   [D] 42 nickels and 14 dimes

Dynamic Item
63. Sara has $5.60 in nickels and dimes. She has three times as many dimes as nickels. How many nickels and how many dimes does she have?

64. During the first 5 weeks of a pledge drive, the Booster Club sold the following number of pledges: 117, 204, 156, 98, and 216. What is the minimum number of pledges that must be sold during the last week of the drive for the club to reach its quota of 160 pledges per week?

65. The sum of two numbers is 78. Three times the lesser number is six less than the greater number. What are the numbers?

66. Four friends are all less than 31 years old. If the friends' ages are ordered from youngest to oldest, the ages increase by 4 years, then 3 years, then 2 years. The mean of their ages is 22. What are their ages?

67. The perimeter of the rectangle shown below is 100 m. Use the figure to find the length and width.

$\frac{1}{2}x + 2$

x

68. Six-sevenths of the tickets to a local community group's annual performance were sold. If 82 tickets were left over, how many tickets were sold?

69. A pizza delivery person made 24 deliveries on Monday, 17 on Tuesday, and 23 on Wednesday. Her store offers a $15.00 bonus to any delivery person who averages at least two dozen deliveries at the end of a 5-day work week. How many deliveries must the driver make the last two days of the week in order to receive the bonus?

70. A cash register drawer contains equal numbers of dimes and quarters and three times as many nickels. If the total value of the coins is $8.00, how many of each type of coin does the drawer contain?

71. Maria has $5.52 with which to buy lunch. What is the maximum amount she can spend on her meal and have enough to leave a 15% tip?

72. The total weight of three containers is 318 g. The median of the weights is 113 g. If the range of the weights is 23 g, what is the mean of the weights?

73. The sum of three consecutive odd numbers is 273. What are the numbers?

CHAPTER 11

Lesson 11-6   Objective 1: Graph translations.

Dynamic Item

74. Points (3, 10), (3, 14), (7, 14), and (7, 10) form a quadrilateral. Which
     graph displays the quadrilateral and its dotted translation 6 units to the left
     and 7 units down?

[A]

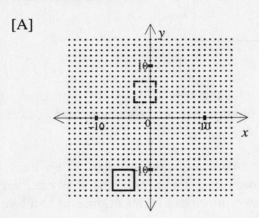

[B]

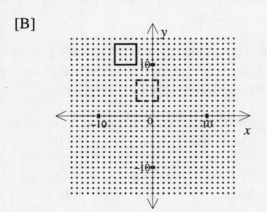

[C]   [D] none of these

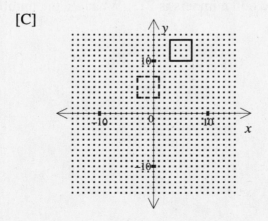

© Prentice-Hall, Inc.

Dynamic Item

75. At the half-time show, a marching band marched in formation. The lead drummer started at a point with coordinates (−1, 3) and moved 5 steps down, and 4 steps right. What are the coordinates of the drummer's final position?

76. How are a translation and an image related?

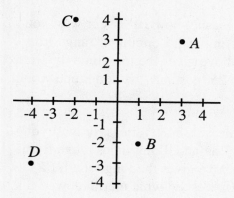

77. Point B above is translated up 4 units. What are its new coordinates?

78. Point D above is translated down 2 units and to the right 5 units. What are its new coordinates?

79. Translate Point A above left 3 units and down 2 units. Then translate the image, Point A', to the left 4 units and down 2 units. What are the coordinates of the image of Point A'?

80. Point C above on the coordinate plane is actually the image of another point which had been translated 2 units to the right and 6 units up. What are the coordinates of this point?

Place	Longitude
Durban, South Africa	30° east
Greenwich, England	0°
Cleveland, Ohio	80° west

Source: National Geographic, <u>Our World</u>

81. Longitude lines (also called meridians) measure how far east or west you are of the prime meridian in Greenwich, England. Longitudes range from 180° east through 180° west. The chart above gives the longitude for a few cities. If you moved Cleveland's position 25° east, at what longitude would it be?

82. Longitude lines (also called meridians) measure how far east or west you are of the prime meridian in Greenwich, England. Longitudes range from 180° east through 180° west. The chart above gives the longitude for a few cities. If you moved Durban's position 40° west, at what meridian would it be?

<u>Lesson 11-6</u>   Objective 2: Write rules for translations.

Dynamic Item

83. Describe the translation of point P(−8, 9) to point P′(−11, 5).

[A] $(x,\ y) \rightarrow (x-3,\ y+4)$ [B] $(x,\ y) \rightarrow (x+3,\ y-4)$

[C] $(x,\ y) \rightarrow (x+3,\ y+4)$ [D] $(x,\ y) \rightarrow (x-3,\ y-4)$

Dynamic Item

84. Describe the translation of point P(−2, −1) to point P′(2, −6).

85. Explain how to find the translation of point B(4,5) to point B'(-2,2).

CHAPTER 11

86. Suppose you wanted to translate *RST* below so that its image is in quadrant I. Identify the translation you might use.

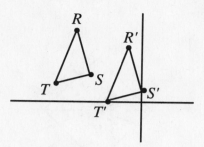

87. Write a translation problem that starts with points B(2,3), C(-4,1), and D(-2,5).

88. Each translation described is $(x,y) \rightarrow (x + 2, y - 3)$ EXCEPT

    [A] $(3,-2) \rightarrow (5,-5)$ [B] $(-4,1) \rightarrow (-2,-2)$

    [C] $(1,-5) \rightarrow (3,-2)$ [D] $(0,4) \rightarrow (2,1)$

89. Each translation described is left 4 down 6 EXCEPT

    [A] $(8,3) \rightarrow (4,-3)$ [B] $(-3,2) \rightarrow (-7,-4)$

    [C] $(0,-6) \rightarrow (-4,0)$ [D] $(4,-1) \rightarrow (0,-7)$

CHAPTER 11

Lesson 11-7   Objective 1: Identify lines of symmetry.

Dynamic Item
90. Which figure shows all lines of symmetry?

[A]

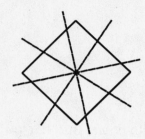

[B]

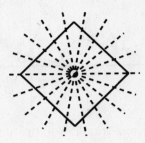

[C]

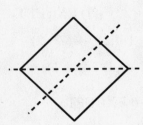

[D]

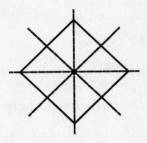

Dynamic Item
91. True or false. The line is a line of symmetry for the shape below.

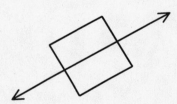

Lesson 11-7   Objective 2: Graph reflections.

Dynamic Item

92. Graph the triangle with vertices (–6, 2), (–2, 2), and (–6, 6). Then, draw its image after a reflection across the *x*-axis.

[A]
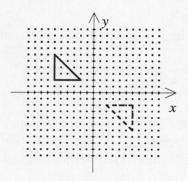

[B]
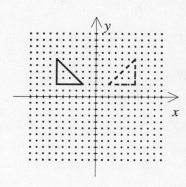

[C]
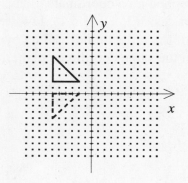

[D]
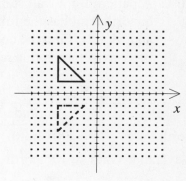

Dynamic Item

93. Find the image of (–3, –6) when it is reflected across the *x*-axis.

94. What is the line of reflection? How does it compare to a line of symmetry?

95. The *x*-axis is the line of reflection for all the following pairs of points EXCEPT

    [A] R(-9,4) → R'(9,-4)   [B] R(1,5) → R'(1,-5)

    [C] R(3,-2) → R'(3,2)   [D] R(-2,-4) → R'(-2,4)

96. The *y*-axis is the line of reflection for all of the following pairs of points EXCEPT

    [A] B(2,-2) → B'(2,2)   [B] B(5,-7) → B'(-5,-7)

    [C] B(-6,2) → B'(6,-2)   [D] B(3,-8) → B'(-3,-8)

97. What is the line of reflection for the points A(2,-9) and A'(2,9)?

98. What is the line of reflection for the points J(-6,-4) and J'(6,-4)?

99. Compare a reflection and a translation. How are they alike? How do they differ?

100. Describe two real-life situations when you would use reflections.

101. Write a problem involving reflection with the solution D'(1,2), E'(-1,-2), F'(4,-3).

102. A pattern for a wall stencil was graphed on a coordinate plane. This quadrilateral has the following vertices: J(2,-1); K(5,1); L(4,4); and M(1,3). Graph the quadrilateral and connect the vertices in order.

103. A pattern for a wall stencil was graphed on a coordinate plane. This quadrilateral has the following vertices: J(2,-1); K(5,1); L(4,4); and M(1,3). Find the coordinates of the reflection of JKLM over the y-axis. Graph this reflection on the same coordinate plane.

Place	Latitude
North Pole	90° north
Cleveland, Ohio	40° north
Equator	0°
South Pole	90° south

104. Latitude measures the distance above or below the equator, in degrees. The chart above lists the latitudes of some places. If you reflected Cleveland's location over the equator, how far south would it be?

105. Latitude measures the distance above or below the equator, in degrees. The chart above lists the latitudes of some places. If you reflected the North pole's location over the equator, how far south would it be?

Lesson 11-8   Objective 1: Identify figures that have rotational symmetry.

Dynamic Item

106. State whether the figure has rotational symmetry.

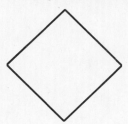

107. Does an eight car Ferris-wheel have rotational symmetry? Explain.

108. How is a rotation of 90° different than a reflection over the *x*-axis?

109. Identify the three different types of transformations and provide a real life example of each.

110. What is the angle of rotational symmetry of a pinwheel that has four blades? Explain.

111. What is the angle of rotational symmetry of a stop sign?

Planet	Period of Rotation
Mercury	59 days
Venus	243 days
Earth	24 h
Jupiter	10 h
Neptune	16 h

112. The chart above shows how long different planets take to rotate. Which planets will make complete rotations in 20 h?

113. The chart above shows how long different planets take to rotate. How many degrees does Jupiter rotate in 2 h?

Lesson 11-8   Objective 2: Rotate figures around a point.

Dynamic Item
114. Draw the rotation image of the figure for a rotation of 180° around turning point D.

[A]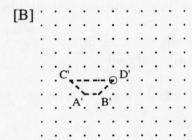

[B]

[C]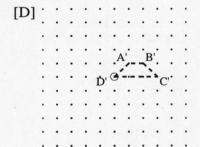

[D]

Dynamic Item

115. Draw the rotation image of the figure under a rotation of 90° clockwise about the rotation center D.

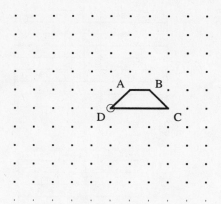

116. Draw a figure with rotational symmetry and tell at which angles of rotation it is symmetric to the original figure.

117. The vertices of *RST* are *R*(–5, 2), *S*(4, 0) and *T*(1, –3). If *R'*(5, 2), *S'*(–4, 0) and *T'*(–1, –3), then the image was formed by a

    [A] none of these   [B] translation.   [C] rotation.   [D] reflection.

118. The vertices of *RST* are *R*(–5, 2), *S*(4, 0) and *T*(1, –3). If *R'*(2, 0), *S'*(–1, –2) and *T'*(2, –5), then the image was formed by a

    [A] reflection.   [B] rotation.   [C] translation.   [D] none of these

119. The vertices of *RST* are *R*(–5, 2), *S*(4, 0) and *T*(1, –3). If *R'*(1, 0), *S'*(5, 5) and *T'*(6, 4), then the image was formed by a

    [A] reflection.   [B] rotation.   [C] none of these   [D] translation.

120. The vertices of *RST* are *R*(–5, 2), *S*(4, 0) and *T*(1, –3). If *R'*(2, 5), *S'*(0, –4) and *T'*(–3, –1), then the image was formed by a

    [A] translation.   [B] rotation.   [C] reflection.   [D] none of these

CHAPTER 11

[1] A

Price Interval	Frequency
$20.01 – $30.00	3
$30.01 – $40.00	5
[2] | $40.01 – $50.00 | 2 |

[3] Both types of graphs have a title, two labeled axes, and use bars to represent various amounts. A histogram differs from a regular bar graph in that it is used to show frequency and that there are no spaces between its bars.

[4] Intervals will vary but may include a difference of one since the range of data is only 6.

[5] 60 students; 14 books

[6] Answers may vary but should include intervals of 3 or 4 units to accommodate the large range of data.

[7] The line plot shows 28 responses from only 24 students. Therefore, it is likely that some students participated in more than one team sport.

[8] D

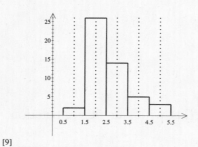

[9]

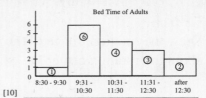

Bed Time of Adults

[10]

Number of Radios	Tally	Frequency
1	I	1
2	III	3
3	IIII	4
4	II	2
5	IIIIII	6
6	III	3
7	I	1

[11]

[12] D

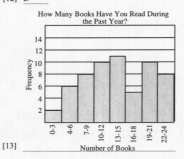

How Many Books Have You Read During the Past Year?

[13]

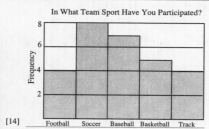

In What Team Sport Have You Participated?

[14]

[15] A

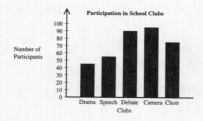

Participation in School Clubs

[16]

[17] A line graph would show how the population changed each year during the ten year period.

[18] A bar graph compares amounts. Examples of data that could be shown on a bar graph will vary but may include amount of time students spend doing certain tasks, amounts of particular product produced in various locations, or even numbers of various lunch offerings purchased in the school cafeteria on a certain day.

[19] A

[20] A bar graph would be used to compare the hourly compensation because you are comparing amounts.

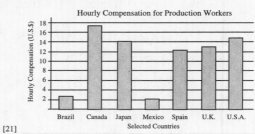

Hourly Compensation for Production Workers

[21]

[22] C

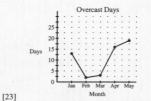

Overcast Days

[23]

[24] This data would best be displayed on a line graph because line graphs show how data changes over time.

[25] D

[26] A line graph would show how the number of lunches changed daily.

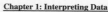

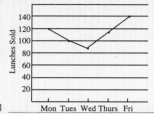

[27]

[28] A line graph shows how the number of monthly rentals changed over time.

[29] The graph shows that during the first month, the video was rented almost daily. During the next two months, rental of the video gradually decreased. The next month will likely show an additional decrease in rental.

[30] D

[31] 792

[32] $22.00

[33] Sample: Double line graph; it is useful for comparing changes in two sets of data over time.

[34] B

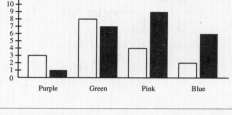
Favorite Color

[35]

[36] It is likely that the number of bus riders will still be more than double the number of walkers.

[37] 35 more students rode buses than walked to school in 1991.

[38] In 1989, the difference between walkers and bus riders was 90 students.

[39] A

[40] A

[41] There are 60 more fiction texts in the library at P.S. 23.

[42] In P.S. 17 there is a difference of 140 texts.

[43] P.S. 17 and P.S. 5 both have a total of 340 fiction and non-fiction texts.

[44] Students should display the data in a double-line graph because it shows how the absences varied over the course of the week.

[45] Answers may include that more students are absent on Friday than on any other day of the week and that neither gender is routinely absent more often.

[46] C

[47] 9, 7, 6

[48] First, find the sum of the numbers. Then divide the sum by the number of items in the group. This yields the mean or average of the numbers.

[49] An outlier is a data item that is much higher or much lower than the rest of the data. A median is the middle value of a set of numbers arranged in numerical order.

[50] The median is 90%. Arrange the grades in numerical order, find the middle two items, and determine their average.

[51] B

[52] C

[53] The median is 9.

[54] The data has two modes: 8 and 9.

[55] The mean of this data is 8.6.

[56] The median is 20.

[57] The mode is 10 and the mean is 18.75. Their difference is 8.75.

[58] A

[59] Numbers used were $30, $40, $30, $50, $70; explanation should include mean, median or mode. (answers will vary)

[60] Since the data is not numerical, one would use the mode.

[61] The outlier of this data is 3 since it is much lower than the rest of the data.

[62] A

[63]
Final Exam Grades

```
5 | 0 3 6 7 9
6 | 1 2 3 4 5
7 | 2 5 6 7 8 9
8 | 0 4
9 | 1 8
```

[64] The stems represent the most general value of the data items while the leaves represent the more detailed value of the data items.

[65] The mode is the greatest number of repeated leaves and its stem. The median is the middle leaf and its stem.

```
10 | 0
 9 | 1 2 3 4 5 7 7
 8 | 8 8
 6 | 4 9
```

[66] The stems are the tens place while the leaves are the ones place.

[67] The median is 96 and the mode is 97.

[68] A

[69] B

[70] The stems represent whole kilometers while the leaves represent tenths of a kilometer.

[71] 35 people participated in the walk. 22 people traveled more than 14 kilometers.

[72] The mean is 14.7 and the median is 14.8.

[73]
```
4 | 0 6
3 | 2
2 | 0 1
1 | 2 5 7 9
0 | 6
```
4 | 0 means 4.0

[74] A

[75] a)
```
0 | 1 3 5 7 8
1 | 5 9 6
2 | 2 2 3 5 7 8 8 9
```
b) mean: 17.375, range: 28

[76] The mode is 15.2 kilometers while the range is 5.2 kilometers.

[77] The range is 4.0 and the mean is 2.28.

[78] B

[79] 220

[80] (a) Read the problem and analyze the information given.
(b) Decide on a strategy to solve the problem.
(c) Try out the strategy.
(d) Think about how you solved the problem.

[81] A logic table is a visual way of showing the information gathered. It helps in analyzing each piece of information individually and identifying the way the information is related.

[82] Tables may vary. Sean scored the most goals, then Mia, Erika, and Chris.

[83] 47,832

[84] 92%

[85] 61,502

[86] 35 points

[87] 6 books

[88] 1919

[89] 1901

[90] A

[91] not a random sample

[92] A random sample is a sample in which each object of the population has an equal chance of being included.

[93] It is often impossible to poll or survey an entire population. Instead, samples are surveyed to gain enough information to draw valid conclusions.

[94] Biased questions are unfair questions. Biased questions can lead to assumptions and invalid responses which would negate the results of a survey.

[95] No, because the clerk is polling only those females who have identified their favorite lipstick manufacturer.

[96] No, the sample is only indicative of those students who buy lunch and probably feel the quality of food is average or better. If they felt the quality of food was poor they would most likely bring lunch.

[97] The results will not indicate the information Dana seeks to identify because she is only polling people who visit the sporting goods store. This is not a random sample of her community. Also, her question asks what is the best team rather than the favorite team.

[98] No, because the twelve-year-olds who go to that restaurant like that kind of food.

[99] B

[100] biased

[101] Answers will vary but may include, "Which subject do you dislike more--Math or Science?" This is biased in that it assumes that the respondent dislikes both subjects.

[102] Answers may include standing outside the cafe and asking every person who leaves between 5 and 6 P.M., "What drink did you order with your dinner?"

[103] Answers may vary but may include standing outside a public office building such as the police station or post office and polling individuals who are of voting age.

[104] The second graph; the scale on the horizontal axis distorts the relative lengths of the bars on the graph.

[105] The first graph; the scale on the vertical axis distorts the relative heights of points on the graph.

[106] At first glance it appears that the cost of a pizza at Big Al's is about half the cost of a pizza at Mama Mia's and about two-thirds the cost of a pizza at Luigi's Cafe.

[107] Big Al's would benefit most from this graph because it misleads a viewer into believing that a Big Al's pizza costs much less than a pizza at the other two restaurants.

[108] The graph should be redrawn with the vertical axis beginning with $0.

[109] The graph does not indicate the size of a large pizza at each restaurant.

[110] B

[111] range

[112] The results are biased due to his sample population (all students) and the manner in which he asked the question.

[113] One needs to know the amount of coffee each container holds.

[114] Answers may vary. Sample: Disagree, because a graph can be accurate but misleading.

[115] While the advertisers cannot print lies about their products, they can deliberately omit certain facts and highlight other facts in order to create a certain image of their products.

[116] B

[117] about 110

[118] A correlation is a trend that exists among data. It shows the existence of a broad relationship between the variables being studied.

[119] The scatter plot shows a positive correlation. This means that as the value of one set of data increases, the values of the other set of data also increase.

[120] C

[121] B

[122] B

[123] The points in a scatter plot having no correlation would be randomly dispersed among the graph and would not illustrate any type of relationship among the data.

[124] Answers will vary but should include labels of "Temperature" and "Number of Cones Sold" because these are the two variables being compared. Intervals used for each axis will likely be groups of four.

[125] The scatter plot shows a positive correlation. This means that as temperature increases so does the number of ice cream cones sold.

[126] No correlation. This means that there is no relationship between the number of movies attended during the past 6 months and performance on a math test.

[127] A

[128]

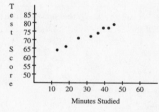

Minutes Studied

[129] The graph should have 7 points: (76, 42), (80, 66), (84, 72), (88, 87), (92, 90), (96, 92), (100, 94). Scales should be 76-100 and 0-100.

[130] Graph should show 7 points: (1, 88), (2, 88), (3, 98), (4, 98), (5, 84), (6, 100), (7, 100). Scale of y-axis should be 0-100 in 10s.

ANSWERS

[1] B

[2] 3.002, 3.02, 3.029

[3] Compare the place values of the digits in each number given. Rewrite the order.

[4] a. Answers may include 2.61; 2.62; 2.63; 2.64; 2.65.
b. Answers may include 15.1; 15.2; 15.3; 15.4; 15.5.

[5] B

[6] D

[7] $0.081 < 0.180 < 0.8 < 0.810 < 0.82$

[8] 98.642

[9] No. Because 3 of the percentages would round up to 20%.

[10] A

[11] 0.34

[12] Answers may vary in explanation. You pay 8 cents on $1.30 because 7.8 cents does not exist and is rounded up to 8 cents.

[13] For both you must look at the rounding place and the digit to the right for deciding on rounded answer. When rounding whole numbers, you add zeros after rounding place in answer. When rounding decimals, you eliminate digits in your answer once you've rounded to the place mentioned.

[14] thousandth, 11.056; ten-thousandth, 0.3217; hundredth, 67.01

[15] Purchase new equipment and books and cancel classes for the day.

[16] B

[17] Estimates may vary. 20

[18] Add the front digits and then adjust the estimate by adding the next column of numbers to the right to the front digit part of the estimate.

[19] Rounding: round to the nearest front digit. Front-end: add the front digits, naming the place value and adjust by adding the digits to the right of the front-end digits.

[41] a. 4.3 years; b. 9 years; c. 4.7 years

[42] D

[43] True. The addition property of zero.

[44] Changing order and groupings of addends make mental addition easier.

[45] Commutative property of addition states that changing the order of the addends does not alter the sum. No, the order of the numbers in subtraction cannot be changed.

[46] Since $65.021 - 65.021 = 0$, the answer is 82.6514.

[47] D

[48] C

[49] There are 29 students in his class.

[50] a. Read problem.
b. What do I need to find?
c. What information can I use?
d. What information do I not need?
e. What operation should I use?
f. Set up and solve.

[51] Sometimes details are provided which have nothing to do with solving the problem.

[52] Answers may vary. Samples: How many days each week does Jessi practice something? How many hours per week does Jessi practice piano?

[53] D

[54] C

[55] Unnecessary information: Peter has 5 brothers and sisters. Peter worked for 5 hours each day.

[56] Too little information

[57] Answers may include: $3.78 for 2 jars of chunky or $3.98 for 2 jars of creamy or $3.88 for 1 jar of each type of peanut butter.

[58] 46

[20] C

[21] ($142 x 4) = $568.

[22] a. $3 + 44 + 16 = 63; 63 + 1.3 = 64.3$
b. $13 + 36 + 125 = 174; 174 + 1 = 175$

[23] Answers may vary. 3000

[24] C

[25] Two compatible numbers which are numbers easy to divide mentally.

[26] Answers may vary, but should include that for estimating to find quotients, your goal is to divide two compatible numbers. Therefore, $4800 \div 60$ would be a better choice.

[27] A

[28] a. Answers will vary, but may include: $160 - 120 = 40$, rounded to nearest ten.
b. Answers will vary, but may include: $190 \times 20 = 3800$, rounded to nearest ten.

[29] You could buy 9 music videos with the money you've earned.

[30] Creamy peanut butter costs about 10 cents per ounce. Therefore, it is more economical to buy the creamy brand.

[31] 8 was the average score.

[32] C

[33] 542.954

[34] Associative and commutative

[35] A

[36] 44.628 ft

[37] $49.57 < 77.804$

[38] 0.5366 meters

[39] $2,693.99

[40] 19.8%

[59] Not enough information. The chart only shows what 5 of the U.N. members owe. You need to know what each of the other governments owe to solve the problem.

[60] A

[61] 0.05621

[62] D

[63] $1.94

[64] $34.02

[65] 76.5 lb

[66] C

[67] B

[68] 3 g

[69] C

[70] zero property for multiplication

[71] Multiplication can be shown by 3×4.6 or $(3)(4)(6)$ or $3(4)(6)$

[72] equal to the number of decimal places in the product.

[73] Commutative and associative are similar (just different operations). Identity for addition $(a + 0 = a)$; for multiplication $(a \times 1 = a)$. Zero property for multiplication $(a \times 0 = 0)$.

[74] This is the associative property of multiplication which states that rearranging factors when multiplying does not change the product.

[75] C

[76] 0.007

[77] 52.3 mi/h

[78] 88.7%

[79] 0.933 percentage

[80] 45.25 mph

Chapter 2: Applications of Decimals

[81] Answers may vary. About 70¢; round $4.14 to $4.20.

[82] 0.16 L

[83] A

[84] 7.1

[85] C

[86] 0.88 lb

[87] A

[88] Answers may vary. Sample: 4.50 ÷ 0.15

[89] 37

[90] C

[91] $0.7\overline{3}$

[92] A

[93] C

[94] The calculator rounds up the last digit shown on the display when it is possible.

[95] a. $0.\overline{11}$, $0.\overline{22}$, $0.\overline{33}$, $0.\overline{44}$; b. $0.\overline{55}$, $0.\overline{66}$

[96] a. $1.\overline{11}$; b. $2.\overline{22}$; c. $0.8\overline{33}$

[97] a. $2.\overline{33}$; b. 3.6; c. $5.8\overline{33}$

[98] a. 0.3; b. 3; c. 30; d. 300; e. 3000; f. 0.001; 30,000; g. 0.0001; 300,000; h. 0.00001; 3,000,000; i. 0.000001; 30,000,000; j. 0.0000001; 300,000,000

[99] $0.5\overline{0}$ repeating

[100] D

[101] A decimal in which a digit, or a series or digits, keeps repeating.

[102] A terminating decimal is a decimal that stops or terminates; when you divide the remainder is 0.

[103] You can say that when 3 and 9 are denominators, the decimal resulting is a repeating decimal.

Chapter 3: Integers and Equations

[1] B

[2] 66.3

[3] Replace the variable (unknown) with a number and find the value of the expression.

[4] No. If $x = 2$, $y = 3$
$xy = 6$
$2 \cdot 3 = 6$? 23

[5] A

[6] Substitute "2 for x". Then, $3x^2 - 5 =$
$3 \times 2^2 - 5 =$
$3 \times 4 - 5 =$
$12 - 5 =$
7

[7] $P = 2L + 2W$
$P = 2L + 2(L - 2)$
$P = 2(5) + 2(5 - 2)$
$P = 10 + 2(3)$
$P = 16$ ft

[8] 0

[9] D

[10] two times a number

[11] A "variable expression" is a mathematical phrase, using symbols to represent numbers, which is made up of variables, numbers, and operations.

[12] Five less than ten times a number "x".

[13] Answers may vary. One possible solution is $2(s + 8) - 4$ or four less than twice the sum of s and 8.

[14] $\dfrac{6l - 2}{2s}$

Chapter 2: Applications of Decimals

[104] a. $0.6\overline{6}$; b. $0.83\overline{3}$; c. $0.\overline{41}$

[105] $0.\overline{09}$, $0.08\overline{33}$, $0.0\overline{66}$, $0.0\overline{55}$

[106] A

[107] 26.37

[108] $5 \times 64 = (5 \times 60) + (5 \times 4)$
$= 300 + 20$
$= 320$

[109] The left side states that you must multiply each factor, then add. The right side says add the addends, then multiply by the factor "6". When you follow the steps the left side will be equal to the right.

[110] Answers will vary, but should indicate the factor 2 is distributed over the addends.

[111] Answers will vary, but may include: 5(100) + 5(20) + 5(0.5) or 5(60) + 5(60) + 5(0.5)

[112] C

[113] $12.00

[114] Pictures will vary, but should show 52 equal units on either side of the equation.

[115] 225 packs

[116] $20.68

[117] $55.14

[118] $42.72

[119] B

[120] 2

[121] C

Chapter 3: Integers and Equations

[15] a. two more than a number divided by two
b. three less than a number
c. one more than twice a number

[16] $50n$

[17] A

[18]

[19] Answers may vary. They are opposites. -10° is 20° less than +10°. They are both 10 units from 0, and have the same absolute value.

[20] Answers may vary. Absolute value of an integer is the distance from 0 on a number line. -5 cannot be the absolute value; distance is always considered positive.

[21] C

[22] A

[23] −161

[24] a. -18; b. 170; c. -2; d. -1

[25] Numbers increase from left to right.

[26] C

[27]

[28] A. -1; B. +3; C. -4; D. +5

[29] Answer should be a number line with points -2 and +5 marked.

[30] Answer should be a number line with points -5 and +10 marked. Difference = 15

[31] about $2,700

[32] 53°F

[33] C

[34] 2

[35] Answers may vary. Sample: Combining the opposite tiles, 1 positive and 1 negative, makes a zero pair.

[36] D

[37] A

[38] 6,284 m; Answers may vary.

[39] Answers may vary. Problems are alike because the absolute values are the same. Different because the signs are different. Each set is the opposite of the other.

[40] C

[41] –10

[42] Answers may vary. There are too many because we can use different signs. Example: +40 + -16; 20 + 4; 22 + 2

[43] C

[44] D

[45] $|10| + |3| - |2| = 11$

[46] 7 minutes

[47] -2 m, 1 m, 3 m

[48] 6°, -4°; Use 6 positive tiles and 4 negative tiles. Since every pair of positive and negative tiles is zero, the result is +2.

The smallest difference was on Saturday; the largest was on Monday.

[49] D

[50]

[51] D

[52] 110 ft

[53] 185 points

[77] (1500 – 300)/30 = 1200/30 = 40 seconds

[78] –2°F

[79] (–3 + 6 + 9 + 12 + 9 + 12 + –3)/7 = 6°

[80] B

[81] $f = 5$

[82] Answers may vary. Samples: Do the same thing to both sides; keep both sides equal; perform inverse operations to both sides; whatever you do to one side you do to the other.

[83] Answers may vary. Samples: Move farther away or back; dist. × weight = dist. × weight; use additional weight (i.e., 7 pounds on friend's side).

[84] Answers may vary. Too many needed--i.e., 1000 + x = 90; involves decimals 1.2 + x = 7.8.

[85] C

[86] a) 13   b) 13.9   c) 6.7

[87] Answers may vary. Inverse operations "undo" each other, e.g., subtraction and addition. Helps to isolate the variable by "undo"ing operations.

[88] A

[89] D

[90] $x - 17° = 7°$
$x - 17° + 17° = 7° + 17°$
$x = 24°$

[91] $55 + 42 + x = 155$
$97 + x = 155$
$x = 155 - 97$
$x = 58$

[92] Answers may vary. Sample: A bar graph with one bar of length 100 and one bar with length 45.

[93] $x + 975 = 1,500$; 525 m^3

[94] $x + 187 = 384$; $197

[54] D

[55] –11

[56] They can use the plus/minus key and add.

[57] Answers will vary. The "–" represents subtraction and negative.

[58] No. Examples will vary. 5 – 7 = –2; 7 – 5 = +2. Answers should mention the sign.

[59] Add. Examples may vary. 5 – 7; 5 + (–7)

[60] C

[61] $17.00

[62] 105°

[63] 46

[64] 14,494 feet

[65] D

[66] 36

[67] Answers will vary. A negative times a negative equals a positive. Examples may vary.

[68] A

[69] –$0.14; (7)(–$0.02) = –$0.14

[70] 50 because 5(100) + 90(–5) = 50

[71] D

[72] +55

[73] When you divide 2 integers with the same sign the quotient is positive. When you divide 2 integers with different signs the quotient is negative. The same is true for multiplication.

[74] Yes. 10(+0.30) + 10(–0.45) + 10(+0.25) = 3.00 + –4.50 + 2.50 = 1.0

[75] A

[76] a. $100.00; b. $200.00; c. $250.00; d. $400.00

[95] $x + 315 = 358$; 43 games

[96] C

[97] a) 2   b) 3.1

[98] Answers may vary. Alike--both use same variables and constants. Different--one is addition and the other is multiplication--different values when solved.

[99] B

[100] C

[101] $\frac{1}{6}x = 22$ pounds; $x = 132$ pounds

[102] $0.35x = 3.85; $x = 11$

[103] 200 minutes

[104] $2m$

[105] C

[106] 36

[107] Answers may vary. You can multiply both sides of an equation by anything and it is still equal.

[108] The first number is negative. If the product is negative, the factors have to have different signs.

[109] Answers may vary. He divided -100 by 5. Possible corrections: Show each step; explain that he needs the inverse operation.

[110] $3x = 12$; $\frac{1}{3} \times x = 12 \times \frac{1}{3}$; $x = 4$; Next year: 3(5) = 13; 15 = 13; No.

[111] $y = 2x$

[112] C

[113] $x + 15 = 18$

ANSWERS

Example: Julie had a $25 "good student" discount on her car insurance. She paid $175 for the insurance. How much was the insurance bill before
[114] the discount?

Answers may vary. Sample: a. Reword if needed; b. Identify the variable;
[115] c. translate into 2 equal mathematical expressions using an = sign.

Answers may vary. Sample: a. A number MINUS six IS four. b. Seven INCREASED BY a number EQUALS negative ten. c. The PRODUCT of three and a number IS THE SAME AS fifteen. d. A number DIVIDED BY
[116] TWO EQUALS negative eight.

[117] A

[118] C

[119] 5 less than is translated to –5. The expressions should be $12 = n - 5$.

2 hours   meet   2 hours

(n+3) mph   28 miles   (n) mph

[120] Rates 5.5 and 8.5 mi/h.

[121] 133 times; no; There is only one value of x in which $3x + 1 = 400$.

[122] 420 calories

Answers may vary. Sample: $x = 2,680 + 2,560$; Sound travels at a rate of
[123] 5,200 m/s through steel.

[124] $30x$

[125] $x + 22$

[126] A

[127] –7

Add -11 to both sides of the equation, then divide by 3 to find that t
[128] equals -7.

Add -3 to both sides of the equation, then multiply both sides by 4 to find
[129] that j equals -40.

[130] C

Chapter 4: Fractions and Number Theory

[1] B

[2] Diagrams may vary.

Models may vary. Sample: a pie cut into five even pieces with 3 pieces missing or a row of five students in which 2 students are wearing
[3] eyeglasses.

[4] No, because the circle is not divided into three equal portions.

Answers may vary. Sample: purchasing an amount of lunch meat or a
[5] length of fabric.

Answers may vary. Example: 1/3 work, 7/24 sleep, 1/16 eating, 1/8
[6] leisure, 3/16 other

[7] B

[8] B

[9] D

[10] $4\frac{5}{7}$

[11] C

[12] D

[13] heavy rain

[14] ▨▨▨▨▨▨□□□□

[15] 4 h

[16] ▨▨▨▨▨▨□□□□
▨▨▨▨▨▨□□□□

[17] A

[18] 1, 2, 3, 6, 9, 18, 27, 54

[19] 3 and 7 are factors of 21; 21 is a multiple of 3 and 7.

[131] D

[132] Answers may vary. Sample: $6x + 4 = 52$.

Answers may vary. Sample: $\frac{y}{3} + 4 = 2$.

[133]

[134] $6 + 3x = 18$; $x = 4$

$\frac{10+n}{4} = 5$; the number is -20

[135]

$\frac{p}{6} + 5 = -11$; $p = 96$

[136]

[137] $y + \$16{,}433 = $ Masters' Income

[138] Midwest = $(x + 5)\%$; South = $(x - 4)\%$; Northeast = $(x + 9)\%$

[139] A

henley   henley   henley   v - neck   v - neck   v - neck
[140] purple   blue   yellow   purple   blue   yellow

Chapter 4: Fractions and Number Theory

Yes; whenever a number is multiplied by 1 it is both a factor and a multiple of itself. For example, 1 and 10 are factors of 10 and 10 is a
[20] multiple of 1 and 10.

A factor is a number that divides another number with no remainder. A multiple of a number is the product of that number and any nonzero whole
[21] number.

[22] B

[23] C

[24] B

[25] A

[26] 60 dancers

[27] 3 tables of 5 and 8 tables of 8

[28] D

[29] Answers may vary. Examples: $\frac{10}{18}, \frac{15}{27}, \frac{20}{36}$

One method is to multiply both the numerator and denominator of a fraction by the same number. Another method is to divide the numerator and denominator by the same number. $\frac{4}{10}, \frac{10}{25}, \frac{8}{20}$, and $\frac{6}{15}$ are all
[30] equivalent fractions to $\frac{2}{5}$.

[31] $\frac{55}{210}$ or $\frac{11}{42}$

[32] $\frac{40}{210}$ or $\frac{4}{21}$

[33] D

[34] $\frac{2}{3} > \frac{1}{2}$

Rename the unlike fractions as like fractions by changing the unlike
[35] fraction to an equivalent fraction.

[36] Compare the numerators.

ANSWERS

[37] B

[38] Both scores are the same, since 32 out of 40 is $\frac{8}{10}$ or $\frac{4}{5}$ and 24 out of 30 is also $\frac{8}{10}$ or $\frac{4}{5}$.

[39] $\frac{3}{7} = \frac{30}{70}$; $\frac{7}{10} = \frac{49}{70}$. Lauren made the greater fraction of goals.

[40] Justin's family

[41] New Jersey and Pennsylvania

[42] C

[43] $\frac{18}{13}$, $\frac{27}{32}$, $\frac{13}{21}$, $\frac{9}{34}$

[44] Answers may vary. Sample: $\frac{1}{2}$, $\frac{2}{4}$, $\frac{4}{8}$.

[45] Answers may vary. Sample: $\frac{2}{3}$, $\frac{5}{8}$

[46] A

[47] Max rode farther because $1\frac{2}{3}$ is 1.666..., which is greater than 1.6.

[48] Iowa, New Jersey and Pennsylvania, New York, Florida, Mississippi

[49] A

[50] 32

[51] Power of 10^6; 10^5; 10^4; 10^3; 10^2.

[52] The product of the two exponential expressions with the same base is the base to the power of the sum of the 2 exponents. $13^6 \times 13^2 = 13^8$

[53] $3^3 \cdot 5^2 \cdot 4^2$; $4x^3y^3$

[54] A

[55] 3018.24

[56] 3.2^2 is read "3.2 to the second power." It means that 3.2 is used as factor two times. $3.2 \times 3.2 = 10.24$.

[57]
a. Do all operations within parentheses.
b. Next, work with all exponents.
c. Multiply and divide (left to right)
d. Add and subtract (left to right)

[58] 16 + 2(3)
16 + 6 = 22

[59] Answers may vary, but may include 6^2 and 7^2.

[60] D

[61] C

[62] $22.33 = 5(0.89) + 6(2.98)$

[63] $(1.5 + 2.2 + 1.8 + 1.9) \div 4 = 7.4 \div 4 = 1.85$ min.

[64] D

[65] Answers may vary, but final numbers should match sample.

[66] A prime number has only two factors, 1 and the number itself. A composite number has more than two factors. An example of a prime number is 3. An example of a composite number is 6.

[67] composite

[68] composite

[69] composite

[70] prime

[71] B

[72] 6 members

[73] 3 shelves

[74] Rows of 13

[75] A

[76] 8

[77] B

[78] $\frac{1}{10}$

[79] Divide both the numerator and the denominator by the same factor (non-zero number).

[80] B

[81] A

[82] $\frac{4}{50}$ or $\frac{2}{25}$

[83] $\frac{10}{50}$ or $\frac{1}{5}$

[84] Chicago Cubs, Atlanta Braves, Texas Rangers; $\frac{24}{50}$ or $\frac{12}{25}$

[85] Toronto Blue Jays; $\frac{7}{50}$

[86] B

[87] $\frac{3}{4}$

[88] Using the divisibility test for 9 you find that $\frac{27}{144}$ can be reduced to $\frac{3}{16}$.

[89] No, because if he had used the GCF he would have had to divide the numerator and denominator only once.

[90] Using the GCF of the numerator and the denominator when simplifying a fraction will produce the fraction in simplest form.

[91] D

[92] A

[93] D

[94] 2 red marbles, 6 blue marbles, 4 green marbles

[95] $1.00

[96] 12

[97] D

[98] When the fifth student leaves the kitchen

[99] 420 customers

[100] 4 students

[101] D

[102] 900-1,000 people

[103] Answers include paying 1 night rental for each of three different movies, paying for 3 nights rental for one movie and 1 night rental for a second movie, or paying for 2 nights rental for two different movies.

[104] 84

[105] A

[106] $\frac{25}{7}$

[107] If $a > b$, then the fraction is improper.

[108] Answers may vary.

[109] C

[110] A

[111] 241 slices

[112] 10 times

[113] $5\frac{1}{4}$ h; $\frac{21}{4}$ h

Chapter 4: Fractions and Number Theory

[114] C

[115] $2\frac{1}{2}$

[116] Divide the denominator into the numerator. The remainder becomes the fractional part of the mixed number.

[117] Answers may vary.

[118] C

[119] C

[120] $8\frac{3}{4}$ h

[121] C

[122] 0.95

[123] Divide the numerator by the denominator.

[124] When changing a fraction to a decimal and the remainder equals 0, your answer is a terminating decimal. When the remainder is not equal to 0, your answer is a repeating decimal.

[125] Answers may vary. Sample: 0.376, 0.38, 0.39. Any decimal between 0.375 and 0.4 is acceptable.

[126] A

[127] math: $\frac{9}{25}$ or 0.36; Spanish: $\frac{6}{25}$ or 0.25; science: $\frac{2}{5}$ or 0.4

[128] Jenn has the most and Lori has the least. (Jenn: 0.4, Rick: 0.375, Lori: 0.357)

[129] $\frac{1}{11}$ = 0.09; $\frac{2}{11}$ = 0.18; $\frac{3}{11}$ = 0.27; $\frac{4}{11}$ = 0.36. $\frac{5}{11}$ would be 0.45; $\frac{6}{11}$ would be 0.54.

Chapter 4: Fractions and Number Theory

The pitchers below are ranked beginning with the pitcher with the best pitching record.

Pitcher and Team	W	L	Fraction	Decimal
David Cone, NY	20	3	$\frac{20}{23}$	0.870
Doug Drabek, Pittsburgh	22	6	$\frac{22}{28}$	0.786
Bob Tewksbury, St. Louis	16	5	$\frac{16}{21}$	0.762
Mike Bielecki, Chicago	18	7	$\frac{18}{25}$	0.720
John Smiley, Pittsburgh	20	8	$\frac{20}{28}$	0.714
Jose Rijo, Cincinatti	15	6	$\frac{15}{21}$	0.714
Dwight Gooden, NY	15	7	$\frac{15}{22}$	.0682

[130]

[131] C

[132] $3\frac{1}{20}$

[133] Answers may vary. Sample: Sports records are easier to compare using decimals instead of fractions.

[134] C

[135] $3\frac{1}{2}$% Answers may vary: Sample: because $\frac{45}{100} < \frac{50}{100}$

[136] Answers may vary. Sample: it's easier to compare decimals, because you don't have to worry about common denominators.

Chapter 5: Applications of Fractions

[1] A

[2] 8

[3] Estimate sums and differences involving fractions by deciding whether each of the fractions is closest to 0, $\frac{1}{2}$, or 1. To estimate the sums and differences of mixed numbers, round to the nearest whole number.

[4] Answers may vary. Samples: $\frac{3}{8}$ and $\frac{7}{16}$ or $\frac{6}{10}$ and $\frac{12}{25}$.

[5] Accept reasonable estimates. Sample: about $4\frac{1}{2}$ lb.

[6] Accept reasonable estimates. Sample: about 27 lb; yes, they should have enough fruit for 100 people, since $27 \div \frac{1}{4}$ is more than 100.

[7] About 6 inches

[8] B

[9] 7

[10] Round each mixed number to the nearest whole number for finding the product of mixed numbers. Then, use compatible numbers for estimating the quotient of mixed numbers.

[11] Answers may vary. Samples: $6\frac{2}{3}$ and $\frac{3}{8}$ or $41\frac{3}{4}$ and $\frac{2}{9}$.

[12] C

[13] D

[14] About 6 inches

[15] Yes. You would only need about 18 c of cooked rice which should be enough if the box contains enough rice for making 25 c of cooked rice.

[16] About 40 inches

[17] B

[18] $\frac{25}{60}$

Chapter 5: Applications of Fractions

[19] Use the LCD to make fractions equivalent to the originals. Add or subtract and write your answer in lowest terms.

[20] Find a common denominator by multiplying the two denominators.

[21] Answers may vary. Sample: $\frac{5}{8}$, $\frac{2}{3}$, $\frac{7}{12}$

[22] Answers may vary.

[23] C

[24] C

[25] $\frac{43}{48}$

[26] $\frac{1}{6}$ cup

[27] 24; it is the LCM of 8 and 12.

[28] D

[29] $8\frac{14}{15}$

[30] $15\frac{9}{20}$ miles

[31] $5\frac{7}{12}$ yards

[32] No.

[33] Answers may vary. Sample: Rename the improper fraction in the sum as a mixed number, than add the whole number part to the sum of the other whole numbers.

[34] $6\frac{1}{6}$ cups

[35] B

[36] $3\frac{29}{56}$

[37] C

262 ■ Middle Grades Math Course 2

© Prentice-Hall, Inc.

ANSWERS

[38] $7\frac{1}{4}$ hours

[39] Marissa, $\frac{3}{8}$ mi

[40] $1\frac{11}{24}$ yd

[41] $\frac{3}{8}$ lb

[42] B

[43] $\frac{5}{14}$

[44] If you add or subtract the same value from both sides of an equation, the equations remain equivalent.

[45] Add $\frac{3}{4}$ to both sides and solve for "n".

[46] Answers may vary, but may include $15\frac{2}{3} - 6\frac{1}{5}$.

[47] B

[48] C

[49] $x - 8\frac{1}{2} = 7$; $x = 15\frac{1}{2}$ years old

[50] $4\frac{1}{3} - 2\frac{3}{4} = n$; $1\frac{7}{12}$ yds $= n$

[51] $x - \frac{1}{2} = 54$; $54\frac{1}{2}$ or $54.50

[52] B

[53] $\frac{11}{20}$

[54] Answers may vary, but may include $2\frac{5}{6} + 3\frac{2}{5}$

(a) $n = 12\frac{3}{4} - 4 = 8\frac{3}{4}$

[55] (b) $n = 2\frac{1}{2} + 1\frac{5}{6} = 3\frac{8}{6} = 4\frac{1}{3}$

[56] $h + 2\frac{1}{4} = 9$; $h = 6\frac{3}{4}$ hrs

[57] $x + \frac{1}{8} = 24$; $53\frac{7}{8}$ or $23.875

[58] C

[59] $\frac{4}{9}$

[60] For multiplying fractions: simplify; then multiply numerators and multiply denominators. For multiplying fractions and whole numbers: rewrite whole number as a fraction with a denominator of 1 and proceed as above.

[61] Multiplying the fractions is a lot easier and the answer is usually in lowest terms.

[62] B

[63] C

[64] $80.00

[65] 8 boys; 24 girls

[66] 40 apples, 2 c sugar, 4 tsp. cinnamon, $1\frac{1}{3}$ c raisins, 2 c water, 2 tbsp butter

[67] C

[68] $32\frac{1}{7}$

[69] Change each mixed number to an improper fraction, simplify, multiply numerators and denominators.

[70] Multiply two whole numbers, then the whole number and the fractional part of the mixed number and add.

[71] $231\frac{1}{8}$ mi

[72] 3:30 P.M. (Ben worked for $2\frac{1}{2}$ h.)

[73] $77.63

[74] A

[75] $\frac{3}{35}$

[76] Reciprocals are two numbers whose product is 1. Examples will vary, but may include $\frac{2}{3}$ and $\frac{3}{2}$.

[77] Answers may vary. Samples: sewing or construction measurement.

[78] No. Zero does not have a reciprocal since $\frac{1}{0}$ is not defined.

[79] B

[80] $\frac{7}{16}$

[81] Convert each to improper fractions, then divide by multiplying the dividend by the reciprocal of the divisor.

[82] C

[83] A

[84] Yes; there is enough for 50.2325... pairs. $(2 \cdot 15 \cdot 3 \cdot 15) \div 21\frac{1}{2} = 50.2325...$

[85] $2\frac{2}{3} \div \frac{1}{3}$; $\frac{8}{3} \div \frac{1}{3} = 8$ friends

[86] 4 pieces

[87] $5\frac{1}{5}$ servings

[88] chicken: $\frac{1}{2}$ lb; potato: $\frac{1}{2}$ potato

[89] 26 full packages; You can multiply $2\frac{1}{2}$ by 16 and divide by $1\frac{1}{2}$.

[90] C

[91] 7:00 am

[92] D

[93] D

[94] $457.33

[95] 11/19 deposit $60.00; balance: $457.33
11/19 debit $100.00; balance: $367.33

[96] $9.35

[97] 11

[98] 7

[99] 2:35 P.M.

[100] 3:05 P.M.

[101] 1:00 P.M.

[102] A

[103] 4 quarts

[104] Answers may vary but may include comparison shopping or adapting a recipe. Methods described should include multiplying when changing from a larger unit to a smaller unit or dividing when changing from a smaller unit to a larger unit.

[105] a. foot or meter b. ton c. gallon or liter

[106] C

[107] A

[108] 64 ft

[109] Mark walked farther. The difference between the lengths of their walks is 73 yards.

ANSWERS

[110] Ingredients for 12 servings: $1\frac{1}{2}$ c barley, $1\frac{1}{2}$ c onion, $1\frac{1}{2}$ c celery, $\frac{3}{4}$ c leeks, $4\frac{1}{2}$ ham hocks, 1 gal 1 qt 1 c $\left(5\frac{1}{4}\text{ qt}\right)$ chicken stock, 1 pt 1 c $\left(1\frac{1}{2}\text{ pt}\right)$ heavy cream.

[111] A

[112] 6,000 lb

[113] Divide 80 by 16 to find the answer of 5 pounds.

[114] Examples may include estimating the weight of a child but measuring the amount of medicine given to the child.

[115] $3.51

[116] No. There is only 7 oz of spaghetti left and Lindsay needs 9 oz for another meal.

[117] Miami collected about 458,941 tons.

[118] A

[119] $\frac{13}{24}$

[120] Multiply both sides by 2 to find that $m = 16$.

[121] By using an inverse operation, you can solve the equation by multiplying or dividing to isolate the variable.

[122] Answers may vary. Samples: $2x = \frac{10}{4}$ or $\frac{x}{2} = \frac{5}{8}$.

[123] D

[124] 75 miles

[125] 16 pounds

[126] $\frac{4}{5}n = 28$; 35

[127] The height of the Apatosaurus is 21 m and its length is 9 m. ($14 = \frac{2}{3}l$; $12 = 1\frac{1}{3}h$)

[128] B

[129] $\frac{1}{56}$

[130] Divide both sides by 3 to find that x = 3.

[131] C

[132] The Pentaceratops is 3 m tall.

[133] The length of the Euophocephalus is 6 m and its height is 2 m. ($10 = 1\frac{2}{3} \cdot l$; $6 = 1\frac{1}{2} \cdot h$)

ANSWERS

[1] D

[2] $\frac{6}{13}$

[3] A ratio is a comparison of two numbers. Sample: The comparison of boys to girls in a classroom.

[4] False. The ratio is one-fourth. The student compared the shaded area and nonshaded area to get one-third. He should have compared shaded area to total area.

[5] 1:3

[6] A

[7] Right-handed to left-handed = 16:4, 8:2, or 4:1. Right-handed to classroom total = 16:20, 8:10, or 4:5.

[8] 24:6 or 4:1

[9] 24:30 or 4:5

[10] C

[11] Examples: 4 to 16, $\frac{4}{16}$, 1 to 4, $\frac{1}{4}$

[12] 1.7

[13] 0.6

[14] $\frac{325}{500} = \frac{13}{20}$

[15] $\frac{155}{500} = \frac{31}{100}$

[16] C

[17] A rate is a ratio that compares two quantities measured in different units. The rate in the example is fourteen questions per ten minutes.

[18] No. Some years she could have visited her aunt more than once, and she may not have made a visit in other years.

[19] A unit rate is the rate for one unit of a given quantity. The unit rate in the example is 1.4 questions per minute.

[20] A

[21] D

[22] 165.7 mi/h

[23] $3.40

[24] $2.95

[25] 1.05 pts./game

[26] 0.45 goals/game

[27] $n = \frac{1}{16}$

[28] 273 parts/h

[29] B

[30] $19.60 for 8 cans of salsa

[31] The 36-ounce box is the better buy costing 9.7¢/oz. The 18-ounce box costs 9.9¢/oz.

[32] Yes.

[33] D

[34] $4 = \frac{4}{1}$. The cross products equal 16.

[35] Solve the cross products to arrive at $n^2 = 64$. The square roots of 64 and n^2 equals 8.

[36] The cross products of the two ratios are not equal, and therefore are not proportions. Examples of changes to form a proportion are change the 39 to 38 or change the 19 to 19.5.

[37] B

[38] Answers will vary. Sample $99 \times 36 = 33n$; $3,564 = 33n$; $n = 108$. Students may also notice that $99 = 33 \times 3$. If they multiply 36×3, they get 108.

[39] A

[40] $27\dfrac{9}{13}$

[41] $\dfrac{54}{13};\dfrac{4}{1}$. The two ratios form a proportion.

[42] D

[43] 16

[44] $n = 3.5;\ \dfrac{35}{70}$ or $\dfrac{17.5}{35.0};\ 50\%$

[45] Answers may vary. Sample: $\dfrac{1}{n} = \dfrac{n}{4};\ 4 = n\ ;\ 2 = n.$

[46] $n = -12;\ \dfrac{-6}{16},\ \dfrac{-15}{40}$

[47] $n = 45.5;\ \dfrac{24}{26}$

[48] $\dfrac{3}{4} = 75\%$

[49] n must be negative because the ratio $\dfrac{24}{n}$ must be negative to equal $\dfrac{-8}{11}$.

[50] B

[51] 64°

[52] No. Since no mention was made that the corresponding angles are congruent, the figures aren't necessarily similar.

[53] No. Since no mention was made of the sides' lengths, the figures aren't necessarily similar.

[54] Answers will vary but may include: the stars are similar, the longer stripes are similar and the shorter stripes are similar. They are also congruent.

[55] No. The stripes adjacent to the stars and the stripes at the bottom of the flag have congruent widths, but different lengths, and therefore are not similar.

[56] C

[57] $WX = 4$

[58] A

[59] D

[60] 12

[61] 6

[62] 27

[63] 18

[64] K.C. Chiefs and T.B. Buccaneers

[65] No. The Dolphins' rectangle is $\dfrac{20}{19}$ higher than the one representing the Giants, but the width of both rectangles is the same.

[66] B

[67] 96 m

[68] Answers will vary but should include mention of proportion, that it can be either an enlargement or a reduction.

[69] Distances on the map approach the actual distances.

[70] Delaware would be closest, Texas would be farthest.

[71] Answers may vary. Example: If the scale were the same for both pocket maps, one would be too large to use or too small to read.

[72] C

[73] B

[74] 110 miles

[75] 290 miles

[76] 36 in.²

[77] 10 in.

[78] 120

[79] 130

[80] D

[81] 70%

[82] Answers will vary but may include: math class takes up 17% of my school day; I spend 30% of my day asleep.

[83] 100%. Explanations will vary but may include all possible scenarios in the weather pattern include rain.

[84] 4%. A 5 × 5 graph contains 25 squares. $\dfrac{1}{25} = 4\%$.

[85] 20%

[86] 4%

[87] 25%

[88] A

[89] 90%

[90] 36% must be removed from the board (100 - 64 = 36). To reduce the length and width, you reduce the sides from 10 to 8, removing 20%.

[91] C

[92] D

[93] $\dfrac{1}{4}$

[94] $75\%\ \left(\dfrac{6}{8}\right)$

[95] $120\%\ \left(\dfrac{12}{10}\right)$

[96] D

[97] $\dfrac{99}{100}$

[98] Decimals and percents, which represent a portion of the number 1 are most alike. Fractions can represent a portion of any number.

[99] A fraction would be the most clear representation of this example. $\dfrac{3}{24}$, or $\dfrac{1}{8}$, of a day is more clearly understood than 12.5% or 0.125.

[100] 33.3%

[101] 66.7%

[102] $1\dfrac{\dot{1}}{2}$

[103] C

[104] 0.47%

[105] Since $\dfrac{8}{24}$, or $\dfrac{1}{3}$, relates to no precise decimal or percent, using a fraction would be the only exact measurement.

[106] Answers may vary. A fraction would be the easiest to justify as the denominator indicates the actual number of total items in the sample, $\dfrac{1}{50}$ and $\dfrac{1}{13}$.

[107] C

[108] B

[109] $\dfrac{1}{100}$

[110] $\dfrac{3,202}{25,255};\ 0.127;\ 12.7\%$

[111] $\dfrac{21,508}{64,859};\ 0.332;\ 33.2\%$

[112] A

[113] 35 weeks

[114] 10,000 squares. Explanations may vary. Example: 100 × (10 × 10) is usually easier to solve mentally than 100 × 100.

[115] The sum of any three numbers across, down or diagonally add up to fifteen. Solve an equation such as $x + 9 + 2 = 15$ to find the value of x. Solve an equation such as $y + 8 + 1 = 15$ to find the value of y.

[116] Drawing diagonals will create four triangles. By adding four congruent triangles to the square, you can double the size and remain a square.

ANSWERS

The area of the square = 5 × 5 = 25. The radius of the circle is $\frac{1}{2}(\sqrt{25+25})$ or approximately 3.5. The area of the circle

[117] $(\pi r^2) = \pi(3.5^2) = 38.5$. $38.5 - 25 = 13.5$.

[118] A

[119] D

[120] 1.5 miles

[121] 2, 4, 6

[122] 7. One quarter, two dimes, four pennies.

[123] 6. 321, 312, 213, 231, 123, 132.

[124] B

[125] 15.86

[126] If 72% live in rural areas, then 28% must live in urban areas. 28% of 6.6 million is 1.848 million people. (Source: USA Today, 10/18/93)

[127] B

[128] C

[129] A

[130] $15.73

[131] $61.56

[132] The price in March was $75, $5 less than the original price.

[133] A

[134] About 15%

[135] $18.81

[136] The $95 skis

[137] D

[138] 42%

[158] 7%

[159] 183%

[160] 2%

[161] 4.2%

[162] C

[163] 9% decrease

[164] 167%. The change is five pieces from three pieces, or $\frac{5}{3}$.

[165] 5% decrease; about $2.76 billion

[166] A

[167] 20% decrease

[168] $900

[139] No. You must also know the tax rate to determine the total amount you must pay for the wreath, tax and shipment.

[140] By cross multiplication, the answer is 10.7% of a cup.

[141] 6%. Explanations may vary, but may include: divide 12.72 by 12.00 and subtract 1 or subtract the purchase price from the total price and divide by the purchase price.

[142] D

[143] A

[144] 1.1% ($\frac{1}{88}$) (Source: The World Almanac 1991)

[145] 33%

[146] C

[147] 120

[148] 66%

[149] 77%

[150] 10 (120% of 50 = 60; 60 - 50 = 10)

[151] $\frac{1,536}{1,600}$. Explanations may vary. Examples may include 4% of 1,600 did not graduate high school. 1,600 - 64 = 1,536.

[152] $\frac{1}{50}$, Florida

[153] D

[154] 10%

[155] 50%. During the first ten minutes, Mario ate two pieces. During the following five minutes, he ate one piece. The increase is $\frac{1}{2}$ of the pieces already eaten, or 50%.

[156] The change is an increase of approximately 6.4%. The dates of decrease include 9/14 and 9/19 as they drop below 740.

[157] B

Chapter 7: Investigating Geometry

[1] C

[2] 64

[3] Answers will vary, but should include the four phases of the moon (full, quarter, half, new) and their fractional equivalents $\left(1, \frac{1}{4}, \frac{1}{2}, 0\right)$.

[4] Answers may vary, but should include that a honeycomb is a pattern of repeating hexagons.

[5] 8 miles; Explanations should reflect students' understanding of Dave's training "pattern."

[6]

[7] A

[8] D

[9] Answer should be a three-fourths-shaded circle and a completely shaded circle.

[10] 12 cm

[11] A 2 × 2 set of dots and a single dot.

[12]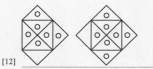

[13] 680

[14] Answers may vary. Sample: 800, if student assumes that the figures double every ten years and uses 50 as the figure for each doubling.

[15] C

[16] acute

[17] Divide 180° by 6. At 5 minutes past, the angle would be 30°.

[18] 2:00 and 10:00

[19] 60°

[20] A

[21] 61°

[22] Check students' answers. They should mention that the complementary angle is 10° and the supplementary angle is 100°.

[23] Yes, if they share a vertex and one side.

[24] B

[25] B

[26] Draw two adjacent right angles (90° each). The result is a pair of supplementary angles with no obtuse angles.

[27] ∠EBA, ∠EBD

[28] ∠ABD, ∠CBD, and ∠ABE, ∠EBC

[29] Acute, 20°

[30] Obtuse, 110°

[31] B

[32] scalene

[33] Yes. They are both acute, since the sum of both angles must be 90°.

[34] No. An obtuse angle is greater than 90°. Two would total more than 180°, which is more than the total angles of a triangle.

[35] Disagree. The triangle can be acute (70°, 70°, 40°) or obtuse (40°, 40°, 100°).

[36] 30 steps. ∠ABC = 60°. The two other angles must be equal, because it is an isosceles triangle. 180°−60°=120°. $\frac{120°}{2}=60°$; therefore, the triangle is equilateral, and the third side must equal 30 steps.

[37] C

[38] B

[39] acute

[40] C

[41] 86°

[42] ∠A = 75°, ∠C = 15°

[43] Two possible answers: 50°, 50°, 80° or 20°, 80°, 80°

[44] 30°, 30°, 120°

[45] A. 38°; B. 92°; C. 60°

[46] 2 isosceles triangles

[47] C

[48] 15 games

[49] Answers may vary. Samples: in order to buy the right amount of materials, to have an idea of what the finished product should look like.

[50] Answers will vary, but may include angles formed by an open door, an open book, or by arms held in different positions.

[51] B

[52] C

[53] Diagram should show 3 dimes, 1 nickel, and 3 pennies, for a total of 7 coins.

[54] 40

[55] 50°, 30°, 100°

[56] Three miles

[57] Two right triangles--all four angles of a rectangle are right angles, leaving one 90° angle in each of the triangles.

[58] 6 angles; 2 acute angles

[59] B

[60] JK = CD, KL = DE, JL = CE, ∠J = ∠C, ∠K = ∠D, ∠L = ∠E

[61] Answers may vary, but students should mention that the corresponding angles of the triangles should have congruent angles and similar size.

[62] No. An equilateral triangle has three 60° angles, a right triangle has a 90° angle.

[63] Yes. A triangle with lengths of three sides known will always have the same angles.

[64] No. Triangles with congruent corresponding angles can have non-congruent sides. Therefore, not congruent.

[65] C

[66] D

[67] ΔEDF

[68] ΔDEF

[69] ΔFED

[70] ∠R; ∠P

[71] 6

[72] Two acute triangles

[73] D

[74] nonagon

[75] Answers may vary depending on the types of figures mentioned and description by sides and/or angles, and may include: trapezoid, parallelogram, rectangle, rhombus, square.

[76] No. A trapezoid has only one pair of parallel sides and a square must have two pairs of parallel sides.

[77] Rectangle

[78] 360°−(∠A + ∠B + ∠C)

[79] Octagon

[80] Rectangles and rhombus

[81] A

[82] rectangle, square, quadrilateral, parallelogram, rhombus

[83] A

[84] A

[85] 70° and 110°

[86] Two quadrilaterals

[87] Pentagon

[88] Neither can have a measure of 90°.

[89] $\overline{RT}$

[90] C

[91] CD has both points on Circle A and passes through center point A.

[92] $\overline{AB}$ has one endpoint on the circle and the other endpoint at the center.

[93] 60°; $\overline{AB}=\overline{AC}$, because the length of all radii are equal. If $\overline{BC}=\overline{AC}$, all segments are equal, creating an equilateral triangle.

[94] No. Neither endpoint of $\overline{BC}$ occupies the center.

[95] Answers may vary, but students should mention that the tire is a circle, the spokes are like radii, etc.

[96] $\overline{AC}$, $\overline{AB}$, $\overline{AD}$

[97] diameter

[98] B

[99] octagon

[100] B

ANSWERS

[101] A

[102] △BAD

[103] 30°

[104] 90°

[105] C

[106] $510

[107] Answers will vary but may include: Other countries produced many more vehicles in 1990 than in 1950; the U.S. dominance of world production is much less in 1990 than in 1950.

[108] Answers may vary, but should indicate that Europe is producing more vehicles with a higher percent of the world total in 1990 than in 1950.

[109] 74%

[110] 26%

[111] 76%

[112] 50%

[113] 48%

[114] Answers may vary. Example: Someone other than Ted and Alice was using the car at least 8% of the time the car was in use.

[115] D

[116]

[129] They would both be acute angles because an angle less than 90° (acute) which is divided in half must also be less than 90°.

[130] They would both be acute angles because an angle less than 180° and more than 90° (obtuse) which is divided in half must be less than 90°.

[131] C

[117] Check graph for appropriate sizes or labels. The explanation should include Canada in the "other" column.

[118] Answers will vary, but should show a continued upward trend for Europe and Japan.

[119]

[120] The angle bisected must be a straight angle.

[121] A midpoint divides the segment into two congruent segments.

[122] D

[123] B

[124] $\overline{DB}$ or $\overline{BD}$, $\overline{GE}$ or $\overline{EG}$, $\overline{CA}$ or $\overline{AC}$

[125] 1 cm × 4 cm

[126]

[127]

[128] D

[1] A

[2]

[3] No. The length of the rubber band may change as it used. This would make the estimate less exact than if a string were used.

[4] The three-foot string would be better because it would require fewer string placements to measure the perimeter.

[5] Explanations may vary. Examples: Advantage of rounding to the foot is that the estimate can be done quickly; disadvantage is that it won't be as accurate as rounding to the nearest inch. Advantage of rounding to the nearest inch is greater accuracy; disadvantage is that it is more time consuming.

[6] B

[7] 6 ft

[8] 27 cm

[9] D

[10] 8 cm^2

[11] Answers may vary. Since the overlapping circles appear to be similar in size, and the area of one circle = $\pi 3^2 = 28.26$ cm^2, the estimate should be somewhat less than 56.5 cm^2. An acceptable range is 47 cm^2 – 54 cm^2.

[12] A

[13] 2.25 ft^2

[14] Approximately 37.5 cm^2

[15] D

[16] 134.4 km

[17] No. Since most rectangles have two sides of different lengths, multiplying one side by four will result in an inaccurate measurement.

[18] Yes. All squares are rectangles and therefore can use this equation.

ANSWERS

[19] B

[20] A

[21] This parallelogram must also be a square. If $A = 36$ cm^2 and $b = 6$ cm, then $h = 6$ cm.

[22] $P = 44$ in. The equation to determine the area of a square is $A = s^2$. $121 = s^2$, $11 = s$. If each side is 11 inches, then $P = 44$ in.

[23] 60 cm^2

[24] 40 cm

[25] 36 in.^{2}

[26] 0.5 m

[27] 980 yd^2

[28] 115.2 m

[29] D

[30] 112 yd^2

[31] Answers may vary. Examples: (1) both triangles will have 12 in. by 6 in. dimensions. The area would then be $\frac{1}{2}(12 \times 6) = 36$ in.^{2} (2) the area of the rectangle is 72 in.^{2}. Two equal triangles created by the diagonal would each have an area of 36 in.^{2}.

[32] B

[33] $A = 10$ in.^{2}; the triangle should be a right triangle with height of 4 in. and a base of 10 in.

[34] 32 in.^{2}

[35] Answers may include right triangles with base and height combinations of 1 and 6, 6 and 1, 2 and 3, 3 and 2 units.

[36] .25 ft^2

[58] about 63.6 m; about 80.7 m^2

[59] about 28.3 m

[60] D

[61] 7

[62] Yes. If the addition or multiplication of any two whole numbers always results in a whole number, then the same must be true of any whole number's square.

[63] The square would be 12 in. by 12 in., or 144 square inches.

[64] The difference between one square and the next will be 2 more than the difference preceding it. (1, 4, 9, 16, 25; differences are 3, 5, 7, 9 etc.)

[65] $l = 1$, $m = 4$. Conclusion: n^2 = n • n, therefore n = 9.

[66] Answers will be one of the following: 1,1,1; 2,4,16 or 3,9,81. The explanation should show an understanding of squares and square roots.

[67] A

[68] 64 in.^{2}

[69] $4(\sqrt{100}) + 4(\sqrt{64}) = 4(10 + 8) = 72$ ft

[70] A = 8, B = 2, C = 6, D = 3

[71] A

[72] 3 and 4

[73] A

[74] 9 mm

[75] Answers may vary. Numbers should be between 196 and 225.

[76] D

[77] 15.23

[78] The congruent sides must be the triangle's legs and the hypotenuse must be longer than the legs in order to satisfy the equation $a^2 + b^2 = c^2$.

[37] A

[38] 110 dm^2

[39] Answers may vary. Trapezoid should have a height of 4". The sum of the bases should be 5".

[40] C

[41] 30 cm^2

[42] 3.5 units

[43] 190 cm^2

[44] B

[45] A

[46] You would divide the circumference by 3.14 (pi) to determine the diameter.

[47] Answers may vary. Sample: the circumference of (circle)A is half that of (circle)B and one-third that of (circle)C. You would double (circle)A's diameter to get (circle)B's (127.4 in.) and triple (circle)A's diameter to get (circle)C's (191.1 in.).

[48] A

[49] 32 cm

[50] 50

[51] A

[52] 803.84 ft^2

[53] D

[54] The stake represents the center of the circle and the thirty foot rope represents the radius. $\pi 30^2 = 2,826$ ft^2

[55] 1:2, 1:4, 1:9

[56] 5 in.

[57] 25

[79] You can use the Pythagorean Theorem to find the length of the side. Write an equation: side^2 + x^2 = diagonal^2. Now solve to find x, the missing side of the rectangle.

[80] The third side must be 20 in. to justify the equation $15^2 + 20^2 = 25^2$. If 15 and 25 were both legs, the hypotenuse would be $\sqrt{850}$, which cannot be converted to a whole number.

[81] Answers may vary. Examples: 3,4,5; 6,8,10; 9,12,15; etc.

[82] C

[83] A

[84] 12 ft

[85] 96 ft^2

[86] 48 ft

[87] 20 cm

[88] Approx. 448 miles (450 is acceptable).

[89] D

[90] yes

[91] No. Answers may vary. Sample: $\sqrt{(6^2 + 10^2)} \neq \sqrt{15^2}$

[92] B

[93] $\sqrt{74}$ ft; 8.602 ft

[94] The longest distance would be one of the two diagonals of the rectangle. The diagonal would represent a hypotenuse with legs of 40 and 20 ft. $40^2 + 20^2 = D^2$, $1600 + 400 = 2000$, $2000 = D^2$, $\sqrt{2000} = 44.7$, the longest distance one could travel in a straight line would be approximately 45 ft.

[95] $90^2 + 90^2 = C^2$

[96] Use the equation $9^2 + N^2 = 15^2$ and solve for N. The result is 12.

[97] Answers may vary. 8,6 or 7,7.

ANSWERS

[98]   C

[99]   216 cm^2

[100] 75 in.

[101] $\frac{1}{2}$ ft^2, 72 in.^{2}

[102] 67 m or 74 yd.

[103] 5 meters

[104] D

[105] Face *DCGH*, face *EFGH*, and face *BCGF*

[106] Yes. If $\overline{AB}$ is parallel to $\overline{EF}$, and $\overline{EF}$ is parallel to $\overline{HG}$, then $\overline{AB}$ must be parallel to $\overline{HG}$.

[107] C

[108] C

[109] C

[110] Answers may vary: cereal box, pitched roof on a house, book, suitcase, and so on.

[111] 6 rectangles, 2 hexagons

[112] A

[113] No. A circle lies in a plane and has only two dimensions.

[114] The base is a quadrilateral and the other four faces are triangles.

[115] 5

[116] Answers may vary. Sample: They both have faces that are polygons. A prism has 2 parallel bases, a pyramid has only 1 base.

[117] Answers may vary. Sample: They both come to a point. A cone has a curved surface; all the surfaces of a pyramid are polygons.

[118] Check student's drawing of a triangular pyramid.

[119] C

[134] 90 m^3

[135] The volumes are the same. 3 in. × 6 in. × 7 in. = 126 in.^{3} and 2 in. × 7 in. × 9 in. = 126 in.^{3}

[136] The base of the box must be a 20 cm × 20 cm square and the height must be 17.5 cm because there are three boards with a thickness of 0.5 each and two spaces of 8 cm between these boards. The volume is 20 cm × 20 cm × 17.5 cm or 7,000 cm^3.

[137] Answers may vary. Samples: 6 cm × 5 cm × 10 cm or 5 cm × 4 cm × 15 cm.

[138] Answers may vary. Samples: 6 in.×5 in.×5 in. or 2 in.×5 in.×15 in.

[139] D

[140] C

[141] 3 in.

[142] 16 mm

[143] 6 cm

[144] 216 in.^{3}

[145] B

[146] 5319.16 ft^3

[147] 4 in.

[148] 1692 m^3

[149] C

[150] 162 and 163

[151] Yes. If you are given a number (81 or 256 for example) you can calculate the square root. By calculating the square root of the square root you have determined n^2 from n^4 ($\sqrt{81} = 9$, $\sqrt{9} = 3$, $3^4 = 81$).

[152] The two calculations are (1) 50 × 50 × 50 and 40 × 40 × 40. If 54,872 is between the two products, then the student is correct. The student is not correct because 40 × 40 × 40 is greater than 54,872 (64,000>54,872). Note: The sides are 38 cm in length.

[120] 1,350 m^2

[121] The total surface area of the box is 65.5 ft^2, so you need two rolls.

[122] It would be a cube. The angles of a rectangular prism are right angles. If the sides are congruent, then all the faces must be squares.

[123] 4. A triangular pyramid would have a three-sided base and three triangles extending from the sides to a common point.

[124] Answers will vary, but may include a prism (cube) with sides of 5cm.

[125] C

[126] 132 ft^2

[127] 110 cm^2

[128] D

[129] 263.76 m^2

[130] about 152 cm^2

[131]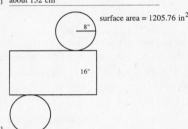
surface area = 1205.76 in^2

[132] The cylinder with the radius 8 has a greater surface area. The formula for the surface area of a cylinder is $2\pi rh + 2\pi r^2$ The first part is the same for both cylinders, so the cylinder with the greater radius will have the greater surface area.

[133] D

[153] 2nd prism. The 1st prism's length = $V \div HW = \frac{70}{10} = 7$. The length of the 2nd prism = $V \div HW = \frac{64}{8} = 8$.

[154] D

[155] B

[156] By guessing the middle number of the remaining possible numbers, you reduce the remaining possibilities by half. Your first guess of 5 would reduce the search to four numbers if David's response is "lower," or five numbers if his response is "higher." If "higher" then your next guess would be 8. The remaining possibilities would be 6, 7 and 9, 10. A wrong guess with either of these two combinations would result in your knowing the number. The lowest number of guesses needed to ensure a correct guess would be four.

[157] 12

[158] *l* = 9 in., *w* = 3 in., *h* = 3 in.

[159] 4 cm^2

[160] 32 ft. (384 in.)

ANSWERS

[1] A

[2] 0.6

[3] Two acceptable explanations are: (1) Jamal could be running successive hot streaks, and (2) Jamal is improving P(make a basket) as he is learning how to throw the basketball.

[4] Isiah would have to throw one-hundred free throws in this particular afternoon. A reasonable explanation for the change in probabilities in the later experiments is that fatigue may set in with each succeeding throw, affecting the probability.

[5] Answers may vary, but should indicate that Choice A will yield the highest number of points in the long run. Choice A has a $\frac{1}{4}$ probability to earn four points. Choice B has a $\frac{1}{8}$ probability to earn six points, and Choice C has a $\frac{1}{16}$ probability to earn ten points.

[6] B

[7] D

[8] $\frac{1}{16}$. The outcome of each event in this series is independent, so regardless of the outcomes of the first six tosses, the probability that the final four will be tails is $\frac{1}{16}$.

[9] C

[10] 0.044

[11] 48%

[12] 40%

[13] They are equal.

[14] Sample answer: Throw the cube 10 times and record the numbers; if 6 turns up, throw again. Record the outcomes. If each of the numbers 1–5 comes up at least once, count that trial as successful. Then repeat the experiment 50 times. The number of successful trials divided by 50 is the probability.

[15] Answers may vary. The table shows that 1 trial had 8 twice, so the probability is 1/5. The results would be different if there were more trials, if the spinner is fair.

[16] C

[17] Answers may vary. Example: Toss a coin until you get 5 heads in a row, and record the number of tosses needed. Repeat the experiment several times and divide the sum of the tosses needed by the number of trials.

[18] The probability would be extremely slight because although different combinations are probable at the beginning of this series, the probability of repeating an already-thrown combination becomes increasingly high as the series proceeds.

[19] A simulation is the development of a model appropriate to a given problem, and the completion of enough trials to generate data to solve the problem.

[20] B

[21] A

[22] C

[23] 14. Even though the probability of drawing 13 consecutive spades is extremely low, you cannot be absolutely certain of drawing another suit.

[24] 1,920

[25] $400

[26] $0.30

[27] $31.00

[28] A

[29] a. $\frac{1}{6}$ b. $\frac{53}{330}$

[30] Answers will vary. Examples are the toss of a coin and the month in which someone in class was born.

[31] $P = \frac{1}{2}$. Explanations may vary, but should indicate that a fair coin has equal chance of an outcome of heads or tails. The tosses will not necessarily alternate tails and heads.

[32] C

[33] The probability of Sara rolling a higher number is $\frac{3}{6}$, a lower number, $\frac{2}{6}$, and the same number, $\frac{1}{6}$.

[34] $\frac{9}{16}$

[35] $\frac{1}{16}$

[36] 72%

[37] D

[38] 83%

[39] The complement of a 60% chance of rain is a 40% chance of no rain.

[40] No. P(2 tails) = 25%, P(2 heads) = 25%. These two probabilities add up to only 50%. The complement to P(2 tails) is P(2 heads or 1 head and 1 tail), 25% + 75%.

[41] B

[42] A

[43] {(1,1), (1,2), (1,3), (1,4), (2,1), (2,2), (2,3), (2,4), (3,1), (3,2), (3,3), (3,4), (4,1), (4,2), (4,3), (4,4)}

[44] Answers may vary, but may include that each stage represents a different portion of the possible outcomes which make up a sample space.

[45] The sample space in a tree diagram is lined vertically or horizontally. The sample space in a grid is grouped vertically and horizontally.

[46] A grid is the easier to construct because it involves much less work to construct in this example, as the drawn diagrams will show.

[47] C

[48] Yes. Even though there are three possible outcomes for two heads and a tail, there is only one that follows the conditions Millie set.

[49] A

[50] 90,000,000

[51] B

[52] 72

[53] 36

[54] a. 6; b. 36; c. 216

[55] $\frac{30}{36}$ or $\frac{5}{6}$

[56] $\frac{6}{36}$ or $\frac{1}{6}$

[57] $\frac{1}{36}$

[58] B

[59] $\frac{3}{64}$

[60] No. The outcome of one toss has no effect on the outcome of any other toss.

[61] Events would be dependent if you did not return picked marbles to the bag. Events would be independent if each picked marble were returned to the bag before each succeeding event.

[62] 7; $P = \frac{1}{6}$. Explanations may vary.

[63] D

[64] $\frac{1}{100}$

ANSWERS

[65] $\dfrac{1}{1000}$

[66] 72% or $\dfrac{72}{100}$

[67] $\dfrac{1}{4}$ or 25%

[68] $\dfrac{1}{6}$

[69] C

[70] $\dfrac{6}{91}$

[71] D

[72] If the first card picked is a club, the probability of the second card being a club is $\dfrac{12}{51}$. If the first card is not a club, then the probability is $\dfrac{13}{51}$.

[73] 1. a home game; 2. a winning game

[74] C

[75] $_7P_3 = 210$

[76] Examples may vary. A possible answer may be that counting your change in a particular order may ensure you of receiving the correct amount.

[77] D

[78] 24

[79] 753, 735, 573, 537, 375, 357; 6 numbers

[80] 120

[81] 205 (120 five-letter, 60 four-letter, 20 two-letter, 5 one-letter)

[82] 288 cars

[83] 24 ways

[84] Answers may vary. Sample: In trying to decide how to schedule several different errands.

[105] The marked deer counted and total deer counted would each increase by four. The estimate of deer population would decrease.

[106] −1.5°C

[107] 1,173

[108] $\dfrac{32}{1212} = \dfrac{60}{x}$; gives $x = 2{,}272.5 \approx 2{,}273$
$\dfrac{32}{1212} = \dfrac{120}{x}$; gives $x = 4{,}545$
As you can see by solving the proportions above, when the total number of deer marked is doubled, the total population estimate is doubled as well.

[109] $\dfrac{42}{1417} = \dfrac{54}{x}$; gives $x = 1{,}822$ $\dfrac{21}{1417} = \dfrac{54}{x}$; gives $x = 3{,}644$
As you can see from solving the proportions above, when the number of marked deer counted is halved the estimated population doubles.

[110] The people would have to be a random sampling of the population.

[111] Answers may vary. Examples: conduct your survey at an ocean beach resort, or in a retirement community.

[85] 120 ways

[86] A

[87] 15

[88] A group of items in a particular order is a permutation. A group of items in no particular order is a combination.

[89] It is possible by using a different set of pictures in each combination, such as 1, 2, 3, 4; 1, 2, 3, 5; 1, 2, 4, 5; 1, 3, 4, 5, etc.

[90] It is not possible. There can only be one combination of all four pictures.

[91] A

[92] 6

[93] 45

[94] D

[95] 6 ways

[96] 10 handshakes. Combination, because the order in which people shake hands doesn't matter.

[97] 5 different sets

[98] A

[99] 800

[100] Yes. As sample sizes increase, they will tend to be more accurate.

[101] No. Since any particular condition would affect marked and unmarked deer equally, the same proportions of deer should be observed under any condition.

[102] 1984--2,536; 1985--1,821. Answers will vary and may include (1) extreme weather conditions reducing the population; (2) more hunting permits distributed in 1985 than in 1984; (3) a possible "hot streak" in 1984 or "cold streak" in 1985 of marked deer counted, etc.

[103] D

[104] D

Chapter 10: Patterns and Functions

[1] A

[2] Start with 5 and add 2 repeatedly.

[3] Answers will vary. Sample: "Start with 1 and add 2, add 3, add 4, and so on".

[4] A

[5] B

[6] 128

[7] C

[8] D

[9] 162, 486, 1458

[10] Both types of sequences contain a series of terms arranged according to a pattern. They differ in whether the pattern is determined by repeated addition (arithmetic sequence) or repeated multiplication (geometric sequence).

[11] A sequence that is neither arithmetic nor geometric is made up of terms and the terms are arranged according to a particular pattern.

[12] Answers will vary. Sample: "Start with 1 and multiply by 2 repeatedly" and "Start with 0 and 4 repeatedly".

[13] 8

[14] Arithmetic sequence. Start with 1 and add 2 repeatedly.

[15] Start with 1 and add 8 repeatedly. The second Wednesday falls on October 9, third Thursday falls on October 17, and fourth Friday falls on October 25.

[16] Start with $4.50 and add $0.50, add $0.75, add $1.00, and so on.

[17] In the sixth year of employment, a worker receives an hourly rate of $9.50.

[18] B

[19] 3.03×10^3

ANSWERS

[20] Answers will vary. Sample: Expressing the vast distances which exist among objects resting outside the Earth's atmosphere in standard form would result in extremely large numbers. Scientific notation provides astronomers with a shortened way of expressing such numbers.

[21] Answers will vary. Letters should describe identifying a factor greater than or equal to 1 but less than 10, multiplying by the appropriate power of 10, and writing the power of 10 using an exponent. The number expressed in scientific notation is 6.2×10^7.

[22] Yes because the greater the exponent, the larger the power of 10 factor.

[23] D

[24] 8.49×10^4 miles (Mercury's diameter is 3,100 miles while Jupiter's diameter is 88,000 miles. Therefore, their difference is 84,900 miles.)

[25] Pacific Ocean - 6.41863×10^7; Atlantic Ocean - 3.342×10^7

[26] 1.301×10^4

[27] 4.161×10^4

[28] A

[29] 419,000

[30] Responses should indicate that the theory is wrong. For example, 4,230,000 expressed in scientific notation is 4.23×10^6, not 4.23×10^4.

[31] B

[32] A

[33] 253

[34] 25 squares

[35] 31 games

[36] Bob makes 1.83 item/min. William makes 1.75 item/min.

[37] 18 and 19

[38] 24 lunches

[39] 6 weeks; Adam will be able to purchase the bond after saving for 5 weeks. Carol will be able to purchase the bond after saving for 11 weeks.

[40] 120

[41] 2 workers

[42] 52 students

[43] 37, 39, 41

[44] C

[45] $499.38

[46] Answers will vary but should demonstrate an understanding of the terms "rate" and "interest."

[47] Questions will vary but should include queries about interest rate, penalties for withdrawals, and account maintenance charges.

[48] $742

[49] C

[50] $591

[51] 6 years

[52] $2314.41

[53] $4527.71

[54] $140.71

[55] A

[56] C

[57] $126.53

[58] About $3,900

[59] A

[60]

input	1	2	3	4	5
output	11	18	25	32	39

[61] A function is a relationship between each member of one set paired exactly with one member of another set. A rule describes a relationship.

[62] Table, rule, graph

[63] (3,12), (4,16), (5,20) The graph would be a straight line with a constant rise of 4 units.

[64] Rule: $3x + 1$

[65] B

[66] B

[67] $d = 70t$

[68] 160 miles

[69] $4.25; $8.50 Earnings = Hours × $4.25

[70] Whale: $d = 20t$; Barracuda: $d = 30t$

[71] The barracuda would have traveled a distance of 180 miles. It would take a whale 9 hours to travel this same distance.

[72] B

[73]

[74] Output = 1/2 input + 1

[75] C

[76] Car 3--the graph shows that car 3 is covering more distance in any time period.

[77] A

[78]

input (n)	output ($n+2$)
1	3
3	5
7	9

[79] The input is represented by the variable n. Any related output is represented by the variable expression $4n + 5$.

[80]

n	$f(n)$
1	8
2	6
3	4
4	2

[81]

Time (sec)	1	2	3	4	5	6	7
Distance (ft)	16	64	144	256	400	576	784

[82]

	1	2	3	4	5	6	7
Noses	29¢	58¢	87¢	$1.16	$1.45	$1.74	$2.03
Buzzers	79¢	$1.58	$2.37	$3.16	$3.95	$4.74	$5.53

[83] D

[84] $f(n) = n^2$

[85] Answers will vary. Sample: Samuel could set up a function table of hours worked and earnings. He could continue filling it out until he reaches an amount that is at least $121.99.

[86] Answers will vary. Sample: $f(n) = n - 2$ and $f(n) = n - 5$.

[87] D

[88] C

[89] $f(n) = 9 - 2n$

ANSWERS

[90] $f(n) = \$0.75n$

[91] $f(n) = \$2.75n$; $\$11.00$

[92] A

[93] Answers may vary: Gas left in tank during trip down a freeway.

[94] $f(n) = \$3.25n$; $f(n) = \$4.25$

[95] $\$46.75 - \$35.75 = \$11.00$

[96] Answers will vary but should indicate a relationship in which the value of a particular variable decreased over time. Sample: weight of a person on a diet or body temperature of an ill person who began to take medication.

[97] Answers will vary but should be evidenced by the information in the graph. Possible responses include students watch more television on Saturday than any other day, watch less television on Tuesday than any other day, and generally watch more television on weekends than weekdays.

[98] D

[99] D

[100] Answers will vary. Sample: By comparing time point at which each graph ends one can determine that Juan rode at a slower pace than Rita.

[101] Answers may vary:

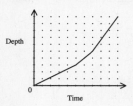

[102] A "flat" segment shows no change in the variable.

[1] D

[2] (−2, −3)

[3] Sentences will vary but may include "The x-axis and y-axis intersect at the origin of a coordinate plane."

[4] Answers will vary. Sample: Start at the origin. Look at the x-coordinate and move that many units left or right. Then look at the y-coordinate and move that many points up or down. Graph a point at this location.

[5] Answers will vary.

[6] D

[7]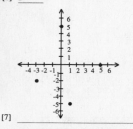

[8] (3,0), (3,2); (−1,2), (−1,0); (2,1), (0,1)

[9]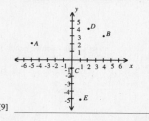

[103] Answers should include compiling data regarding height at each age, drawing two axes, labeling the vertical axis "Change in Height" and the horizontal axis "Age," determining the value of each unit on the graph, plotting the data and connecting the points with a line.

[104] The steeper the line, the faster the rider.

[105]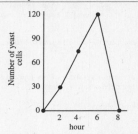

[106] Answers will vary. Sample: Something occurred in the glass dish between hours 6 and 8 that caused the yeast cells to suddenly die.

[10]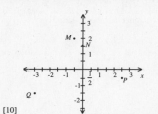

[11] Answers may vary. Sample: (0,6), (-6,0), (0,-6)

[12] B

[13] third quadrant

[14] Answers will vary. Sample: (0, 1), (0, 0), (-2, 0)

[15] B

[16] C

[17] C

[18] no

[19] Letters will vary but should describe a linear equation as one in which all its solutions lie in a straight line on a coordinate plane.

[20] Answers may vary. Sample: Substitute the first coordinate for x and the second coordinate for y. If the equation is true, then the ordered pair is a solution of the equation.

[21] Answers will vary but may include $x + y = 8$.

[22] Tables will vary. Sample:

x	$y = 4x - 1$	(x, y)
1	3	(1,3)
−1	−5	(−1,−5)
2	7	(2,7)
−2	−9	(−2,−9)
0	−1	(0,−1)

[23] Answers may vary. Sample: $(0,\frac{1}{2})$ and $(1,2\frac{1}{2})$

Tables will vary. Sample:

x	$y=\frac{1}{2}x+2$	(x,y)
1	$2\frac{1}{2}$	$(1,2\frac{1}{2})$
−1	$1\frac{1}{2}$	$(-1,1\frac{1}{2})$
2	3	$(2,3)$
−2	1	$(-2,1)$
0	2	$(0,2)$

[24]

Tables will vary. Sample:

Canada				Austria		
x	$y=x(3.0)$	(x,y)		x	$y=x(1.5)$	(x,y)
1	3	$(1,3)$		1	1.5	$(1,1.5)$
2	6	$(2,6)$		2	3	$(2,3)$
3	9	$(3,9)$		3	4.5	$(3,4.5)$
4	12	$(4,12)$		4	6	$(4,6)$
5	15	$(5,15)$		5	7.5	$(5,7.5)$

[25]

[26] C

[27]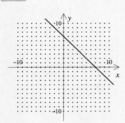

Answers will vary but should indicate the value of a in the equation $y=ax$
[37] is greater than 5.

Answers will vary. Sample: the amount of rain the region generally
[38] receives and the roof structures already used in the region.

[39] D

[40] C

The slope of Line t is 3 and the slope of Line r is −2. So Line t has the
[41] steepest slope.

[42] $y=-3x$; the slope is −3

[43] $\frac{1}{4}$

[44] $-\frac{1}{2}$

[45] $2;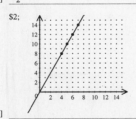

[46] Slope = 2. The slope is the same as the rate of savings.

[47] B

[28] C

[29] D

[30] D

[31] D

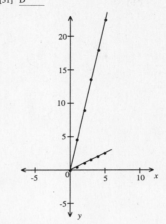

[32] United States; Turkey; see graph.

[33] C

[34] $-\frac{2}{9}$

Use the following ratio to determine the slope of the line:
[35] $\dfrac{\text{difference in } y\text{-coordinates}}{\text{difference in } x\text{-coordinates}}; \dfrac{-4-5}{-1-2}; \dfrac{3}{1}$

[36] The slope is $-\frac{1}{2}$ because the value of a in the equation $y=ax$ is the slope.

[48]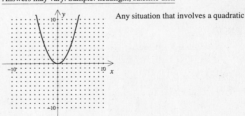

Both are graphs of an equation and show sets of ordered pairs. They differ
in that the ordered pairs that make up a parabola lie in a curved line while
[49] those that make up a linear equation lie in a straight line.

All three equations would be parabolas. The parabola for each of the first
two equations would lie in quadrants I and II while the parabola for the
[50] third equation would lie in quadrants III and IV.

[51] Answers may vary. Sample: headlight, satellite dish

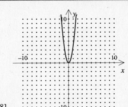

Any situation that involves a quadratic

[52] equation.

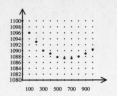

[53] _____

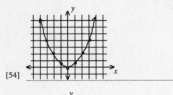

[54] _____

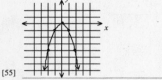

[55] _____

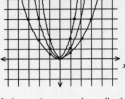

[56] In the equation $y = mx$, the smaller the value of m, the wider the parabola.

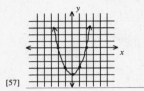

[57] _____

[58] C _____

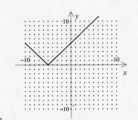

[59] _____

[60] C _____

[61] C _____

[62] A

[63] 16 nickels and 48 dimes

[64] 169 pledges

[65] 18 and 60

[66] 17, 21, 24, and 26

[67] length is 32 m; width is 18 m

[68] 492 tickets

[69] at least 56 deliveries in the last two days

[70] 16 quarters ($4.00), 16 dimes ($1.60), 48 nickels ($2.40)

[71] $4.80

[72] 106 g

[73] 89, 91, 93

[74] C

[75] $(3, -2)$

[76] A translation is performed by sliding a point, line or shape into a new position without turning it or flipping it over. The new shape is its image.

[77] (1,2)

[78] (1,-5)

[79] (-4,-1)

[80] (-4,-2)

[81] 55° west

[82] 10° west

[83] D

[84] $(x, y) \rightarrow (x + 4, y - 5)$

[85] Determine the change in the x-coordinate ($4 \rightarrow -2$ or a change of -6) and in the y-coordinate ($5 \rightarrow 2$ or a change of -3). The translation is $(x,y) \rightarrow (x - 6, y - 3)$.

[86] Answers will vary but may include $(x,y) \rightarrow (x + 8, y)$.

[87] Answers may vary. Check students' work.

[88] C

[89] C

[90] D

[91] true

[92] D

[93] $(-3, 6)$

[94] The line of reflection is the axis over which the image crossed. It is similar to a line of symmetry in that it represents the dividing line between the mirror images.

[95] A

[96] A

[97] Since the y-coordinate of the points has changed, the line of reflection is the x-axis.

[98] Since the x-coordinate of the points has changed, the line of reflection is the y-axis.

[99] Both a reflection and a translation are types of images of a figure by making changes to the coordinates of the figure and both can be represented on a coordinate plane. In a reflection, the new image is reflected across an axis while in a translation the new image is shifted along an axis.

[100] Answers may vary.

[101] Answers may vary.

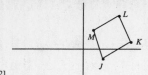

[102]

J'(-2,-1), K'(-5,1), L'(-4,4), M'(-1,2);

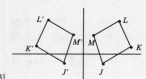

[103] _____

[104] 40° south _____

[105] 90° south _____

[106] yes _____

Yes, an eight car Ferris-wheel does have rotational symmetry because it can be rotated to a new position and still look identical to its original
[107] position. _____

[108] In the rotation, the figure is turned rather than flipped across the axis.

Translation = moving a piece of furniture from one location to another, Reflection = symmetrical sides of the human body; Rotation = a centrifuge
[109] or Tilt-A-Whirl ride at an amusement park _____

[110] The angle of rotation is 90 degrees since $\frac{360}{4} = 90$.

[111] 45° _____

[112] Jupiter, Neptune _____

[113] 72° _____

[114] B _____

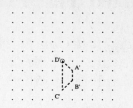

[115] _____

[116] Answers may vary. _____

[117] D _____

[118] C _____

[119] C _____

[120] B _____

Standardized Test Practice Exercises on the Software

Your *Prentice Hall Computer Item Generator with Standardized Test Practice* software includes a special feature—practice exercises that have been correlated to the mathematics objectives of the standardized tests below.

	Level of Prentice Hall *Middle Grades Math*		
	Course 1	Course 2	Course 3
California Achievement Tests, 5th Ed. (CAT5)	Level 16	Level 17	Level 18
Comprehensive Tests of Basic Skills (CTBS), Terra Nova	Level 16	Level 17	Level 18
Iowa Tests of Basic Skills (ITBS), Form M	Level 12	Level 13	Level 14
Metropolitan Achievement Tests, 7th Ed. (MAT7)	Intermediate 1	Intermediate 2	Intermediate 3
Stanford Achievement Test, 9th Ed. (SAT9)	Intermediate 2	Intermediate 3	Advanced 1
TAAS	Grade 6	Grade 7	Grade 8
NC End-of-Grade	Grade 6	Grade 7	Grade 8

The pages that follow show the objectives for the various standardized tests and the numbers of the items in the software that address each objective. You can use this information as an aid in creating worksheets and practice tests. You can also use the numbers to order worksheets or tests via Prentice Hall's exclusive Dial-A-Test® service. (See page vii for details.)

Test Objective	Standardized Test Practice Item Numbers
Computation	
Add, subtract, multiply, and divide decimals	1.1, 1.2, 1.3, 1.4, 1.5, 1.6
Add, subtract, multiply, and divide fractions	1.7, 1.8, 1.9, 1.10, 1.11, 1.12
Add, subtract, multiply, and divide integers	1.13, 1.14, 1.15, 1.16, 1.17
Percents	1.18, 1.19
Order of operations	1.20, 1.21, 1.22
Concepts and Applications: Numeration	
Fractional part	1.23, 1.24, 1.25
Recognize numbers	1.26, 1.27
Compare numbers	1.28, 1.29, 1.30, 1.31, 1.32, 1.33
Expanded notation	1.34
Place value	1.35, 1.36
Estimate, round	1.37, 1.38, 1.39, 1.40, 1.41
Concepts and Applications: Number Theory	
Number properties	1.42, 1.43, 1.44, 1.45, 1.46
Divisibility	1.47, 1.48
Equivalent forms	1.49, 1.50, 1.51, 1.52, 1.53, 1.54, 1.55, 1.56
Multiples	1.57, 1.58
Odd, even numbers	1.59
Prime, composite numbers	1.60, 1.61
Concepts and Applications: Data Interpretation	
Graphs	1.62, 1.63, 1.64, 1.65, 1.66, 1.67, 1.68
Probability, statistics	1.69, 1.70, 1.71, 1.72, 1.73, 1.74
Table, chart, diagram	1.75, 1.76, 1.77
Pre-solution (too much, not enough information)	1.78, 1.79, 1.80

STANDARDIZED TEST PRACTICE

CAT5 Level 17 (Continued)

Test Objective	Standardized Test Practice Item Numbers
Concepts and Applications: Pre-Algebra	
Find the missing element in an equation	**1.81, 1.82, 1.83, 1.84, 1.85, 1.86, 1.87**
Use ratio, proportion to solve problems	**1.88, 1.89, 1.90, 1.91, 1.92, 1.93**
Function, pattern	**1.94, 1.95, 1.96, 1.97, 1.98, 1.99, 1.100**
Percents	**1.101, 1.102, 1.103, 1.104**
Apply problem-solving strategies	**1.105, 1.106, 1.107, 1.108, 1.109, 1.110, 1.111, 1.112**
Concepts and Applications: Measurement	
Money	**1.113, 1.114**
Time	**1.115, 1.116, 1.117**
Temperature	**1.118**
Length	**1.119, 1.120, 1.121, 1.122, 1.123, 1.124**
Area	**1.125, 1.126, 1.127, 1.128, 1.129, 1.130, 1.131**
Volume, capacity	**1.132, 1.133, 1.134, 1.135**
Concepts and Applications: Geometry	
Symmetry	**1.136, 1.137**
Angles	**1.138, 1.139, 1.140**
Triangles	**1.141, 1.142, 1.143, 1.144, 1.145, 1.146**
Congruence	**1.147, 1.148, 1.149**
Properties of plane figures	**1.150, 1.151, 1.152**
Transformation	**1.153, 1.154**
Visualization	**1.155, 1.156**
Logical reasoning	**1.157, 1.158, 1.159**

STANDARDIZED TEST PRACTICE

CTBS Terra Nova Level 17

Test Objective	Standardized Test Practice Item Numbers
Number and Number Relations	
Demonstrate an understanding of number, number sense, and number theory by ordering numbers, representing numbers in equivalent forms, identifying relationships, interpreting numbers in real-world situations, and applying number concepts in real-world situations.	2.1, 2.2, 2.3, 2.4, 2.5, 2.6, 2.7, 2.8, 2.9, 2.10, 2.11, 2.12, 2.13, 2.14, 2.15, 2.16, 2.17, 2.18, 2.19, 2.20, 2.21, 2.22, 2.23, 2.24, 2.25, 2.26, 2.27, 2.28, 2.29, 2.30, 2.31, 2.32, 2.33, 2.34, 2.35, 2.36, 2.37, 2.38, 2.39, 2.40, 2.41, 2.42, 2.43, 2.44, 2.45, 2.46, 2.47, 2.48, 2.49
Computation and Numerical Estimation	
Demonstrate proficiency in computation procedures, solve real-world computation problems, apply estimation strategies, and determine reasonableness of results.	2.50, 2.51, 2.52, 2.53, 2.54, 2.55, 2.56, 2.57
Measurement	
Demonstrate an understanding of measurement systems, units, and tools by describing, calculating, or estimating size, location, and time; by using the concepts of perimeter, area, volume, capacity, weight, and mass; and by identifying appropriate degrees of accuracy. Solve problems involving principles of measurement, rate, and scale.	2.58, 2.59, 2.60, 2.61, 2.62, 2.63, 2.64, 2.65, 2.66, 2.67, 2.68, 2.69, 2.70, 2.71, 2.72, 2.73, 2.74, 2.75, 2.76, 2.77, 2.78, 2.79, 2.80
Geometry and Spatial Sense	
Demonstrate spatial sense and an understanding of geometry by visualizing and identifying two- and three- dimensional objects, classifying shapes, recognizing symmetry, using transformations, applying geometric formulas, and evaluating properties of geometric figures.	2.81, 2.82, 2.83, 2.84, 2.85, 2.86, 2.87, 2.88, 2.89, 2.90, 2.91, 2.92, 2.93, 2.94, 2.95, 2.96, 2.97, 2.98, 2.99, 2.100, 2.101, 2.102, 2.103
Data Analysis, Statistics, and Probability	
Analyze, interpret, and evaluate data in various forms; and apply the concepts and processes of data analysis, statistics, and probability to real-world situations.	2.104, 2.105, 2.106, 2.107, 2.108, 2.109, 2.110, 2.111, 2.112, 2.113, 2.114, 2.115, 2.116, 2.117, 2.118, 2.119, 2.120, 2.121, 2.122, 2.123
Patterns, Functions, Algebra	
Recognize and extend patterns.	2.124, 2.125, 2.126, 2.127, 2.128, 2.129, 2.130

STANDARDIZED TEST PRACTICE

CTBS Terra Nova Level 17 (Continued)

Test Objective	Standardized Test Practice Item Numbers
Demonstrate an understanding of functional relationships, algebraic processes, variables, and inequality.	2.131, 2.132, 2.133, 2.134, 2.135, 2.136, 2.137, 2.138, 2.139, 2.140, 2.141, 2.142, 2.144, 2.145, 2.146, 2.147, 2.148
Recognize algebraic representations of problem situations and apply algebraic methods to solve real-world problems.	2.149, 2.150, 2.151, 2.152, 2.153, 2.154, 2.155

Problem Solving and Reasoning

Test Objective	Standardized Test Practice Item Numbers
Select and apply problem-solving strategies, identify necessary information, use patterns and relationships to evaluate situations, apply inductive and deductive reasoning and spatial and proportional reasoning, and solve a variety of non-routine, real-world problems.	2.156, 2.157, 2.158, 2.159, 2.160, 2.161, 2.162, 2.163, 2.164, 2.165, 2.166

Communication

Test Objective	Standardized Test Practice Item Numbers
Relate daily vocabulary to mathematical terminology; and relate models, diagrams, and pictures to mathematical ideas.	2.167, 2.168, 2.169, 2.170, 2.171

Decimals

Test Objective	Standardized Test Practice Item Numbers
Add, subtract, multiply, and divide decimals.	2.172, 2.173, 2.174, 2.175, 2.176, 2.177, 2.178

Fractions

Test Objective	Standardized Test Practice Item Numbers
Add, subtract, multiply, and divide fractions.	2.179, 2.180, 2.181, 2.182, 2.183, 2.184, 2.185, 2.186, 2.187

Integers

Test Objective	Standardized Test Practice Item Numbers
Add, subtract, multiply, and divide integers.	2.188, 2.189, 2.190, 2.191, 2.192, 2.193, 2.194, 2.195, 2.196, 2.197

Percents

Test Objective	Standardized Test Practice Item Numbers
Solve computational problems involving percents.	2.198, 2.199, 2.200, 2.201, 2.202, 2.203, 2.204, 2.205, 2.206, 2.207, 2.208, 2.209, 2.210, 2.211, 2.212, 2.213

Order of Operations

Test Objective	Standardized Test Practice Item Numbers
Solve computational problems involving the standard order of operations.	2.214, 2.215, 2.216

STANDARDIZED
TEST PRACTICE

ITBS Form M Level 13

Test Objective	Standardized Test Practice Item Numbers
Concepts: Numeration and Operations	
Properties of number system	3.1, 3.2, 3.3, 3.4, 3.5, 3.6, 3.7
Classify numbers: divisibility	3.8, 3.9, 3.10, 3.11, 3.12, 3.13
Standard form	3.14, 3.15
Scientific notation	3.16, 3.17, 3.18, 3.19
Use negative numbers	3.20, 3.21, 3.22, 3.23, 3.24, 3.25, 3.26
Numerical patterns	3.27, 3.28, 3.29, 3.30, 3.31, 3.32
Perform fundamental operations	3.33
Concepts: Geometry	
Classify figures	3.34, 3.35, 3.36, 3.37, 3.38
Identify figures	3.39, 3.40, 3.41, 3.42, 3.43, 3.44, 3.45
Patterns	3.46, 3.47, 3.48
Properties	3.49, 3.50, 3.51, 3.52, 3.53, 3.54, 3.55
Area	3.56, 3.57, 3.58, 3.59, 3.60, 3.61, 3.62, 3.63
Concepts: Measurement	
Estimate measurements	3.64, 3.65
Identify appropriate units	3.66, 3.67
Weight	3.68
Concepts: Fractions/Decimals/Percents	
Interpret representations	3.69, 3.70, 3.71, 3.72, 3.73, 3.74, 3.75, 3.76, 3.77, 3.78, 3.79, 3.80, 3.81, 3.82, 3.83, 3.84, 3.85, 3.86, 3.87, 3.88
Compare and order	3.89, 3.90, 3.91, 3.92, 3.93, 3.94
Perform fundamental operations	3.95, 3.96, 3.97, 3.98, 3.99, 3.100, 3.101, 3.102, 3.103, 3.104, 3.105
Apply ratio	3.106, 3.107, 3.108, 3.109, 3.110, 3.111, 3.112, 3.113, 3.114
Concepts: Probability and Statistics	
Apply probability concepts	3.115, 3.116, 3.117, 3.118, 3.119, 3.120, 3.121, 3.122, 3.123

STANDARDIZED TEST PRACTICE

Test Objective	Standardized Test Practice Item Numbers
Central tendency	3.124, 3.125, 3.126, 3.127, 3.128, 3.129
Variability	3.130
Concepts: Equations and Inequalities	
Relational symbols	3.131, 3.132
Solve equations	3.133, 3.134, 3.135, 3.136, 3.137, 3.138, 3.139, 3.140, 3.141, 3.142
Estimation	
Standard rounding	3.143, 3.144, 3.145
Order of magnitude	3.146, 3.147
Compensation	3.148, 3.149, 3.150, 3.151, 3.152
Problem Solving	
One-step problems	3.153, 3.154, 3.155, 3.156, 3.157
Multi-step problems	3.158, 3.159, 3.160, 3.161, 3.162, 3.163
Problem-solving strategies	3.164, 3.165
Data Interpretation	
Read amounts	3.166, 3.167, 3.168, 3.169, 3.170, 3.171, 3.172
Compare quantities	3.173, 3.174, 3.175, 3.176
Interpret relationships	3.177, 3.178, 3.179, 3.180, 3.181, 3.182, 3.183, 3.184, 3.185, 3.186, 3.187, 3.188
Math Computation	
Whole numbers	3.189, 3.190, 3.191, 3.192, 3.193, 3.194, 3.195
Fractions	3.196, 3.197, 3.198, 3.199, 3.200, 3.201, 3.202, 3.203
Decimals	3.204, 3.205, 3.206, 3.207, 3.208, 3.209, 3.210, 3.211, 3.212

MAT7 Intermediate 2

Test Objective	Standardized Test Practice Item Numbers
Concepts	
Numeration	4.1, 4.2, 4.3, 4.4, 4.5, 4.6, 4.7, 4.8, 4.9, 4.10, 4.11, 4.12, 4.13, 4.14, 4.15, 4.16, 4.17
Number theory	4.18, 4.19, 4.20, 4.21, 4.22, 4.23, 4.24, 4.25, 4.26, 4.27
Patterns and relationships	4.28, 4.29, 4.30, 4.31, 4.32, 4.33, 4.34, 4.35, 4.36, 4.37, 4.38, 4.39
Measurement	4.40, 4.41, 4.42, 4.43, 4.44, 4.45, 4.46, 4.47
Geometry	4.48, 4.49, 4.50, 4.51, 4.52, 4.53, 4.54, 4.55, 4.56, 4.57, 4.58, 4.59, 4.60, 4.61, 4.62, 4.63, 4.64, 4.65, 4.66, 4.67
Algebra	4.68, 4.69, 4.70, 4.71, 4.72, 4.73, 4.74, 4.75, 4.76, 4.77, 4.78, 4.79, 4.80, 4.81, 4.82, 4.83, 4.84
Problem Solving	
Solution sentences	4.85, 4.86, 4.87, 4.88
Estimation	4.89, 4.90, 4.91, 4.92, 4.93, 4.94
Statistics and probability	4.95, 4.96, 4.97, 4.98, 4.99, 4.100, 4.101, 4.102, 4.103, 4.104, 4.105, 4.106, 4.107, 4.108, 4.109, 4.110
Strategies	4.111, 4.112, 4.113, 4.114, 4.115, 4.116, 4.117, 4.118, 4.119, 4.120, 4.121, 4.122, 4.123, 4.124, 4.125, 4.126, 4.127, 4.128, 4.129, 4.130, 4.131, 4.132
Procedures	
Operations with whole numbers	4.133, 4.134, 4.135, 4.136
Operations with decimals and fractions	4.137, 4.138, 4.139, 4.140, 4.141, 4.142, 4.143, 4.144, 4.145, 4.146, 4.147, 4.148, 4.149, 4.150, 4.151, 4.152, 4.153

STANDARDIZED
TEST PRACTICE

Test Objective	Standardized Test Practice Item Numbers
Measurement	
Determine measurements indirectly from scale drawings.	5.1, 5.2, 5.3
Convert between units within the same system.	5.4, 5.5, 5.6, 5.7
Measure length.	5.8, 5.9
Determine measurements indirectly from similar figures.	5.10, 5.11, 5.12, 5.13
Estimation	
Identify reasonableness.	5.14, 5.15, 5.16, 5.17
Use estimation in operations with decimals and money.	5.18, 5.19, 5.20, 5.21, 5.22
Use estimation in operations with whole numbers.	5.23, 5.24
Use estimation in operation with fractions and mixed numbers.	5.25, 5.26, 5.27
Use estimation in problems with percents.	5.28, 5.29
Problem Solving Strategies	
Identify missing information.	5.30, 5.31
Solve problems using non-routine strategies.	5.32, 5.33, 5.34, 5.35, 5.36
Number and Number Relationships	
Compare and order fractions.	5.37, 5.38, 5.39, 5.40
Identify alternative representations of a fraction or mixed number.	5.41, 5.42, 5.43, 5.44, 5.45
Identify equivalent fractions, including lowest terms fractions and improper fractions.	5.46, 5.47, 5.48, 5.49, 5.50
Identify an integer that is greater than or less than a negative integer.	5.51, 5.52, 5.53
Identify integers on a number line.	5.54, 5.55
Identify alternative representations of a decimal.	5.56, 5.57, 5.58
Number Systems and Number Theory	
Identify the place value of a digit in a decimal.	5.59

STANDARDIZED TEST PRACTICE

SAT9 Intermediate 3 (Continued)

Test Objective	Standardized Test Practice Item Numbers
Identify the place value of a digit in a whole number.	**5.60**
Identify whole numbers expressed in expanded notation.	**5.61**
Distinguish between numbers with only two factors (primes) and numbers with more than two factors (composites).	**5.62, 5.63**
Identify powers and square roots.	**5.64, 5.65, 5.66, 5.67**
Identify numbers expressed in scientific notation.	**5.68, 5.69, 5.70, 5.71**

Patterns and Functions

Identify missing elements in number patterns.	**5.72, 5.73, 5.74**
Identify the output of functions (number machines).	**5.75, 5.76, 5.77, 5.78, 5.79**
Solve a problem involving rate or proportion.	**5.80, 5.81, 5.82, 5.83, 5.84**

Algebra

Identify a solution sentence equivalent to a problem expressed in words.	**5.85, 5.86, 5.87, 5.88, 5.89, 5.90**
Identify equivalent expressions that represent associative, commutative, distributive, and identity properties.	**5.91, 5.92, 5.93, 5.94**
Solve linear equations.	**5.95, 5.96, 5.97, 5.98, 5.99, 5.100, 5.101**

Statistics

Determine measures of central tendency and dispersion.	**5.102, 5.103, 5.104, 5.105, 5.106, 5.107**
Extrapolate from a circle graph.	**5.108, 5.109**
Extrapolate from a table.	**5.110, 5.111, 5.112**
Read and interpret tally charts.	**5.113, 5.114, 5.115**
Read and interpret multiline graphs.	**5.116, 5.117, 5.118**

Probability

Determine combinations and permutations.	**5.119, 5.120, 5.121, 5.122**
Identify probabilities.	**5.123, 5.124, 5.125, 5.126, 5.127**
Predict outcomes.	**5.128, 5.129, 5.130, 5.131**

STANDARDIZED TEST PRACTICE

Test Objective	Standardized Test Practice Item Numbers
Geometry	
Classify angles.	5.132, 5.133, 5.134, 5.135, 5.136, 5.137
Identify radius and diameter.	5.138
Identify transformations: translations, rotations, reflections.	5.139, 5.140, 5.141, 5.142, 5.143
Calculate area of plane figures.	5.144, 5.145, 5.146, 5.147, 5.148, 5.149
Identify coordinates.	5.150, 5.151, 5.152, 5.153
Calculate circumference.	5.154, 5.155, 5.156
Calculate volume.	5.157, 5.158, 5.159
Identify parallel and perpendicular lines.	5.160, 5.161
Computation, Using Symbolic Notation	
Multiplication and division of whole numbers	5.162, 5.163, 5.164
Operations with rational numbers	5.165, 5.166, 5.167, 5.168, 5.169, 5.170, 5.171, 5.172, 5.173
Computation in Context	
Operations with whole numbers in context	5.174, 5.175, 5.176, 5.177
Multiple operations in context	5.178, 5.179, 5.180
Operations with decimals, money, percents in context	5.181, 5.182, 5.183, 5.184, 5.185, 5.186
Operations with fractions and mixed numbers in context	5.187, 5.188, 5.189
Rounding	
Round to estimate and solve problems.	5.190, 5.191, 5.192

STANDARDIZED TEST PRACTICE

TAAS Grade 7

Test Objective	Standardized Test Practice Item Numbers
Concepts: The student will demonstrate an understanding of number concepts.	
Compare and order integers and nonnegative rational numbers.	6.1, 6.2, 6.3, 6.4, 6.5, 6.6, 6.7, 6.8, 6.9, 6.10
Round whole numbers and decimals.	6.11
Determine relationships between and among fractions, decimals, and percents.	6.12, 6.13, 6.14, 6.15, 6.16, 6.17, 6.18, 6.19, 6.20, 6.21, 6.22, 6.23, 6.24, 6.25, 6.26, 6.27
Use exponential notation with zero or positive exponents only.	6.28, 6.29, 6.30, 6.31
Use scientific notation.	6.32, 6.33, 6.34, 6.35
Concepts: The student will demonstrate an understanding of mathematical relations, functions, and other algebraic concepts.	
Recognize and use rational number properties and inverse operations.	6.36, 6.37, 6.38, 6.39, 6.40
Determine missing elements in patterns.	6.41, 6.42, 6.43, 6.44, 6.45, 6.46, 6.47, 6.48
Apply ratio and proportion.	6.49, 6.50, 6.51, 6.52, 6.53, 6.54, 6.55, 6.56, 6.57, 6.58
Solve simple equations involving decimals and fractions.	6.59, 6.60, 6.61, 6.62, 6.63, 6.64, 6.65, 6.66
Identify ordered pairs on the coordinate plane and solution sets in one dimension.	6.67, 6.68, 6.69, 6.70
Evaluate algebraic expressions.	6.71, 6.72
Concepts: The student will demonstrate an understanding of geometric properties and relationships.	
Recognize properties of 2- and 3- dimensional figures.	6.73, 6.74, 6.75, 6.76, 6.77, 6.78, 6.79, 6.80, 6.81, 6.82, 6.83, 6.84, 6.85, 6.86, 6.87, 6.88
Apply similarity, congruence, and symmetry.	6.89, 6.90, 6.91, 6.92, 6.93, 6.94
Recognize basic geometric constructions.	6.95, 6.96
Concepts: The student will demonstrate an understanding of measurement concepts using metric and customary units.	
Use metric and customary units.	6.97, 6.98, 6.99, 6.100, 6.101, 6.102, 6.103, 6.104, 6.105

STANDARDIZED
TEST PRACTICE

TAAS Grade 7 (Continued)

Test Objective	Standardized Test Practice Item Numbers
Find area and volume.	6.106, 6.107, 6.108, 6.109, 6.110, 6.111, 6.112, 6.113, 6.114, 6.115, 6.116

Concepts: The student will demonstrate an understanding of probability and statistics.

Use permutations and combinations.	6.117, 6.118, 6.119, 6.120, 6.121
Find the probability of simple events.	6.122, 6.123, 6.124, 6.125, 6.126, 6.127, 6.128, 6.129, 6.130, 6.131
Find the mean, the median, and the mode.	6.132, 6.133, 6.134, 6.135, 6.136, 6.137

Operations: The student will use addition to solve problems.

Add rational numbers (fractions, decimals, and integers).	6.138, 6.139, 6.140

Operations: The student will use subtraction to solve problems.

Subtract rational numbers (fractions, decimals, and integers).	6.141, 6.142, 6.143, 6.144

Operations: The student will use multiplication to solve problems.

Multiply rational numbers (fractions, decimals, and integers).	6.145, 6.146, 6.147, 6.148

Operations: The student will use division to solve problems.

Divide rational numbers (fractions, decimals, and integers).	6.149, 6.150, 6.151, 6.152, 6.153

Problem Solving: The student will estimate solutions to a problem.

Estimate solutions emphasizing decimals and percents.	6.154, 6.155, 6.156

Problem Solving: The student will determine solution strategies and will analyze or solve problems.

Identify strategies for solving problems using operations with fractions, decimals, and percents.	6.157, 6.158, 6.159, 6.160, 6.161, 6.162, 6.163, 6.164, 6.165, 6.166, 6.167, 6.168
Identify strategies for solving problems requiring the use of geometric concepts.	6.169, 6.170, 6.171
Analyze or solve problems through the use of similarity, congruence, and symmetry.	6.172, 6.173

STANDARDIZED TEST PRACTICE

© Prentice-Hall, Inc.

TAAS Grade 7 (Continued)

Test Objective	Standardized Test Practice Item Numbers
Analyze or solve problems using probability and statistics concepts.	6.174, 6.175
Determine methods for solving and solve measurement problems.	6.176, 6.177
Make predictions.	6.178

Problem Solving: The student will express or solve problems using mathematical representation.

Formulate equations/inequalities.	6.179, 6.180, 6.181, 6.182, 6.183, 6.184, 6.185, 6.186
Analyze or interpret graphs, charts, tables, and maps and use the information derived to solve problems.	6.187, 6.188, 6.189, 6.190, 6.191, 6.192, 6.193, 6.194

Problem Solving: The student will evaluate the reasonableness of a solution to a problem situation.

Evaluate reasonableness.	6.195, 6.196, 6.197

NC End-of-Grade 7

Test Objective	Standardized Test Practice Item Numbers
The learner will demonstrate an understanding and use of real numbers.	
Use models to represent positive and negative rational numbers.	**7.1, 7.2, 7.3, 7.4, 7.5, 7.6, 7.7, 7.8**
Compare and order rational numbers in meaningful contexts.	**7.9, 7.10, 7.11**
Express whole numbers in scientific notation; convert scientific notation to standard form.	**7.12, 7.13, 7.14, 7.15**
Use exponential notation to express prime factorization of numbers less than 100.	**7.16**
Within meaningful contexts use estimation techniques with rational numbers; justify the strategy chosen.	**7.17, 7.18**
Develop the meaning of the square and the square root of a number; estimate square root and find square roots on the calculator.	**7.19**
In meaningful context, relate concepts of ratio, proportion, and percent.	**7.20, 7.21, 7.22, 7.23, 7.24, 7.25**
The learner will demonstrate an understanding and use of geometry.	
Make constructions of perpendicular and parallel lines using straightedge and compass.	**7.26**
Use the properties and relationships of geometry to solve problems.	**7.27, 7.28, 7.29, 7.30, 7.31, 7.32, 7.33, 7.34, 7.35, 7.36, 7.37, 7.38**
Use models to develop the concept of the Pythagorean Theorem.	**7.39, 7.40, 7.41, 7.42, 7.43**
Identify applications of geometry in the environment.	**7.44, 7.45**
Given models of 3-dimensional figures, draw representations.	**7.46, 7.47, 7.48, 7.49**
Given the end, side, and top views of 3-dimensional figures, build models.	**7.50**
Graph shapes and congruent figures on a coordinate plane.	**7.51, 7.52, 7.53**
The learner will demonstrate an understanding and use of patterns, relationships, and pre-algebra.	
Describe, extend, analyze and create a wide variety of patterns to investigate relationships and solve problems.	**7.54, 7.55, 7.56, 7.57, 7.58, 7.59, 7.60, 7.61, 7.62, 7.63**

Test Objective	Standardized Test Practice Item Numbers
Use concrete materials as models to develop the concept of operations with variables.	7.64, 7.65
Use concrete, informal and formal methods to model and solve simple linear equations.	7.66, 7.67, 7.68, 7.69, 7.70, 7.71, 7.72, 7.73, 7.74, 7.75, 7.76, 7.77
Investigate and evaluate algebraic expressions using mental calculations, pencil and paper and calculators where appropriate.	7.78, 7.79, 7.80, 7.81

The learner will demonstrate an understanding and use of measurement.

Apply measurement concepts and skills as needed in problem solving situations.	7.82, 7.83, 7.84, 7.85, 7.86, 7.87, 7.88, 7.89, 7.90, 7.91, 7.92, 7.93, 7.94, 7.95, 7.96, 7.97, 7.98, 7.99, 7.100
In measurement situations make judgments about degree of precision needed and reasonableness of results.	7.101, 7.102
Use models to develop the concept and formula for surface area for rectangular solids and cylinders.	7.103, 7.104
Use models to develop the concept of volume for prisms/cylinders as the product of area of the base and height.	7.105, 7.106, 7.107, 7.108, 7.109, 7.110

The learner will solve problems and reason mathematically.

Use an organized approach and a variety of strategies to solve increasingly complex non-routine problems.	7.111, 7.112, 7.113, 7.114, 7.115, 7.116, 7.117, 7.118
Use calculators and computers in problem solving situations as appropriate.	7.119, 7.120, 7.121, 7.122
Discuss alternate strategies, evaluate outcomes, make conjectures and generalizations based on problem situations.	7.123, 7.124, 7.125, 7.126
Use concrete or pictorial models involving spatial reasoning to solve problems.	7.127, 7.128
Identify and solve problems that require proportional reasoning.	7.129, 7.130, 7.131, 7.132, 7.133, 7.134, 7.135, 7.136, 7.137, 7.138
Solve problems involving interpretation of graphs, including inferences and conjectures.	7.139, 7.140, 7.141, 7.142

The learner will demonstrate an understanding and use of graphing, probability, and statistics.

Create, compare, and evaluate both orally and in writing different graphic representations of the same data.	7.143, 7.144, 7.145

STANDARDIZED TEST PRACTICE

Test Objective	Standardized Test Practice Item Numbers
Construct a box plot (box and whiskers) by ordering data, identify the median, quartiles, and extremes.	7.146
Evaluate appropriate uses of different measures of central tendency.	7.147, 7.148, 7.149, 7.150, 7.151
Draw inferences and construct convincing arguments based on analysis of data.	7.152, 7.153, 7.154, 7.155
Investigate and recognize misuses of statistical or numeric information.	7.156
Show all possible outcomes by making lists, tree diagrams and frequency distribution tables.	7.157, 7.158, 7.159, 7.160
Explain the relationship between experimental results and mathematical expectations.	7.161
Find the probability of simple events using experiments, random number generation, computer simulation, and theoretical methods.	7.162, 7.163, 7.164, 7.165, 7.166, 7.167, 7.168, 7.169, 7.170, 7.171
Use permutations and combinations in applications.	7.172, 7.173, 7.174, 7.175

The learner will compute with real numbers.

Select appropriate operations, strategies, and methods of solving a variety of application problems using positive rational numbers, and justify the selection.	7.176, 7.177, 7.178
Estimate and solve problems using ratios, proportions, and percent, selecting and using appropriate method, explaining the process.	7.179, 7.180, 7.181, 7.182
Apply concepts of ratio, proportion, and percent to real life situations such as consumer applications, science and social studies.	7.183, 7.184, 7.185, 7.186, 7.187, 7.188, 7.189, 7.190, 7.191
Use real world examples or models to represent multiplication and division of integers; record and explain procedures used.	7.192, 7.193, 7.194
Use operations with integers in relevant problem situations.	7.195, 7.196, 7.197, 7.198

STANDARDIZED
TEST PRACTICE

<u>Macintosh</u>

System Requirements

PH Computer Item Generator will run on any Mac with a 68030 or better processor, at least 8MB of RAM, System 7.0 or later, at least 5MB of hard drive space available, and a printer.

Installation

- Insert the Prentice Hall *Computer Item Generator with Standardized Test Practice* CD into your CD-ROM drive.
- Open the PHCIG CD icon.
- Double-click **Install PHCIG**.
- Follow the instructions on screen.

You can choose either "Standard" or "Custom" installation. Choose "Custom" only if you are re-installing a portion of the PH Computer Item Generator software.

The installation program will prompt you to choose a location for the folder containing the PH Computer Item Generator software.

After installation is complete, your computer will re-start. You can now use Prentice Hall *Computer Item Generator with Standardized Test Practice*. For detailed instructions, consult the User's Guide by opening the CIG User's Guide icon.

<u>Windows</u>

System Requirements

PH Computer Item Generator will run on a PC with a 66 MHz 486DX or better processor, at least 8MB of RAM, VGA color graphics display, at least 5MB of hard drive space available, and a Windows-compatible printer. **NOTE**: PH Computer Item Generator requires a math coprocessor; it will not run with a 486SX processor.

Installation with Windows 95

- Insert the Prentice Hall *Computer Item Generator with Standardized Test Practice* CD into your CD-ROM drive.
- Click the **Start** button.
- Choose **Run...** from the **Start** menu.
- Type **X:\SETUP** (where X is the letter of your CD-ROM drive).
- Click the **OK** button.
- Follow the instructions on screen.

Installation with Windows 3.1

- Insert the Prentice Hall *Computer Item Generator with Standardized Test Practice* CD into your CD-ROM drive.
- Choose **Run...** from the **File** menu.
- Type **X:\SETUP** (where X is the letter of your CD-ROM drive).
- Click the **OK** button.
- Follow the instructions on screen.

You can choose a "Complete" or "Custom" installation. Choose "Custom" only if you are re-installing a portion of the PH Computer Item Generator software.

The setup program will prompt you for the directory and program folder names for PH Computer Item Generator. We suggest you accept the defaults provided.

After installation is complete, your computer will re-start. You can now use Prentice Hall *Computer Item Generator with Standardized Test Practice*. For detailed instructions, open the PH CIG User's Guide in the PH Computer Item Generator program group.